PLUTARCH: ON THE MALICE OF HERODOTUS

"I am astonished, my dear," said Mrs Bennet, "that you should be so ready to think your children silly. If I wished to think slightingly of any body's children, it should not be of my own however."

"If my children are silly I must hope to be always sensible of it."

"Yes – but as it happens, they are all of them very clever."

Jane Austen
Pride and Prejudice

ARIS AND PHILLIPS CLASSICAL TEXTS

PLUTARCH

Malice of Herodotus

A. J. Bowen

Aris & Phillips is an imprint of Oxbow Books

First published in the United Kingdom in 1992. Reprinted 2015 by
OXBOW BOOKS
10 Hythe Bridge Street, Oxford OX1 2EW

and in the United States by
OXBOW BOOKS
908 Darby Road, Havertown, PA 19083

Paperback Edition: ISBN 978-0-85668-569-9

A CIP record for this book is available from the British Library

For a complete list of Aris & Phillips titles, please contact:

UNITED KINGDOM
Oxbow Books
Telephone (01865) 241249
Fax (01865) 794449
Email: oxbow@oxbowbooks.com
www.oxbowbooks.com

UNITED STATES OF AMERICA
Oxbow Books
Telephone (800) 791-9354
Fax (610) 853-9146
Email: queries@casemateacademic.com
www.casemateacademic.com/oxbow

Oxbow Books is part of the Casemate Group

Printed and bound by CPI Group (UK) Ltd, Croydon, CR0 4YY

Contents

Preface

In composing this translation and commentary for Plutarch's *The Malice of Herodotus* I have had in mind chiefly its use to students of the Persian wars. Some of them may find here more than they need, and some perhaps less than they want: if more, that is because there are things to say about Plutarch as well as about Herodotus and the wars; if less, that is because I have tried not to discuss Herodotean issues unless Plutarch is involved. Otherwise the work would have grown too large. I have therefore assumed, as Plutarch plainly did, that readers of it are reasonably acquainted with Herodotus.

I was drawn to start this work by teaching for the paper in the J.A.C.T. Ancient History syllabus called 'Herodotus and the Conflict of Greece and Persia'. I have been helped to complete it in many ways: by the books and articles listed, and, no doubt, by others unlisted; by some periods of study at the British School in Athens, and by the Faculty of Classics at Cambridge in the shape of travel grants and other help; by Professor E.W. Handley and Drs J.T. Killen and P.C. Millett of that faculty; by Professor R.J.A. Talbert of the University of North Carolina and by Professor H.B. Rosén of the Hebrew University of Jerusalem in correspondence; by Dr P.A. Cartledge of Clare College, Cambridge, who read a first draft and made many corrections and suggestions; and very greatly by Professor M.M. Willcock of University College, London, who read subsequent drafts and always improved them (both of these two have been encouraging and neither is responsible for faults that remain, which are mine); and finally, or rather, initially, by several classes of pupils at Shrewsbury School. To all of them, my thanks.

The Schools, Shrewsbury   Anthony Bowen
Jesus College, Cambridge   February 1992

Introduction

1. Plutarch seems to have lived a singularly agreeable life. He was born in Chaeronea in Boeotia a little before 50 A.D. in the time of the emperor Claudius. The Romans had mostly left Greece alone since the devastations of the civil wars nearly a century earlier, and slowly it had recovered some prosperity. Its politics were now quite parochial, but its culture had prevailed, in the western Mediterranean as earlier in the east. Greece had educated Rome, and the Roman authorities were essentially sympathetic to it.

2. Plutarch's family was well-to-do, and had been locally established for at least three generations. The area was fertile, and from Chaeronea, a small settlement of some historic note, there was ready access to Athens and to Delphi, and to the gulf of Corinth for travel by sea. In 54 Claudius was succeeded by Nero, a genuine philhellene, who passed nearly two whole years in Greece, from 66 to 68. By then Plutarch had become a student in the Academy at Athens, which Plato had founded over four centuries earlier. Rhetoric was the staple of ancient education, but Plutarch also studied Platonism. Platonists mistrusted rhetoric, but the training in persuasive speech gave Plutarch forms of expression which came as easily to his writing as did Platonic forms of thought to his mind. Both may be seen in this work.

3. When Nero fell in 68, the horrors of a civil war loomed again; this time the competing Roman generals kept their quarrels out of Greece, and Vespasian the victor soon restored order. Plutarch accepted a leading role in his community, having audience of the Roman authorities in Greece and travelling several times to Rome, where he displayed his talents as a speaker (in Greek, not Latin; he never perfected his command of Latin: see *Life of Demosthenes* 2). He and his family by way of a Roman friend, L. Mestrius Florus, received Roman citizenship. He travelled also to Egypt. But the reign of Domitian cast an increasing shadow; philosophers were expelled from Rome in 93. Then in 96 Domitian was murdered, and the world grew brighter.

4. By now Plutarch was more than middle-aged. His political activities diminished; his travelling was mostly limited to visits to Delphi, where *c.*95 he had been made one of the two chief priests, an honour he particularly esteemed. In semi-retirement he took up his pen in earnest. Amid his books and friends and pupils, and in the comfort of an affectionate family life, he produced in the score or more years that remained to him works which lived on and later helped to educate Europe, in particular the famous *Lives*. Plutarch's reputation is not now what it was from the Renaissance to the nineteenth century (and even later). Rousseau wrote (*Reveries* 1782), 'Among the small number of books that I occasionally reread, it is Plutarch who most of all holds my attention and benefits me .... He is almost the only author of whom I can say that I have never read him without some profit.' More surprisingly, Harry S. Truman, President of the United States, said, 'I've read Plutarch through many times .... They just don't come any better than old Plutarch. He knew more about politics than all

the other writers I've read put together.'[1] Biography remains a flourishing genre. In Plutarch's case, the ease of his narrative and the importance and interest of many of his chosen characters sustain the currency of his *Lives* still. Above all, Plutarch has a talent for presenting character through anecdote. As H.J. Rose says (*A Handbook to Greek Literature*[4], London 1951, 409), ironically in view of the present work, Plutarch had 'such love of a good story, combined with power to tell it effectively, as had hardly been found since Herodotus.'

5. Plutarch wrote a great deal. In addition to the *Lives*, there are many essays and letters and conversation pieces, collectively called the *Moralia*. The name is derived from the content of the first few pieces as arranged in Maximus Planudes' collection of the late thirteenth century, but the word is not out of place for any of Plutarch's writings. In those that survive, which are perhaps fewer than half of the original total, the author appears as an amiable and serious man, of diverse intellectual interests, and prodigiously well read. He does not have the critical faculty of a scholar, but he has achieved something different from most scholars, in being read by men and women of affairs and of no affairs, with pleasure and profit, for generations. Before he died, in 120 or soon after, he had received an honorary consulship, for services to literature as would be said nowadays, and another philhellene was emperor, Hadrian, who backed his sentiments with practical aid. The Mediterranean world had moved into an era of prosperity and stability: to quote Edward Gibbon, 'If a man were called to fix the period in the history of the world, during which the condition of the human race was most happy and prosperous, he would, without hesitation, name that which elapsed from the death of Domitian to the accession of Commodus' (180 A.D.).

6. The essay *The Malice of Herodotus* is rather an oddity among Plutarch's works. It is seriously meant, but is hard to read in its original spirit now, and it is not amiable. Plutarch was not alone in the ancient world in attacking Herodotus, but Herodotus survives the attack comparatively unscathed; Plutarch does not. Some critics, seeking to rescue the author, have doubted he wrote it; but style and language, and especially the range and nature of references to other writers, make Plutarch's authorship certain (see Lachenaud 114). Some suggest it was a youthful *jeu d'esprit*, too zealously preserved; but its purpose is sustained, and the rhetoric is mature and arises naturally out of the author's intent . In any case, Plutarch's writing all seems to belong to his later years: though some of it can be ordered, particularly the *Lives*, very little of it can be dated (see Jones 1966). If Alexander its addressee is rightly identified (see 1/854En)[2], then it too belongs to these later years. In addition, Plutarch's mention (32/866B) of a projected *Life of Leonidas* ties it in to the whole project of the parallel *Lives*, which were not begun till 96. It would make sense if the moment to write this work came when Plutarch was preparing his *Lives of Themistocles* and *Aristeides*, as suggested by Wardman (189); but the attitude towards Herodotus in this work and in the

---

[1] See Sansone, 1–3.

[2] References to the text usually give both chapter and the general reference (for which see prefatory note in the commentary). n draws attention to a note in the commentary.

various *Lives* which owe material to Herodotus[3] is so different that, whatever the impulse, this work was plainly written as a separate piece.

7. Though the date and context of writing are not clear, the cause is. Plutarch declares his purpose at once, which is to rescue the good name of his ancestors the Boeotians, and of the Corinthians, and of all those others traduced in Herodotus' *Histories*. He also claims to be rescuing truth.

8. Plutarch was fond of Chaeronea, but in relation to the scope and dispassion of Herodotus' work, and for a citizen of the Roman empire, his parochialism is surprising. Other causes of writing are worth a look. Plutarch did not trust Herodotus' style, and he had Platonic warrant for his suspicion (1/854En), but there is no literary animosity, and elsewhere Plutarch shows admiration for Herodotus as a writer (see 43/874B, and the passage quoted in the note *ad loc.*).

9. A more promising cause is religious disapproval. Herodotus' treatment of Heracles clearly upset Plutarch (13 & 14): perhaps Heracles' ancestral links with Thebes aroused Plutarch's patriotism. More seriously, the oracular authorities at Delphi had evidently expected a Persian victory and advised accordingly. Herodotus reveals the defeatism without condemnation or condonation; that could have made a good stick with which to beat Herodotus, but there are only two protests against Herodotus' treatment of Delphi, one in 23 and the other in 40, and neither is important. The corruption of the oracle engineered by Cleomenes in order to oust his fellow king Demaratus, of which Herodotus gives much detail, is passed over in silence.

10. If Plutarch were a historian, we might have looked for historical rivalry, such as may be detected as early as Thucydides (1.21 & 23), whom Plutarch greatly admired. Plutarch was not a historian; and yet, in his understanding and misunderstanding of history lies not so much the cause as the condition of his writing this work. As Russell remarks (*CR* 80 (1966) 182), "*de Malignitate* contains in its opening sections one of the most revealing accounts of the principles of ancient historiography that we possess".

11. Herodotus and Thucydides differ in aim, in topic and in treatment. What Plutarch could see in Thucydides was a more or less single narrative line, a ruthless pruning of detail, and a firm view of the motives of collective human action. In Herodotus the many stories eddy in a broad stream, and the causes of things are many too. Plutarch's romantic puritanism was not at ease with Herodotus' catholic and generous relativism. In Herodotus' day new patterns of thought were still in the making; Herodotus is difficult to categorise precisely because his own thoughts were still forming. Plutarch lived in an older world, and the firm line taken by thinkers like Thucydides and Plato had helped to make it so. In writing his *Lives* Plutarch borrowed freely and often without acknowledgement, as though he and Herodotus were kindred spirits; if, in the end, we return to Plutarch's own explanation of why he wrote this work, it is because that points truly to the intellectual gap which lies between them.

12. There are external differences too. Herodotus was born and brought up on the fringe of the Greek world; he was probably not entirely Greek by descent (23/860En), and for much of his life he was a homeless nomad (35/868An:

[3] See notes in 1/855A, 3/855C, 5/855E, 6/856A, 7/856B, 11/856F, 12/857A, 15/857F, 18/858D, 27/862D (twice), 34/867B and 868A, 37/869D, 38/869F, 39/870B, 40/871C and 42/872A and B.

Lucian, who lived about three generations later than Plutarch, describes in *How to write History* 41 the ideal historian: one desirable quality is statelessness). These things may have helped to produce his sense of detachment, or what Plutarch saw as his lack of Hellenic patriotism (12/857A). But in Herodotus' world, Greek versus Greek was still a much more absorbing contest than Greek versus other, as Thucydides' choice of topic attests; local loyalties were the fiercest. Plutarch's parochialism is more inward-looking; he could hardly understand the powerful rivalries of the old city states. Politically and intellectually, Plutarch's world was essentially one; that of Herodotus was kaleidoscopic.

13. The form of Plutarch's work is simple. First he declares his aim, with elegant warning of the difficulty of countering Herodotean guile-in-style, but before proceeding to his task he sets up a theoretical base for it by listing sorts of malice. They are mostly illustrated, the examples being drawn from his copious store of historical anecdote; he is careful not to take examples from Herodotus (the one in 5 concerning Themistocles belongs to that gentleman's post-Herodotean career). The list is perhaps such a one as was made in the schools, to help student orators: by reference to it the apprentice could classify his rival's arguments and so deal with them methodically in his turn. There is a semi-forensic air to the whole work. But when the list is done, in 10 (and it has its own interest: see Russell, quoted above), Plutarch more or less ignores it. It provides neither the intellectual nor the formal framework of the attack that ensues. It turns out to be more of a defensive starched front, as though Plutarch felt the temerity of his undertaking, and wished to look respectable at its beginning.

14. The preface is a tenth part of the whole. The main body of the work, from 11 to 42, has uncertain form initially (see 18 & 19 below), but starts to settle in 15 and establishes coherence and focus in 19. Plutarch might have proceeded in accordance with his preface, treating Herodotus' malice by its types (see 1/855B); he might have proceeded by topic: there are traces of this approach in 11–14, where questions of origin are raised, and in 36, where Herodotus' various references to Naxos are gathered in one; but the way of least preparation was to take the issues in Herodotean order. From 15 onwards, with three exceptions, this is what he does: a glance at the index of passages cited makes it plain. The three exceptions are 25, 28 and 30; all are slight re-orderings, and two are well justified (see 25/861Dn). At the end is a summary chapter, 43. The four great battles of 480 and 479 are given explicitly the prominence they have already had implicitly, and Plutarch finishes by returning to the deceptiveness of Herodotus' charm with which he began.

15. In challenging Herodotus Plutarch has basically two approaches. At first he can do little more than quote what Herodotus says and deny it; the argument from silence and the argument from implausibility or impropriety are in heavy use. Herodotus' early material is, in a sense, prehistoric: Plutarch cannot counter it with alternative facts. He quotes his first alternative source in 20, the historian Charon of Lampsacus, and from then on a more serious sort of challenge can be mounted. From then on, too, Herodotus is quoted more thoroughly: the work settles to a pattern. Whole sentences from Herodotus are copied or paraphrased,

good lengths of text which Plutarch obviously excerpted and kept to hand. The practice he refers to in 457D and 464F, of making notes as he read, rescues him from the shaky start. The unfortunate corollary is that, as he wrote, he apparently had only his excerpts to consult and not a full text of Herodotus; hence, no doubt, many of his subsequent errors of detail.

16. If the formal shape of the work is due to Herodotus, the emotional rhythm is Plutarch's. His moments of greatest protest and indignation are not always his best pieces of argument: the three chapters on Thermopylae, 31–33, are notably bad, both as history and in observation of Herodotus, though 32 is an interesting measure of how the legend of Thermopylae had developed. But 39, in which the record of Adeimantus and the Corinthians at Salamis is righted, is coherently and effectively organised. There are high points also in 22, 27, 28 and 42. I have chosen 22 to be the subject of some literary comment in 37 below. The combination of Herodotean order and varying Plutarchan intensity has a major part to play in creating the impression of a work with pace, progression and proportion.

17. Four items merit closer study here. They are the uncertain start in 11–14, Plutarch's use of Herodotus, his use of the other sources, and Plutarch as a writer himself.

18. Plutarch starts 11 with the story of Io. He seems to be adopting at once the procedure noted above as simplest, of making his points as the topics arise in Herodotus. What Plutarch says about Io in no way contradicts Herodotus; he quotes, not quite accurately, a notorious sentence and repeats it with different inaccuracy, making it the springboard for further attack which rapidly loses control: he finally blames Herodotus for a story about Aristomenes the Messenian which Herodotus never tells! Then for three chapters he picks items mostly out of book two, dodging here and there in it as if he were picking his matter by topic, but patently working from memory; one item (in 13) comes from book one, and one (in 14) from book six. All, roughly, are on the topic of origins. In 13 he seems to quote five times, but there are only eight words of Herodotus all told; the longer quotations in 12 and 14 both diverge some way from Herodotus' text. There is still virtually no argument, only independent assertion; the assertion at the end of 12 about Helen and Menelaus is not followed up; he misses a piece of Herodotean irony. He lacks steady aim and method. It seems he realised it.

19. He could have scrapped the section: it has no relevance to his main concern, the great battles of 480 and 479. He could have revised it: Plutarch's interest in religion was real, and Herodotus' fascination with Egypt produced something which is more a contribution to ethnography than to the history of memorable deeds promised in his prologue. In leaving it at least Plutarch learnt something about method; for he went back to Herodotus, it seems, and read him through again for the bits he wanted, this time making excerpts. Pelling (31) has a useful paragraph on the physical difficulties of reference and research among papyri. Plutarch went back to book one, skimmed through book three, and started his serious work in book five (see Index of Plutarch's citations). He still did a certain amount from memory; one-word or two-word quotations continue to occur for a few more chapters. Inaccuracies also remain: in 16 he puts words in

the mouth of Megacles' daughter which Herodotus does not; in 17 he misrepresents what Herodotus says about Othryades; in 18 he overlooks a distinction made between Croesus' different dedications; in 19 he brings together two passages forty lines apart. Such things continue throughout the work, and it often seems coarse and hurried; valid criticisms of Herodotus are not pursued effectively, and other criticisms are made invalid by misrepresentation as much as by misunderstanding.

20. Plutarch's practice in quotation of Herodotus is symptomatic of this. A line or two of Homer or Sophocles or Pindar can easily be quoted from memory; so too a phrase from Plato or even Herodotus himself; perhaps an epigram of Simonides. In educated circles such things were commonplace, and perfect accuracy was not at a premium. But chunks of Herodotus up to sixty words long, written in an antique dialect, are not quoted from memory: they have been excerpted, to be copied into the work as required. It is surprising to find that they are not copied exactly.

21. Three sorts of change are, on the face of it, trivial. First, Plutarch regularly normalizes some of Herodotus' Ionicisms: he rejects psilosis, he adds the temporal augment and paragogic nu, and he adds iota to the aorist stems and to the perfect passive stem of δείκνυμι. Second, he often omits Herodotus' connecting particle at the head of a quotation; in 22/859E he replaces δέ with a γάρ of his own; sometimes he preserves the particle when it would be easier to be rid of it; his practice is not consistent. Third, having frequent occasion to say 'Herodotus says ...' he sometimes converts original direct statement from its indicatives to the infinitives of indirect speech; there are examples in 19, 20, 34, 42 and elsewhere. There are a few other changes which lie between adaptation to context and light paraphrase, like ἦν for ἐών in 23/860D. Paraphrase proper is another thing: since then Plutarch is not quoting, his fairness to the sense is what matters, and in paraphrase he is pretty fair. Examples may be found in 22 and 39, and lesser ones in 34 and 36 and elsewhere.

22. The third of the changes mentioned above is, unfortunately, often misleading. (It is also impossible to represent in English!) Herodotus often uses the infinitives of indirect speech in his own narrative in order to show that he is telling a story which may be no more than a story. Plutarch's infinitives may mark adaptation of original indicatives or be quotation of original infinitives, but with their original status now obscured. The situation is complicated by Herodotus' willingness to use infinitives after the verb λέγειν, 'to say'; standard classical Greek did not. In this way Plutarch may blur important distinctions. In 39 he even moves in the opposite direction: Herodotus' infinitives for the story about Adeimantus become indicatives in Plutarch!

23. Six times Plutarch declares, with various formulae, 'I quote'. Twice he is introducing quotations from Charon of Lampsacus, the only historian apart from Herodotus to be quoted verbatim in evidence (see 24/861Cn). The other four introduce quotations from Herodotus. In 31/865E he quotes from 7.220.4; in 35/868B from 8.30; in 37/869DE he has a long quotation from 8.57–8, in three pieces, the first and third prefaced by 'I quote'. Whatever the general carelessness of the ancient world may be in quotation, here we might reasonably

look for accuracy; but it is not there, even after the normalization of Ionicisms mentioned.

24. It is a little disconcerting. There were the excerpts, to hand. Perhaps Plutarch's text of Herodotus was not in the same line of manuscript descent that has produced our medieval exemplars. On three occasions possible textual variants may point in that direction (see notes in 19/859A, 22/860A and 23/860E); better evidence should come from the papyri of Oxyrhynchus and elsewhere. When Hude produced the third edition of his Oxford Classical text in 1927, there were twelve papyri to be cited. In the succeeding sixty years, that number has been a little more than doubled[4], but nothing has been found to change the original estimate of their significance. Their texts coincide comfortably with the testimony of the medieval MSS. But *P. Oxy.* 1092 briefly offers something very different. The top five lines of column ix are in a different handwriting and have an alternative version of the text a little lower down the column (2.162.5). Only half-lines survive, but in those five half-lines word order is different three times and there is syntactical variation possibly of the sort which Plutarch can produce (see A.S. Hunt, *Oxyrhynchus Papyri* VIII London 1911, which has a photograph; G. Rudberg's attempt in *Eranos* 39 (1941) 145–7 to play down the difference is unconvincing). If Plutarch's own text was as erratic as that one briefly is, all would be explained. On the whole, however, it is simpler to say that he was careless, since that deals not only with his variations of text but also with much casual error, like the sequence of events after the sack of Sardis (24/861C), the number of towns wrecked in Phocis (35/868B), and the number of Naxian ships at Salamis (36/869A).

25. Otherwise (apart from Charon), Plutarch does not quote: he merely mentions his alternative authorities. It is time to look at them. [5] Those cited in the preface are not relevant to the real business of the essay, but they establish the impression of a well read man moving comfortably in all genres of literature and in easy command of what he wants. There are Plato and Sophocles, and another, anonymous, tragedian; Thucydides, Ephorus and Theopompus, the three best known historians apart from Herodotus; the Syracusan historian Philistus; Aristoxenus, known chiefly as a writer on music; and Philip V of Macedon with a memorable saying. Unnamed are the comic poets of Athens like Aristophanes. It is a various and catholic collection, and makes a convincing start to the work.
26. From 11 to 19 no one at all is cited; Plutarch has to make all the running himself for the early stuff, and the lack of evidence is one reason for the relatively unconvincing impression made in this part of the work. Only in 20, with the fate of Pactyes after the Persian conquest of Ionia, is Plutarch able to challenge Herodotus with alternative information. Now the breadth of his reading starts to emerge. Over the remaining chapters he mentions (listed here in alphabetical order) Antenor the Cretan historian, Aristophanes the Boeotian

---

[4] See A.H.R.E. Paap, *de Herodoti reliquiis in papyris et membranis Aegypti servatis* Leiden 1948; R.A. Pack, *The Greek and Latin literary texts from Greco-Roman Egypt* Ann Arbor 1965[2]; B. Hemmerdinger, *Les manuscrits d'Hérodote et la critique verbale*, Genoa 1981, 195–9; and Rosén XLIII.

[5] See Index of references to other literature.

chronicler, Charon of Lampsacus, Dionysius of Chalcis, Diyllus the Athenian, Ephorus of Cyme, Hellanicus of Lesbos, Lysanias of Mallos, Nicander of Colophon, Pindar, Simonides and Thucydides. There are also the Naxian chroniclers as a group and other anonymous groups; possibly Theopompus (see 27/862Dn); the wholly obscure Lacrates the Spartiate; not to mention sayings of Spartans, and unnamed sources for certain alleged events at Thermopylae. Charon and Hellanicus are of Herodotus' own era; Simonides and Pindar lived in the Persian wars themselves; Thucydides is a generation later than Herodotus; the rest are fourth century figures, except for Nicander and probably Antenor; Lysanias is undatable.

27. Of all the prose writers, Thucydides apart, little or nothing has survived. Only therefore when Plutarch uses Thucydides can we judge his judgement in any detail. In 39 Plutarch emerges with credit (see 870Dn); but in 19 (see 858Fn) Thucydides can be used to upset the argument, already unsound, which Plutarch is conducting, and in 5 the appeal to Thucydides' silence is unsound. Plutarch knew his Thucydides well, but since Thucydides' topic overlaps with Herodotus' hardly at all, there is little use he can make of him. Of the others, only Charon is quoted, in 20 and 24: examination of the two passages suggests that if we had a full text of Charon, we should use it only where Herodotus fails.

28. This may suggest that Plutarch has a poor appreciation of his alternative sources. Let us remember, however, that he is not trying to write history: he is arguing a case, and he quotes for the sake of the case. Any genuinely historical points are incidental. More striking is the fact that from all his reading he is able to challenge Herodotus so little.

29. Best evidence would come from the time of the wars itself. Plutarch's one quotation of Pindar is inconclusive in context (34/867C), being something of a Plutarchan commonplace; in fact there is evidence in Pindar which Plutarch might have used to right the Aeginetan record, had he noticed the problem. Simonides, however, is used well. Plutarch quotes him three times, in 36/869C, in 39/871B, and in 42/872DE. In addition there are seven other sets of verses quoted which posterity attributed to Simonides, and Plutarch probably did too (see 36/869Cn). The first of the ten (34/867F) neither disproves Herodotus nor is vital to Plutarch's case; the second (36/869C) supports Herodotus with a detail that Herodotus chose not to make space for; the next five, all in 39, have excellent cumulative effect, though the relevance of the fifth can be challenged. The last three occur in 42; the first of them usefully makes explicit what Herodotus at best implies about the Corinthian contribution at Plataea, and is well worth quotation; the other two are ambivalent, the last on Plutarch's own admission.

30. The quotation of Simonides is one of the best things Plutarch does. He had an inkling of the virtues of epigraphic and other sorts of concrete contemporary evidence (see 7/856Bn). He had read one of the epigrams *in situ* (see 34/867Fn), even though most of them probably came to him as literary evidence. The rest of his evidence challenges Herodotus only on the fringes or in tiny detail.

31. To go in chronological order of events: Antenor and Dionysius of Chalcis are cited together for an event over a century before Xerxes' invasion, the safe return of 300 Corcyrean boys from Samos (22). Charon is quoted for an event a little after 546, the fate of Pactyes (20). The Naxian chroniclers are cited for

events there (36: but the text is disturbed) in 499 and 490. Charon is quoted again (24) for the Athenian part in the attack on Sardis in 498; Lysanias of Mallos is cited at the same time for the role of the Eretrians.

32. Then we come to the events of 480 and 479. Aristophanes the Boeotian and Nicander of Colophon are cited (33) for who led the Theban contingent at Thermopylae: this is the only point at which we may reckon Herodotus is wrong and Plutarch has put him right. Hellanicus and Ephorus are cited for the number of Naxian ships at Salamis (36), but they differ and are probably both wrong. Finally there are the incidents at Thermopylae asserted by Plutarch without citing his authority, for the second of which Ephorus is probably responsible, Leonidas' dream (31), his assault on Xerxes' camp (32), and the Thessalian intervention on behalf of the Thebans (33). There are also the sayings attributed to Leonidas and others (see 32/866Bn).

33. Two historians are cited for events of Herodotus' own lifetime. Diyllus (28) says the Athenians awarded Herodotus a fee of 10 talents, and Aristophanes the Boeotian (31) tells of the Theban refusal to offer him anything.

34. It is a thin haul from the historians. Only Simonides is useful for events of any centrality, the role of the Corinthians at Salamis (39) and at Plataea (42). We have observed above that if Plutarch's interest had been strictly historical, he might have got more out of Pindar. It is worth considering whether there are other sources untapped which were known to him. Damastes of Sigeum is a possible one. Dionysius of Halicarnassus (see 20/859Bn) mentions him as a contemporary of Thucydides, and one scrap of information (*FGrH* 5 F4) indicates that he commented on the medism of the Aleuads of Thessaly (see 31/864D and 35/868Cn). Plutarch mentions Damastes himself, in *Life of Camillus* 19.4. He also mentions Megarian historians in *Life of Themistocles* 10, and Samian historians on some five occasions. Evidence from these two groups might have been relevant in 42, and in 21 and 22, respectively.

35. Let us return to Plutarch the writer. Discussions of Plutarch's style have been based largely, and naturally, upon the *Lives*. There is a useful general survey in Hillyard xxii-xxxiii. In the *Lives* narrative dominates, but, as Hillyard observes (xxxv), 'there are different styles in the *Moralia*.' *The Malice of Herodotus* is a quarrelsome work, and that makes for several differences. Plain narrative is infrequent, but some can be found briefly in 15, 31 and 32, in the story of Pittacus and the tales of Leonidas. Since none of the stories is original to Plutarch, it is worth looking at another brief passage, where Plutarch retells a story of Herodotus in his own words: the summary about the boys from Corcyra in 22. In all of the passages, the phrases are of moderate length, the structure simple and progressive, the vocabulary plain, and the sense clear.

36. A rhetorical training would cover all forms of public utterance, narrative as well as argument. It provided not only much practice in developing and readiness in handling verbal and logical structures, but also much store of literary, historical and philosophical knowledge, from all of which the would-be speaker and writer could select as appropriate. Plutarch had plainly been an apt pupil. In this work the combative element emerges most obviously in the plentiful superlatives, the imperatives, the indignant questions and exclamations, and in several invocations of Herodotus. Three other features common to

Plutarch's writing in general also serve his purposes here, triplets, hyperbaton, and especially pairs of words which are synonyms or virtually so. Plutarch knows also the virtue of a short sentence. None of the chapters where Plutarch's rhetorical skills are most plainly in demand, 22, 27, 28, 31, 39 and 42, contains all the features mentioned, but it is worth looking at one in some detail. (The analysis is necessarily focussed on the Greek; the translation, not being literal, will not always reveal the point under consideration.)

37. In 22 Plutarch fires off his second barrel against Herodotus' account of the Sparto-Corinthian attack on Samos in 525. The chapter has two main parts, and an appendix in which his first barrel turns out to have a little left over!

a) The first pair of sentences establishes, by antithesis of Sparta and Corinth, both the new topic and a rising emotional temperature: the word order at the end shows hyperbaton (πάρεργον ... αἰτίας/διαβολῆς), and chiasmus on the noun pair. The next sentence, headed by its verb with Herodotean double prefix (tellingly echoed later in συμπαροξῦναι) rises in mocking quotation to προθύμως and ὑβρίσματος; then it falls away in standard Greek fashion to ὑπάρξαντος. Then come the facts of the case, in two simple sentences with asyndeton, τούτους matching Κερκυραίων παῖδας, the head phrases, while ἔπεμπε and περιεποίησαν match each other at the ends. But τούτους is cleverly picked up by τοῦθ ', and τοῦθ ' sets up διὰ τοῦτο: the anaphora lifts us out of mere narrative mode, and the renewal of energy takes us through the main sentence into a participial phrase beyond, which finishes unexpectedly and powerfully on ἄνδρας. Part one seems over, but the shorter, sharper sentence which follows also finishes on an up with τὴν πόλιν, and sets up a greater climax. Periander's behaviour made sense: but the Corinthians? Plutarch's indignation erupts in the form of a question into the longest sentence of the chapter; two pairs of abstract nouns give it early body; καὶ ταῦτα quickly sustains the energy, and when it might have ceased at τυραννίδος, that very word is used to generate the further flurry of a genitive absolute phrase, a pair of neuter nouns picked out by πᾶν τε ... καὶ πᾶν, a pair of participles and finally a pair of adjectives with which we return to τυραννίδος.

b) In contrast with that length and volume come two little sentences themselves in contrast with each other by means of μέν and δέ and ὕβρισμα and τιμώρημα. The second is cast as another question: Plutarch maintains his tempo. Now he concedes Herodotus' case as a hypothesis but wittily stands Herodotus' conclusion right on its head, pressing the point home with a chiasmus (ἐλεύθεροι ... δουλεύοντες).

c) So far Plutarch has argued on probability. Part two of his attack brings in the evidence. It starts with a third question, the last of the chapter as δήποτε probably indicates, used like *denique* in Latin, and antithesis is again the structural weapon; but because Plutarch has evidence, he can work with shorter, jabbing sentences as he moves to triumph. The first sentence is elaborately arranged, nevertheless, with two pairs of participles and chiasmus of the main verbs; then comes a classic triplet, the middle unit being the shortest to sustain the pace and structure (Κνιδίων δὲ μέμνηνται), the third containing its own triplet of nouns, and all three headed by nouns bared of the definite article. Two more short sentences complete the revelation; the authorities for it all, themselves a pair, are tacked on in a clause of quietly smirking triumph.

d) Again Plutarch might have ended; but in a further eight lines, which match in pattern the previous ten, the smirk becomes a grin. Samos goes into the witness box itself, for the Archias story, and tacked on in indulgent indignation is Herodotus himself to confirm it.

38. One particular element of fluency, as the stylists of the fourth century had realised, was avoidance of hiatus. Russell, *CR* 80 (1966) 181, speaks of Plutarch's comparative carelessness about hiatus in this work, but comparison with *Life of Pericles*, a careful work of very similar length, does not bear him out. Stadter (1989) liv gives some figures for *Life of Pericles*[6] (in brackets are the corresponding figures for this work): hiatus after καί 64 (50), after the article 65 (67), after περί 6 (8), after ὦ 1 (3), after τί 2 (4), after numbers 3 (1), and after punctuation 5 (2). All instances together, Stadter's total is 167; for this work it is 179, omitting quotations. Greater use of crasis (e.g. τἀγαθοῦ in 4/855D, and likewise elsewhere: Häsler XI comments sensibly on this) and of elision (e.g. πρᾶγμ᾽ in 4/855D and elsewhere) could reduce the incidence of apparent hiatus in both works; but in this work we need to note Plutarch's delicate touch in semi-quotation: hiatus is often a sign that though he is not quoting *in extenso* he still has Herodotus' words very much in mind (see 19 especially); I detect 21 such instances. In addition, proper names liable to cause hiatus, like Herodotus, are more frequent in this work. In sum, Plutarch's care in this work is much the same as in Life of Pericles; in 21/859D there is even a small case-study for avoidance of hiatus in the placing of δέ.

39. A second element of fluency is rhythm. Prose writers avoided the rhythms of verse and developed their own, but they shared with the poets the feeling that rhythm mattered more at the end of a unit. In the twenty or so sentences of 22, five end - ˘ - x (Stadter calls this one especially favoured; A.W. de Groot, quoted by Hillyard (xxiv), says it accounts for 29% of all Plutarch's clausulae), and two more end in a variant of it, - ˘ ˘ ˘ x. Rhythm is thus another factor in choice of vocabulary and shaping of phrases. On the other hand, one sentence in 22 ends in a rhythm which Stadter says Plutarch avoided: - - - x, δουλεύοντες: in context, a deliberate harshness.

40. But the most notable linguistic feature of *The Malice of Herodotus* takes us back to the first words of 22: οὐ μὴν ἀλλά. It is Plutarch's use of particles. Homer and the playwrights use particles in abundance, and Plato in superabundance; they are one of the most striking features of classical Greek at its richest. In later Greek they fell out of use; in modern Greek καί and ἀλλά are virtually the only survivors. The decay is commonly dated to the Hellenistic period, which would make Plutarch's performance with them in this work a virtuoso revival. Stadter (1989) lv remarks 'Plutarch shares the general decline in variety of connecting particles found in Hellenistic Greek. Three particles, δέ, γάρ and οὖν, account for more than 70% of initial sentence connections in the *Pericles*' (δέ 47%, γάρ 13%, οὖν 13%). But Blomqvist 132ff distinguishes between connecting particles and emphatic particles: he finds connecting particles to be as much used in the Hellenistic as in the classical period, but

---

[6]Stadter uses the Teubner text. Since editorial decisions on crasis can make a big difference (Hansen's text shows over 30 crases which Lachenaud's does not), I have used Häsler's text of *Malice of Herodotus* for the comparison here.

emphatic particles, especially δή, are less used. To some extent the change of use reflects a change of genre and style in the surviving literature: less drama and less dialogue. Blomqvist also argues for a concentration on making relationships between whole sentences explicit rather than high-lighting individual moments in sentences. He points additionally (146) to the radical change in the pronunciation of Greek, from a pitch accent to stress (see Allen 94 and 130) but puts the change 'probably ... before the first century A.D.' Allen puts it later: it may have been occurring in Plutarch's own lifetime. If Allen is right, Plutarch was just in time to be in touch with a living tradition; soon afterwards the new stress accent made the emphatic particles redundant, and only educated Atticists could keep them in play.

41. Plutarch was certainly an educated Atticist, but not a linguistic antiquarian. Lesky, *A History of Greek Literature*, London 1966, 825, observes 'Atticism was flourishing when Plutarch wrote but ... he ... proved to be a man of moderation. He joined neither in the pursuit of rare Attic words, nor did he bar elements of Koine[7] from his diction, so that his style belongs to the Hellenistic tradition.' In Plutarch's use of the particles, at least in this work, that judgement is well justified. *The Malice of Herodotus* is an argumentative work, and we should expect not only the attempt to clarify relationships noted by Blomqvist in the connecting particles, but some opportunity to mark individual emphases, the job of the emphatic particles.

42. Let us return to statistics. In this work, omitting the quotations and acknowledging some uncertainty about what is and what is not a new sentence (γάρ is likely to be overrated, since even when it sets up a parenthesis, the preceding stop is usually more than a comma), I reckon that δέ connects 35% of the sentences (over a quarter of those 35% are set up by μέν, but μέν and δέ are more commonly used together within a sentence) and γάρ starts 19%. Asyndeton accounts for a further 6%; ἀλλά, καί and οὖν do 5% each; καίτοι and τοίνυν 4% each; demonstratives 3%. The remaining 14% is shared between relative pronouns and adverbs, εἶτα, καί μήν, μέντοι, ὥσπερ, διό, οὐ μήν ἀλλά, καί γάρ, ἐπεί, δή, ἀλλά δή (which all occur at least twice), ἀλλά γάρ, ἆρ' οὖν, οὐκοῦν, γοῦν, γε μήν, ἤ and ὡς: a generous and lively spread! Particles used for emphasis within a sentence are by contrast five times less numerous than particles used for connection: commonest is καί with its negatives οὐδέ and μηδέ (together over half); then γε and μέν *solitarium*; γοῦν and δή occur thrice each; τοι not at all. More noteworthy are the particles used for structure within a sentence; I count nearly twice as many instances of these as of emphatic particles, and I omit from this count δέ and καί. μέν ... δέ and οὐ/μή ... ἀλλά (and its variants) are much the most frequent; τε ... καί and οὔτε ... οὔτε are also significant. καὶ ταῦτα occurs three times, and ἆρ' οὐκ and ἤ που *in apodosi* once each. Under all headings the use of particles is apt and various.

43. I called this work earlier rather an oddity. Modern readers of it, especially if they are primarily interested in ancient history, are likely to be puzzled, at least at first. It has its contribution to make to our knowledge of ancient history, and

---

[7] See 28/863Fn.

for what there is we are bound to be grateful; but the facts come incidentally, and when Plutarch had read so much that is now lost, when he saw the uses of material evidence, when he knew Herodotus so well, we shall sooner sigh for what this work is not than appreciate what it is. It will surely sharpen and increase our appreciation of Herodotus, and that is well worth while; but it is on its own terms a notable piece of special pleading, the by-work of a man marvellously busy with greater works who yet thought fit to construct this passionate protest against the Father of History. Plutarch writes with fluency and wit and well-sustained energy: the work is an excellent example of the uses and abuses of a literary education.

Note on Text and Translation

Two principal MSS of *The Malice of Herodotus* have survived to us; they show slightly different texts. They are designated B and E, and are both in Paris. E contains all that survives of Plutarch, in a collection begun by the Byzantine scholar Maximus Planudes (1255–1305) shortly before 1300; it was written some time in the fourteenth century (see N.G. Wilson, 'Some notable manuscripts misattributed,' *GRBS* 16 (1975) 95–7). B was written a century later, and contains a selection of Plutarch's work. There is no consensus about the relationship between the two texts.

Modern texts have been established by L. Pearson in 1965 for the Loeb Classical Library, by B. Häsler in 1978 for the Teubner series (replacing that of G.N. Bernardakis), and by G. Lachenaud in 1981 for the Budé series. In 1979 P.A. Hansen produced a text of the work on its own.

It is a difficult text to establish, and in some places impossible: for instance, both MSS indicate gaps (this happens twice in the first ten lines) where the text had at some previous stage become indecipherable for a determinate space; other gaps are suspected though not indicated. I have not sought to establish my own text and have not normally discussed textual questions in the commentary. I have profited most from study of Hansen's work, and would have used his text, but it has several flaws as printed and is in other ways unsuitable for photocopying. Lachenaud's text, which is, with permission, reproduced here, is both sound and suitable, and the translation follows it, except sometimes in the quotation of Herodotus (see below).

For Herodotus I have used the text of C. Hude in the Oxford Classical texts series (third edition 1927), but I have also consulted Vol. I, containing books I to 4, of the new text by H.B. Rosén in the Teubner series (Leipzig 1987–), and have preferred its readings where they differ. Plutarch's quotation of Herodotus is discussed in the Introduction; it is tempting, and perhaps sometimes right, to approximate the quotations to their Herodotean form, but Hansen's warning, expressed several times in his *Apparatus Criticus* and implicit at other points in it, seems to me essentially right: *cave ipsum Plutarchum ex Herodoto corrigas.* I have sometimes in the commentary disagreed with Lachenaud's text for this reason.

In translation my aim has been English which would represent not only the words of the text but something also of Plutarch's energy and flow. It is not, therefore, a word for word translation; nor, I hope, is it unliteral without fair cause. There are four particular problems: irony, which is an important weapon in argument but hard to hear in print; rhetorical devices, such as question and apostrophe, of which English is sparing; long sentences; and quotation of poetry. I have rendered the verses in rhyming decasyllables, except in 42/873C. The quotations of Herodotus are, with permission, from Aubrey de Selincourt's Penguin translation (revised edition 1972); where variations from it occur, either they represent Plutarch's own variations from Herodotus' text or they bring de Selincourt's English closer to it; important variations are dealt with in the commentary. I have done this for the sake of students whose knowledge of

Herodotus is owed to de Selincourt. Quotations of Herodotus (but not paraphrases) are marked in the translation by double inverted commas; of all other authors by single inverted comr as. References to Herodotus, whether by quotation or paraphrase or mere mention, are in round brackets; so too are references for the ten sets of verses as gathered by Campbell under Simonides.

Select Bibliography

Not all books and articles listed here are referred to specifically; those that are, are cited as shown. Other books and articles are cited in full *ad loc.*

ATL	Merritt, B.D., Wade-Gery, H.T. and McGregor, M.F. *The Athenian tribute lists* (4 vols.), Cambridge Mass. and Princeton 1939–53
Allen	Allen, W.S. *Vox Graeca*[3], Cambridge 1987
Barrow	Barrow, R.H. *Plutarch and his times*, London 1967
Bergk	Bergk, T. *Poetae lyrici Graeci*[4] (3 vols.), Leipzig 1878–82
Blomqvist	Blomqvist, J. *Greek particles in Hellenistic prose*, Lund 1969
Browning	Browning, R. *Medieval and modern Greek*, London 1969
Buck	Buck, R.J. *History of Boeotia*, Edmonton 1979
Burn 1960	Burn, A.R. *The Lyric Age of Greece*, London 1960
Burn 1972	Burn, A.R. *Introduction to de Selincourt* (see below)
Campbell	Campbell, D.A. *Greek Lyric III*, Harvard UP 1991 (Loeb library series)
Cartledge 1979	Cartledge, P.A. *Sparta and Lakonia*, London 1979
Cartledge 1982	'Sparta and Samos: a special relationship?' *CQ* 76 (1982) 243–65
Cook	Cook, J.M. *The Persian empire*, London 1983
Dascalakis	Dascalakis, A. *Problèmes historiques autour de la bataille des Thermopyles*, Paris 1962
Davies	Davies, J.K. *Athenian propertied families 600–300*, Oxford 1971
Denniston	Denniston, J.D. *The Greek particles*[2], Oxford 1954
Dover	Dover, K.J. *Greek word order*, Cambridge 1960
Emlyn-Jones	Emlyn-Jones, C.J. *The Ionians and Hellenism*, London 1980
Evans	Evans, J.A.S. *Herodotus explorer of the past*, Princeton 1991
FGrH	Jacoby, F. *Die fragmente der Griechischen Historiker*, Berlin/Leiden 1923–58
FHG	Müller, C. and T. *Fragmenta historicorum Graecorum* (5 vols.), Paris 1841–70
Fornara	Fornara, C.W. *Herodotus, an interpretative essay*, Oxford 1971
Forrest	Forrest, W.G. *History of Sparta 950–192 B.C.*, London 1968
Frost	Frost, F.J. *Plutarch's Themistocles, a historical commentary*, Princeton 1980
G H	*Greece Geographical handbook* (3 vols.), Naval Intelligence Division, 1944

Goodwin	Goodwin, W.W. *Syntax of the moods and tenses of the Greek verb*[2], London 1889
Gould	Gould, J. *Herodotus*, London 1989
Griffith	Griffith, M. *Prometheus Bound*, Cambridge 1983
HCT	Gomme, A.W. and others *Historical commentary on Thucydides* (5 vols.), Oxford 1945–81
H & W	How, W.W. and Wells, J. *A commentary on Herodotus* (2 vols.), Oxford 1928
Hansen	Hansen, P.A. *Plutarch, The Malice of Herodotus*, Amsterdam 1979
Hanson	Hanson, V.D. *The western way of war*, London 1989
Hart	Hart, J. *Herodotus and Greek history*, London 1982
Häsler	Häsler, B. *Plutarchus, The Malice of Herodotus*, Leipzig 1978 (Teubner series: *Moralia* V 2,2)
Hauvette	Hauvette, A. *Hérodote, historien des guerres médiques*, Paris 1894
Helmbold	Helmbold, W.C. and O'Neil, E.N. *Plutarch's Quotations*, Baltimore 1959
Hignett	Hignett, C. *Xerxes' invasion of Greece*, Oxford 1963
Hillyard	Hillyard, B.P. *Plutarch, de Audiendo, a text and commentary*, New York 1981
Hooker	Hooker, J.T. *The ancient Spartans*, London 1980
Hornblower 1983	Hornblower, S. *The Greek world 479–323*, London 1983
Hornblower 1987	Hornblower, S. *Thucydides*, London 1987
Hude	Hude, C. *Herodotus*, Oxford 1927[3] (Oxford Classical Texts series: 2 vols.)
IG	*Inscriptiones Graecae*[3], Berlin 1981–
Immerwahr	Immerwahr, H.R. *Form and thought in Herodotus*, Cleveland 1966
Jones 1918	Jones, W.H.S. and others *Pausanias, Description of Greece* (5 vols.), Harvard UP 1918–55 (Loeb Library series)
Jones 1966	Jones, C.P. 'Towards a chronology of Plutarch's works'. *JRS* 56 (1966) 61–74
Jones 1971	Jones, C.P. *Plutarch and Rome*, Oxford, 1971
Jones 1980	Jones, R.M. *The Platonism of Plutarch*, New York 1980
LSJ	Liddell, H.G. and Scott, R. *A Greek-English Lexicon*[9], rev. Sir H. Stuart Jones, Oxford, 1940
Lachenaud	Lachenaud, G. *Plutarque, de la malignité d'Hérodote*, Paris 1981 (Budé series: *Moralia* XII[1])
Legrand	Legrand, Ph-E. in *Mélanges Gustave Glotz II*, Paris 1932
Legrand 1932	Legrand, Ph-E. and others *Hérodote*, Paris 1932–54 (Budé series; 11 vols.)
Levi 1955	Levi, M.A. *Plutarcho e il quinto secolo*, Milan 1955
Levi 1971	Levi, P. *Pausanias Guide to Greece*, Harmondsworth 1971
Lewis	Lewis, D.M. *Sparta and Persia*, Leiden 1977
Lexicon	Powell, J.E. *Lexicon to Herodotus*, Cambridge 1937
Lloyd	Lloyd, A.B. *Herodotus book II* (3 vols.), Leiden 1975–88

M–L   Meiggs, R. and Lewis, D.M. *A selection of Greek historical inscriptions*, Oxford 1969

Macan   Macan, R.W. *Herodotus books 7–9* (2 vols.), London 1908

Mediterranean Pilot   *Mediterranean Pilot* IV[10], Royal Navy 1987 (Hydrographic Dept.)

Moore   Moore, J.M. *Aristotle and Xenophon on democracy and oligarchy*[2], London 1983

Myres   Myres, J.L. *Herodotus father of history*, Oxford 1953

PG   Burn, A.R. *Persia and the Greeks*[2], London 1984

Parke 1956   Parke, H.W. and Wormell, D.W. *The Delphic oracle* (2 vols.), Oxford 1956

Parke 1977   Parke, H.W. *Festivals of the Athenians*, London 1977

Pearson   Pearson, L. *Plutarch, The Malice of Herodotus*, Harvard UP 1965 (Loeb Library series: *Moralia XI*)

Pelling   Pelling, C.B.R. *Life of Antony*, Cambridge 1988

Podlecki   Podlecki, A.J. *The Life of Themistocles*, Montreal 1975

Powell   Powell, J.E. *The History of Herodotus*, Cambridge 1939

Pritchett 1971   Pritchett, W.K. *The Greek state at war* (5 vols.), Berkeley 1971–91

Pritchett 1982   Pritchett, W.K. *Studies in ancient Greek topography* (4 vols.), Berkeley 1982

Rosén   Rosén, H.B. *Herodotus*, Leipzig 1987- (Teubner series; 2 vols.) vol 1 1–4

Russell   Russell, D.A. *Plutarch*, London 1973

de Sainte Croix   de Sainte Croix, G. *The origins of the Peloponnesian war*, London 1972

Salmon   Salmon, J.B. *Wealthy Corinth* Oxford 1984

Sansone   Sansone, D. *Lives of Aristeides and Cato* (Minor), Warminster 1989

Scott-Kilvert   Scott-Kilvert, I. *The rise and fall of Athens*, Harmondsworth 1960

de Selincourt   de Selincourt, A. *Herodotus the histories*, Harmondsworth 1972

Stadter 1965   Stadter, P.A. *Plutarch's historical methods*, Harvard UP 1965

Stadter 1989   Stadter, P.A. *A commentary on Plutarch's Pericles*, Chapel Hill 1989

Shipley   Shipley, D.G.J. *A History of Samos 800–180 B.C.*, Oxford 1987

Talbert   Talbert, R.J.A. *Plutarch on Sparta*, Harmondsworth 1988

Tarn   Tarn, W.W. 'The fleet of Xerxes' *JHS* 28 (1908) 202–33

Teodorsson   Teodorsson, S-T. *A commentary on Plutarch's Table Talks* vol I, Göteborg 1989

Wardman   Wardman, A.E. *Plutarch's Lives*, London 1974

Wyttenbach   Wyttenbach, D. *Plutarchi Moralia* vol. 8 Index Graecitatis (2 vols.) Oxford 1830

Ziegler   Ziegler, K. *Plutarchos von Chaironeia*, Stuttgart 1964

PLUTARCH: ON THE MALICE OF HERODOTUS

ΠΕΡΙ ΤΗΣ ΗΡΟΔΟΤΟΥ ΚΑΚΟΗΘΕΙΑΣ   854 E

1 Τοῦ Ἡροδότου ⟨τοῦ Ἁλικαρνασσέως⟩ πολλοὺς μέν,
ὦ Ἀλέξανδρε, καὶ ἡ λέξις ὡς ἀφελὴς καὶ δίχα πόνου καὶ
ῥᾳδίως ἐπιτρέχουσα τοῖς πράγμασιν ἐξηπάτηκε · πλείονες
δὲ τοῦτο πρὸς τὸ ἦθος αὐτοῦ πεπόνθασιν. Οὐ γὰρ μόνον,
ὥς φησιν ὁ Πλάτων, « τῆς ἐσχάτης ἀδικίας μὴ ὄντα δοκεῖν
εἶναι δίκαιον », ἀλλὰ καὶ κακοηθείας ἄκρας ἔργον, εὐκολίαν
μιμούμενον καὶ ἁπλότητα δυσφώρατον εἶναι. ⟨Ἐπειδὴ δὲ
κακοηθείᾳ⟩ μάλιστα πρός τε Βοιωτοὺς καὶ Κορινθίους F
κέχρηται, μηδὲ τῶν ἄλλων τινὸς ἀπεσχημένος, οἶμαι προ-
σήκειν ἡμῖν ἀμύνεσθαι ὑπὲρ τῶν προγόνων ἅμα καὶ τῆς
ἀληθείας, κατ' αὐτὸ τοῦτο τῆς γραφῆς τὸ μέρος · ἐπεὶ
τά γ' ἄλλα ψεύσματα καὶ πλάσματα βουλομένοις ἐπεξιέναι
πολλῶν ἂν βιβλίων δεήσειεν. Ἀλλὰ

     δεινὸν τὸ τᾶς Πειθοῦς πρόσωπον,

ὥς φησιν ὁ Σοφοκλῆς, | μάλιστα δ' ὅταν ἐν λόγῳ χάριν 855 A
ἔχοντι καὶ δύναμιν τοσαύτην ἐγγένηται τάς τ' ἄλλας
ἀτοπίας καὶ τὸ ἦθος ἀποκρύπτειν τοῦ συγγραφέως.
Ὁ μὲν γὰρ Φίλιππος ἔλεγε πρὸς τοὺς ἀφισταμένους
Ἕλληνας αὐτοῦ καὶ τῷ Τίτῳ προστιθεμένους ὅτι λειότερον
μέν, μακρότερον δὲ κλοιὸν μεταλαμβάνουσιν · ἡ δ' Ἡροδότου κακοήθεια λειοτέρα μέν ἐστιν ἀμέλει καὶ μαλακωτέρα
τῆς Θεοπόμπου, καθάπτεται δὲ καὶ λυπεῖ μᾶλλον, ὥσπερ
οἱ κρύφα διὰ στενοῦ παραπνέοντες ἄνεμοι τῶν διακεχυ-
μένων.

Δοκεῖ δή μοι βέλτιον εἶναι τύπῳ τινὶ λαβόντας ὅσα
κοινῇ μὴ καθαρᾶς μηδ' εὐμενοῦς ἐστιν ἀλλὰ κακοήθους B
οἷον ἴχνη καὶ γνωρίσματα διηγήσεως, εἰς ταῦτα τῶν

Plutarch: Upon the Malice of Herodotus

1. Many people, my dear Alexander, have been deceived by the style of Herodotus of Halicarnassus: it is so smooth and unlaborious, and it ripples through events so lightly. But even more have been deceived about the man himself. As Plato remarks, 'to seem good without being so is a sign of utter wickedness;' but more than that, to act decent and honest and get away with it is the very pinnacle of malice. Since he has employed malice against the Boeotians and against the Corinthians in F particular while sparing no one else either, I think it becomes my duty to come to the rescue, both for my ancestors and for truth, as far as that aspect of his work goes. It would take many volumes to work through all his fictions and fabrications.

'Persuasion's face,' as Sophocles says, 'is fearsome to behold,' 855 A especially when it is part of a style so charming and effective as to conceal not just an author's historical but especially his personal flaws. Philip of Macedon used to say when Greeks were deserting him and joining Titus that their new collar would chafe less and last longer. The malice in Herodotus is certainly less chafing and gentler than that in Theopompus, but it takes better hold and bites deeper, like winds that come as draughts through cracks compared with those that blow in the open.

Best procedure will be to grasp in outline the things which by common consent serve as signs of a narrative made in malice rather than in open B and honest intent, and then to test each item to be examined against them

ἐξεταζομένων ἕκαστον, ἂν ἐναρμόττῃ, τίθεσθαι.

2 Πρῶτον μὲν οὖν ὁ τοῖς δυσχερεστάτοις ὀνόμασι καὶ ῥήμασιν, ἐπιεικεστέρων παρόντων, ἐν τῷ λέγειν τὰ πεπραγμένα χρώμενος — ὥσπερ εἰ θειασμῷ προσκείμενον ἄγαν ἐξὸν εἰπεῖν τὸν Νικίαν ὁ δὲ θεόληπτον προσείποι, ἢ θρασύτητα καὶ μανίαν Κλέωνος μᾶλλον ἢ κουφολογίαν — οὐκ εὐμενής ἐστιν, ἀλλ᾽ οἷον ἀπολαύων τῷ † σοφῶς † διηγεῖσθαι τοῦ πράγματος.

3 Δεύτερον, ὅτῳ κακὸν πρόσεστιν ἄλλως τῇ δ᾽ ἱστορίᾳ μὴ προσῆκον, ὁ δὲ συγγραφεὺς ἐπιδράττεται τούτου καὶ παρεμβάλλει τοῖς πράγμασιν οὐδὲν δεομένοις, ἀλλὰ τὴν C διήγησιν ἐπεξάγων καὶ κυκλούμενος, ὅπως ἐμπεριλάβῃ ἀτύχημά τινος ἢ πρᾶξιν ἄτοπον καὶ οὐ χρηστήν, δῆλός ἐστιν ἡδόμενος τῷ κακολογεῖν. Ὅθεν ὁ Θουκυδίδης οὐδὲ τῶν Κλέωνος ἁμαρτημάτων ἀφθόνων ὄντων ἐποιήσατο σαφῆ διήγησιν, Ὑπερβόλου τε τοῦ δημαγωγοῦ θιγὼν ἑνὶ ῥήματι καὶ μοχθηρὸν ἄνθρωπον προσειπὼν ἀφῆκε· Φίλιστος δὲ καὶ Διονυσίου τῶν πρὸς τοὺς βαρβάρους ἀδικιῶν ὅσαι μὴ συνεπλέκοντο τοῖς Ἑλληνικοῖς πράγμασιν ἁπάσας παρέλιπεν. Αἱ γὰρ ἐκβολαὶ καὶ παρατροπαὶ τῆς ἱστορίας μάλιστα τοῖς μύθοις δίδονται καὶ ταῖς ἀρχαιολο- D γίαις, ἔτι δὲ πρὸς τοὺς ἐπαίνους· ὁ δὲ παρενθήκην λόγου τὸ βλασφημεῖν καὶ ψέγειν ποιούμενος ἔοικεν εἰς τὴν τραγικὴν ἐμπίπτειν κατάραν

θνητῶν ἐκλέγων τὰς συμφοράς.

4 Καὶ μὴν τό γ᾽ ἀντίστροφον τούτῳ παντὶ δῆλον ὡς καλοῦ τινος καὶ ἀγαθοῦ παράλειψίς ἐστιν, ἀνυπεύθυνον δοκοῦν πρᾶγμα εἶναι, γιγνόμενον δὲ κακοήθως ἄνπερ ἐμπίπτῃ τὸ παραλειφθὲν εἰς τόπον προσήκοντα τῇ ἱστορίᾳ· τὸ γὰρ ἀπροθύμως ἐπαινεῖν τοῦ ψέγοντα χαίρειν οὐκ ἐπιεικέστερον, ἀλλὰ πρὸς τῷ μὴ ἐπιεικέστερον ἴσως καὶ χεῖρον.

to see if they fit.

2. First, it is no honest-minded writer who uses very fierce nouns and verbs in his narrative when soft ones are available, calling Nicias for instance a fanatic when one could say he was rather 'over-inclined to divination', or talking of Cleon's manic boasting rather than of his 'irresponsibility'. For such a writer the pleasure lies in the cleverness of his description.

3. Second, a writer is plainly delighting in his abuse when there is something discreditable on other grounds but irrelevant in a story and he goes for it, foisting it on to his narrative needlessly, and prolonging the C account by a digression just to get in the misfortune or mistake, however inappropriate or futile. Even though Cleon's misdeeds were plentiful, Thucydides gave no clear account of them, and he dealt with Hyperbolus the demagogue in one phrase, calling him 'a wretched character', and leaving it at that. Philistus entirely omitted all those crimes of Dionysius against non-Greeks which were not part of Greek history. Digressions and diversions in a history usually belong in myths and tales of the distant D past, or in paragraphs of praise. Anyone who makes special space for abuse and prejudice seems to be incurring the curse of tragedy, 'for picking out men's miseries'!

4. The opposite of this obviously is omission of good things. That may seem unobjectionable, but if the stuff omitted has a proper place in the narrative, then to omit it is an act of malice. Cold praise is no better than eager censure; rather than no better, it is probably worse.

5 Τέταρτον τοίνυν τίθεμαι σημεῖον οὐκ εὐμενοῦς Ε
ἐν ἱστορίᾳ τρόπου τὸ δυοῖν ἢ πλειόνων περὶ ταὐτοῦ λόγων
ὄντων τῷ χείρονι προστίθεσθαι. Τοῖς γὰρ σοφισταῖς
ἐφεῖται πρὸς ἐργασίαν ἢ δόξαν ἔστιν ὅτε τῶν λόγων
κοσμεῖν τὸν ἥττονα παραλαμβάνοντας· οὐ γὰρ ἐμποιοῦσι
πίστιν ἰσχυρὰν περὶ τοῦ πράγματος οὐδ᾽ ἀρνοῦνται πολλά-
κις εἰς τὸ παράδοξον ἐπιχειρεῖν ὑπὲρ τῶν ἀπίστων·
ὁ δ᾽ ἱστορίαν γράφων ἃ μὲν οἶδεν ἀληθῆ λέγων δίκαιός
ἐστι, τῶν δ᾽ ἀδήλων τὰ βελτίονα δοκῶν ἀληθῶς λέγεσθαι
μᾶλλον ἢ τὰ χείρονα. Πολλοὶ δ᾽ ὅλως τὰ χείρονα παραλεί-
πουσιν· ὥσπερ ἀμέλει περὶ Θεμιστοκλέους Ἔφορος
μὲν εἰπὼν ὅτι τὴν Παυσανίου προδοσίαν ἔγνω καὶ τὰ
πρασσόμενα πρὸς τοὺς βασιλέως στρατηγούς, «ἀλλ᾽ οὐκ Ϝ
ἐπείσθη, φησίν, οὐδὲ προσεδέξατο κοινουμένου καὶ παρα-
καλοῦντος αὐτὸν ἐπὶ τὰς ⟨αὐτὰς⟩ ἐλπίδας·» Θουκυδίδης
δὲ καὶ τὸ παράπαν τὸν λόγον τοῦτον ὡς κατεγνωκὼς
παρῆκεν.

6 Ἔτι τοίνυν ἐπὶ τῶν ὁμολογουμένων πεπρᾶχθαι, τὴν
δ᾽ αἰτίαν ἀφ᾽ ἧς πέπρακται καὶ τὴν διάνοιαν ἐχόντων
ἄδηλον, ὁ πρὸς τὸ χεῖρον εἰκάζων δυσμενής ἐστι καὶ
κακοήθης· ὥσπερ οἱ κωμικοὶ τὸν πόλεμον ὑπὸ τοῦ
Περικλέους ἐκκεκαῦσθαι δι᾽ Ἀσπα|σίαν ἢ διὰ Φειδίαν 856 Α
ἀποφαίνοντες, οὐ φιλοτιμίᾳ τινὶ καὶ φιλονικίᾳ μᾶλλον
στορέσαι τὸ φρόνημα Πελοποννησίων καὶ μηδενὸς ὑφεῖσ-
θαι Λακεδαιμονίοις ἐθελήσαντος. Εἰ μὲν γάρ τις εὐδοκι-
μοῦσιν ἔργοις καὶ πράγμασιν ἐπαινουμένοις αἰτίαν φαύλην
ὑποτίθησι καὶ κατάγεται ταῖς διαβολαῖς εἰς ὑποψίας
ἀτόπους περὶ τῆς ἐν ἀφανεῖ προαιρέσεως τοῦ πράξαντος,
αὐτὸ τὸ πεπραγμένον ἐμφανῶς οὐ δυνάμενος ψέγειν
– ὥσπερ οἱ τὸν ὑπὸ Θήβῃς Ἀλεξάνδρου τοῦ τυράννου
φόνον οὐ μεγαλονοίας οὐδὲ μισοπονηρίας, ζήλου δέ
τινος ἔργον καὶ πάθους γυναικείου τιθέμενοι· καὶ Κάτωνα

5. Fourth mark of unfriendly intent in a historian is to side with the worse E
account of an event when two or more accounts are available. Professors
of rhetoric at times have licence to take on the poorer argument and make
it look good, whether for practice or for show: they are not trying to
persuade for real, and they often admit that they are toiling at
implausibilities just to create an effect. But the historian, properly, should
declare as fact what he knows to be so, and when there is doubt, a better
account should be preferred to a worse. Many historians entirely omit less
creditable versions; in the case of Themistocles, Ephorus says the man
knew of Pausanias' treacherous dealings with the king's generals 'but he F
wasn't persuaded; and when Pausanias let him into the secret and invited
him to share the same hopes, Themistocles wouldn't even entertain the
idea.' Thucydides, on the other hand, has entirely ignored the story,
effectively condemning it.

6. Further, when there is no dispute about what happened but cause and
motive are unclear, anyone going for the worse interpretation shows ill-
will and malice, like the comic poets who claimed the great war was
sparked off by Pericles because of Aspasia, or because of Pheidias, and 856 A
not because of his own proud and combative desire to squash Peloponnesian
arrogance and to yield the Spartans nothing. If a shabby motive is
constructed for deeds of note and acts of renown, and if the insinuation
leads on to inappropriate suspicions about what the doer of the deed
intended personally because it is impossible to attack the deed itself
publicly – compare those who claim that Thebe's murder of the tyrant
Alexander was not an act of high ideals and of hatred for his wickedness
but came of feminine jealousy and passion, or compare those who say

λέγοντες ἑαυτὸν ἀνελεῖν δείσαντα τὸν μετ' αἰκίας θάνατον B ὑπὸ Καίσαρος —, εὔδηλον ὅτι φθόνου καὶ κακοηθείας ὑπερβολὴν οὐ λέλοιπε.

7 Δέχεται δὲ καὶ παρὰ τὸν τρόπον τοῦ ἔργου διήγησις ἱστορικὴ κακοήθειαν, ἂν χρήμασι φάσκῃ μὴ δι' ἀρετῆς κατειργάσθαι τὴν πρᾶξιν, ὡς Φίλιππον ἔνιοι φάσκουσιν· ἂν σὺν οὐδενὶ πόνῳ καὶ ῥᾳδίως ὡς Ἀλέξανδρον· ἂν μὴ φρονίμως ἀλλ' εὐτυχῶς, ὡς Τιμόθεον οἱ ἐχθροί, γράφοντες ⟨ἐν⟩ πίναξιν εἰς κύρτον τινὰ τὰς πόλεις αὐτάς, ἐκείνου καθεύδοντος, ὑποδυομένας. Δῆλον γὰρ ὅτι τῶν πράξεων ἐλαττοῦσι τὸ μέγεθος καὶ τὸ κάλλος οἱ τὸ γενναίως καὶ φιλοπόνως καὶ κατ' ἀρετὴν καὶ δι' αὐτῶν ἀφαιροῦντες. C

8 Ἔστι τοίνυν τοῖς ἀπ' εὐθείας οὓς βούλονται κακῶς λέγουσι δυσκολίαν ἐπικαλεῖν καὶ θρασύτητα καὶ μανίαν, ἐὰν μὴ μετριάζωσιν· οἱ δὲ πλαγίως οἷον ἐξ ἀφανοῦς βέλεσι χρώμενοι ταῖς διαβολαῖς, εἶτα περιιόντες ὀπίσω καὶ ἀναδυόμενοι, τῷ φάσκειν ἀπιστεῖν ἃ πάνυ πιστεύεσθαι θέλουσιν ἀρνούμενοι κακοήθειαν, ἀνελευθερίαν τῇ κακοηθείᾳ προσοφλισκάνουσιν.

9 Ἐγγὺς δὲ τούτων εἰσὶν οἱ τοῖς ψόγοις ἐπαίνους τινὰς παρατιθέντες, ὡς ἐπὶ Σωκράτους Ἀριστόξενος ἀπαίδευτον καὶ ἀμαθῆ καὶ ἀκόλαστον εἰπών, ἐπήνεγκεν « ἀδικία δ' οὐ προσῆν ». Ὥσπερ γὰρ οἱ σύν τινι τέχνῃ D καὶ δεινότητι κολακεύοντες ἔστιν ὅτε πολλοῖς καὶ μακροῖς ἐπαίνοις ψόγους παραμιγνύουσιν ἐλαφρούς, οἷον ἥδυσμα τῇ κολακείᾳ τὴν παρρησίαν ἐμβάλλοντες, οὕτω τὸ κακόηθες εἰς πίστιν ὧν ψέγει προαποτίθεται τὸν ἔπαινον.

10 Ἦν δὲ καὶ πλείονας καταριθμεῖσθαι τῶν χαρακτήρων· ἀρκοῦσι δ' οὗτοι κατανόησιν τοῦ ἀνθρώπου τῆς προαιρέσεως καὶ τοῦ τρόπου παρασχεῖν.

that Cato committed suicide for fear of an undignified death from Caesar   B
–, then obviously we are well beyond normal spite and malice.

7. Historical narrative is also guilty of malice beyond the norm if it says
a success was gained by money and not by courage, as some say of Philip;
or without toil and trouble, as some say of Alexander; or by luck and not
judgement, as his enemies say of Timotheus, drawing pictures to show
the cities tumbling into his lobster-pot of their own accord and him asleep
throughout. Plainly the greatness and glory of deeds are diminished when
the spirit and energy and courage and independence of the doer are taken   C
away.

8. Direct attack upon chosen victims certainly earns a charge of ill-will
and aggressiveness, and of fanaticism unless there is some moderation in
it. But as for those who attack by innuendo, firing from ambush as it were,
and who then turn in their tracks and withdraw, saying they don't
themselves believe what they do want you to believe, by denying malice
they earn a charge of mean-spiritedness to add to their malice.

9. A similar group are those who qualify their attacks with a few words
of approval, like Aristoxenus on Socrates: he called him boorish, ignorant
and mannerless, but added 'There was, however, no evil in him.' People
who can flatter with some skill and force often combine their more   D
plentiful praises with lightly critical remarks; the frankness seasons the
flattery. On the same pattern, malice forks out some praise early on to
make its attacks more convincing.

10. A list of the characteristics of malice could go on, but these are enough
to provide an idea of the fellow's purpose and manner.

11 Πρῶτα δὴ πάντων ὥσπερ ἀφ᾽ Ἑστίας ἀρξάμενος
Ἰοῦς τῆς Ἰνάχου θυγατρός, ἣν πάντες Ἕλληνες ἐκτεθειῶσ-
θαι νομίζουσι ταῖς τιμαῖς ὑπὸ τῶν βαρβάρων καὶ καταλιπεῖν ὄνομα πολλαῖς μὲν θαλάτταις, πορθμῶν δὲ τοῖς E
μεγίστοις ἀφ᾽ αὐτῆς διὰ τὴν δόξαν, ἀρχὴν δὲ καὶ πηγὴν
τῶν ἐπιφανεστάτων καὶ βασιλικωτάτων γενῶν παρασχεῖν,
ταύτην ὁ γενναῖος ἐπιδοῦναί φησιν ἑαυτὴν Φοίνιξι
φορτηγοῖς, ὑπὸ τοῦ ναυκλήρου διαφθαρεῖσαν ἑκουσίως
καὶ φοβουμένην μὴ κύουσα φανερὰ γένηται. Καὶ καταψεύ-
δεται Φοινίκων ὡς ταῦτα περὶ αὐτῆς λεγόντων, Περσῶν
δὲ τοὺς λογίους μαρτυρεῖν φήσας ὅτι ⟨τὴν Ἰοῦν⟩
μετ᾽ ἄλλων γυναικῶν οἱ Φοίνικες ἀφαρπάσειαν, εὐθὺς
ἀποφαίνεται γνώμην τὸ κάλλιστον ἔργον καὶ μέγιστον
τῆς Ἑλλάδος ἀβελτερίᾳ τὸν Τρωικὸν πόλεμον γενέσθαι διὰ
γυναῖκα φαύλην. «Δῆλον γάρ, φησίν, ὅτι, εἰ μὴ αὐταὶ F
ἐβούλοντο, οὐκ ἂν ἡρπάζοντο». Καὶ τοὺς θεοὺς τοίνυν
ἀβέλτερα ποιεῖν λέγωμεν, ὑπὲρ τῶν Λεύκτρου θυγατέρων
βιασθεισῶν μηνίοντας Λακεδαιμονίοις καὶ κολάζοντας
Αἴαντα διὰ τὴν Κασάνδρας ὕβριν· δῆλα γὰρ δὴ καθ᾽
Ἡρόδοτον ὅτι, εἰ μὴ αὐταὶ ἐβούλοντο, οὐκ ἂν ὑβρίζοντο.
Καίτοι καὶ Ἀριστομένη φησὶν αὐτὸς ὑπὸ Λακεδαιμονίων
ζῶντα συναρπασθῆναι, καὶ Φιλοποίμην ὕστερον ὁ τῶν
Ἀχαιῶν στρατηγὸς τὸ αὐτὸ τοῦτ᾽ ἔπαθε, | καὶ Ῥηγοῦλον 857 A
ἐχειρώσαντο Καρχηδόνιοι τὸν Ῥωμαίων ὕπατον· ὧν ἔργον
εὑρεῖν μαχιμωτέρους καὶ πολεμικωτέρους ἄνδρας. Ἀλλὰ
θαυμάζειν οὐκ ἄξιον, ὅπου καὶ παρδάλεις ζώσας καὶ
τίγρεις συναρπάζουσιν ἄνθρωποι· Ἡρόδοτος δὲ κατηγορεῖ
τῶν βιασθεισῶν γυναικῶν, ἀπολογούμενος ὑπὲρ τῶν
ἁρπασάντων.

12 Οὕτω δὲ φιλοβάρβαρός ἐστιν, ὥστε Βούσιριν
ἀπολύσας τῆς λεγομένης ἀνθρωποθυσίας καὶ ξενο-
κτονίας, καὶ πᾶσιν Αἰγυπτίοις θειότητα πολλὴν καὶ

11. Herodotus makes his start on his own hearth, as it were, with Io daughter of Inachus (1.1.3). The universal Greek opinion is that non-Greeks have deified her in their worship, that her fame has bestowed her name on many seas and on major straits, and that she has been the E fountainhead of distinguished royal families. Our excellent author says (5.2) she gave herself up to Phoenician traders when she had been seduced by their captain, with her own consent, and was afraid of the pregnancy starting to show. That, he falsely alleges, is the Phoenician tale of Io. After claiming "learned Persians" (1.1.1) in evidence for the story that Io was carried off by the Phoenicians with other women, he at once reveals his view, that the greatest and most glorious deed of Greece, the Trojan war, was a piece of folly caused by a worthless woman; it is plain, he says F (4.2), that no young woman allows herself to be abducted if she does not wish to be.

Are we then to say that the gods too were acting in folly when they were angry with the Spartans for the violation of the daughters of Leuctrus and when they punished Ajax for his violation of Cassandra? "It is obvious," according to Herodotus, "that no young woman allows herself to be raped if she does not wish to be." And yet he himself says that Aristomenes was carried off alive by the Spartans, and the same thing happened later to Philopoemen the Achaeans' general, and Regulus the 857 A Roman consul was taken alive by the Carthaginians. It would be some task to find better warriors than those! But we must not be surprised: men even carry off leopards and tigers alive, but Herodotus goes for the ruined women and constructs a defence for their raptors.

12. He is such a barbarophile that (2.45) he acquits Busiris of alleged human sacrifice and guest-murder. He says there is a strong sense of religion (37.1 and 65.1) and justice amongst all Egyptians, and he turns

δικαιοσύνην μαρτυρήσας ἐφ' Ἕλληνας ἀναστρέφει τὸ
μύσος τοῦτο καὶ τὴν μιαιφονίαν. Ἐν γὰρ τῇ δευτέρᾳ
βίβλῳ Μενέλαόν φησι παρὰ Πρωτέως ἀπολαβόντα τὴν B
Ἑλένην καὶ τιμηθέντα δωρεαῖς μεγάλαις ἀδικώτατον
ἀνθρώπων γενέσθαι καὶ κάκιστον· ὑπὸ γὰρ ἀπλοίας
συνεχόμενον «ἐπιτεχνήσασθαι πρᾶγμα οὐχ ὅσιον, καὶ
λαβόντα δύο παιδία ἀνδρῶν ἐπιχωρίων ἔντομά σ⟨φεα⟩
ποιῆσαι· μισηθέντα δ' ἐπὶ τούτῳ καὶ διωκόμενον οἴχεσθαι
φεύγοντα νηυσὶν ἰθὺ ἐπὶ Λιβύης. Τοῦτον δὲ τὸν λόγον οὐκ
οἶδ' ὅστις Αἰγυπτίων εἴρηκεν· ἀλλὰ τἀναντία πολλαὶ
μὲν Ἑλένης πολλαὶ δὲ Μενελάου τιμαὶ διαφυλάττονται
παρ' αὐτοῖς.

13 Ὁ δὲ συγγραφεὺς ἐπιμένων Πέρσας μέν φησι
⟨παισὶ⟩ μίσγεσθαι παρ' Ἑλλήνων μαθόντας – καίτοι
πῶς Ἕλλησι Πέρσαι διδασκάλια ταύτης ὀφείλουσι τῆς C
ἀκολασίας, παρ' οἷς ὀλίγου δεῖν ὑπὸ πάντων ὁμολογεῖται
παῖδας ἐκτετμῆσθαι πρὶν Ἑλληνικὴν ἰδεῖν θάλασσαν ; –
Ἕλληνας δὲ μαθεῖν παρ' Αἰγυπτίων πομπὰς καὶ πανηγύ-
ρεις, καὶ τὸ τοὺς δώδεκα θεοὺς σέβεσθαι· Διονύσου δὲ καὶ
τοὔνομα παρ' Αἰγυπτίων Μελάμποδα μαθεῖν καὶ διδάξαι
τοὺς ἄλλους Ἕλληνας· μυστήρια δὲ καὶ τὰς περὶ Δήμητραν τελετὰς ὑπὸ τῶν Δαναοῦ θυγατέρων ἐξ Αἰγύπτου
κομισθῆναι. Καὶ τύπτεσθαι μὲν Αἰγυπτίους φησὶ καὶ
πενθεῖν, ⟨ὃν δ'⟩ οὐ βούλεσθαι αὐτὸς ὀνομάζειν, ἀλλ'
«εὐστόμως κεῖσθαι» περὶ τῶν θείων. Ἡρακλέα δὲ καὶ
Διόνυσον, οὓς μὲν Αἰγύπτιοι ⟨σέβονται⟩, ἀποφαίνων D
θεούς, ⟨οὓς⟩ Ἕλληνες δέ, ἀνθρώπους καταγεγηρακότας,
οὐδαμοῦ ταύτην προὔθετο τὴν εὐλάβειαν· καίτοι καὶ
τὸν Αἰγύπτιον Ἡρακλέα τῶν δευτέρων θεῶν γενέσθαι
λέγει καὶ τὸν Διόνυσον τῶν τρίτων, ὡς ἀρχὴν ἐσχηκότας
γενέσεως καὶ οὐκ ὄντας ἀϊδίους· ἀλλ' ὅμως ἐκείνους
μὲν ἀποφαίνει θεούς, τούτοις δ' ὡς φθιτοῖς καὶ ἥρωσιν

the pollution of murder back upon the Greeks! In the second book (119) he says that Menelaus got Helen back from Proteus, received some fine B presents and then turned very nasty: being kept from sailing by the winds "he devised a wicked deed: he took two Egyptian children and offered them in sacrifice. For this he was hated and was pursued but managed to escape with his ships to Libya." I have no idea what Egyptian produced this tale; in direct contradiction, both Helen and Menelaus are the recipients of many honours in Egypt which still go on.

13. Our historian keeps on at it: he says (1.135) that the Persians learnt "sexual intercourse with boys" from the Greeks (yet how can Persians C owe lessons in this grossness to the Greeks when there is almost universal agreement that they practised castration before they ever saw the Aegean?) and (2.58) that the Greeks learnt "processions and festivals" from the Egyptians, including (2.4.2) the worship of the twelve gods; that the very name of Dionysus was picked up from the Egyptians by Melampus (49.1) who taught it to the rest of the Greeks; that the mysteries and rituals concerning Demeter (171.3) were brought from Egypt by the daughters of Danaus. He says the Egyptians "beat their breasts" in lament, but for what god he will not say (61): "I will say no more" (171.1) about the rites. But he was not at all so scrupulous about Heracles (43 and 145/6) and D Dionysus (145/6): the ones that the Egyptians worship he presents as gods, whereas those the Greeks worship are humans "grown old." And yet he says (145.1) that the Egyptian Heracles belongs to the second set of gods and Dionysus to the third, so that they are not eternal, but have a date of birth. Even so he presents the Egyptian ones as gods whereas the Greek ones he thinks (44.5) should not be offered sacrifice as gods but

ἐναγίζειν οἴεται δεῖν ἀλλὰ μὴ θύειν ὡς θεοῖς. Τὰ αὐτὰ
καὶ περὶ Πανὸς εἴρηκε, ταῖς Αἰγυπτίων ἀλαζονείαις καὶ
μυθολογίαις τὰ σεμνότατα καὶ ἁγνότατα τῶν Ἑλληνικῶν
ἱερῶν ἀνατρέπων.

14 Καὶ οὐ τοῦτο δεινόν · ἀλλ᾿ ἀναγαγὼν εἰς Περσέα Ε
τὸ Ἡρακλέους γένος Περσέα μὲν Ἀσσύριον γεγονέναι λέγει
κατὰ τὸν Περσῶν λόγον · « Οἱ δὲ Δωριέων, φησίν, ἡγεμόνες
φαίνοιντ᾿ ἂν Αἰγύπτιοι ἰθαγενέες ἐόντες, καταλέγοντι τοὺς
ἄνω ⟨ἀπὸ⟩ Δανάης τῆς Ἀκρισίου πατέρας.» Τὸν γὰρ
Ἔπαφον καὶ τὴν Ἰὼ καὶ τὸν Ἴασον καὶ τὸν Ἄργον ὅλως
ἀφῆκε, φιλοτιμούμενος μὴ μόνον ἄλλους Ἡρακλεῖς
Αἰγυπτίους καὶ Φοίνικας ἀποφαίνειν, ἀλλὰ καὶ τοῦτον, ὃν
αὐτὸς τρίτον γεγονέναι φησίν, εἰς βαρβάρους ἀποξενῶσαι
τῆς Ἑλλάδος. Καίτοι τῶν παλαιῶν καὶ λογίων ἀνδρῶν οὐχ
Ὅμηρος, οὐχ Ἡσίοδος, οὐκ Ἀρχίλοχος, οὐ Πείσανδρος, F
οὐ Στησίχορος, οὐκ Ἀλκμάν, οὐ Πίνδαρος, Αἰγυπτίου
ἔσχον λόγον Ἡρακλέους ἢ Φοίνικος, ἀλλ᾿ ἕνα τοῦτον
ἴσασι πάντες Ἡρακλέα τὸν Βοιώτιον ὁμοῦ καὶ Ἀργεῖον.

15 Καὶ μὴν τῶν ἑπτὰ σοφῶν, οὓς αὐτὸς σοφιστὰς
προσεῖπε, τὸν μὲν Θάλητα Φοίνικα τῷ γένει τὸ ἀνέκαθεν
ἀποφαίνεται βάρβαρον · τοῖς δὲ θεοῖς λοιδορούμενος ἐν τῷ
Σόλωνος προσώπῳ ταῦτ᾿ εἴρηκεν · « ὦ Κροῖσε, ἐπιστάμενόν
με τὸ θεῖον πᾶν ἐὸν φθονερόν τε καὶ ταραχῶδες | ἐπειρωτᾷς 858 A
ἀνθρωπηίων πέρι πραγμάτων.» Ἃ γὰρ αὐτὸς ἐφρόνει
περὶ τῶν θεῶν τῷ Σόλωνι προστριβόμενος κακοήθειαν τῇ
βλασφημίᾳ προστίθησι. Πιττακῷ τοίνυν εἰς μικρὰ καὶ οὐκ
ἄξια λόγου χρησάμενος, ὃ μέγιστόν ἐστι τῶν πεπραγμένων
τῷ ἀνδρὶ καὶ κάλλιστον, ἐν ταῖς πράξεσι γενόμενος παρῆκε.
Πολεμούντων γὰρ Ἀθηναίων καὶ Μυτιληναίων περὶ
Σιγείου καὶ Φρύνωνος τοῦ στρατηγοῦ τῶν Ἀθηναίων
προκαλεσαμένου τὸν βουλόμενον εἰς μονομαχίαν, ἀπήντη-

should be worshipped as mortals and heroes. He has said the same (46 and 145/6) of Pan, overthrowing the most solemn and holy truths of Greek religion with Egyptian humbug and fairytale.

14. That is not the worst. He traces Heracles' ancestry back to Perseus E and says (6.54) that according to the Persians Perseus was an Assyrian; (53.2) "If you trace their ancestry back beyond Danae and Acrisius, the Dorian chieftains would turn out to be genuine Egyptians." Epaphus and Io and Iasus and Argus he has completely ignored in his enthusiasm not just to set up an alternative to Heracles in Egypt (2.43.1) and another in Phoenicia (44.3/4) but to get our own one – third in time anyway, he says! – out of Greece and in amongst foreigners. And yet, of the learned men of old, not Homer not Hesiod not Archilochus not Peisander not Stesichorus F not Alcman not Pindar mentioned an Egyptian or a Phoenician Heracles: they all know of one Heracles only, the Heracles of Boeotia and Argos.

15. Then there are the Seven Sages, whom he called "sophists" (1.29.1). Thales he represents (170.3) as a Phoenician by remote origin, non-Greek again. Solon he makes serve as his mouthpiece for abuse of the gods as follows (32.1): "'My lord, I know god is envious of human prosperity and likes to trouble us; and you question me about the lot of man.'" By forcing 858 A upon Solon his own ideas about the gods he compounds his blasphemy with malice. Pittacus he mentioned (27.2) for trifles not worth mentioning, and omitted the man's best and biggest deed in spite of having the opportunity (5.94/5) to put it in. Athens and Mytilene were at war over Sigeum, and Phrynon the Athenian general had issued an open challenge

σεν ὁ Πιττακὸς καὶ δικτύῳ περιβαλὼν τὸν ἄνδρα ῥωμαλέον
ὄντα καὶ μέγαν ἀπέκτεινε· τῶν δὲ Μυτιληναίων δωρεὰς
αὐτῷ μεγάλας διδόντων, ἀκοντίσας τὸ δόρυ τοῦτο μόνον Β
τὸ χωρίον ἠξίωσεν ὅσον ἐπέσχεν ἡ αἰχμή· καὶ καλεῖται
μέχρι νῦν Πιττάκειον. Τί οὖν ὁ Ἡρόδοτος, κατὰ τὸν τόπον
γενόμενος τοῦτον; ἀντὶ τῆς Πιττακοῦ ἀριστείας τὴν
Ἀλκαίου διηγήσατο τοῦ ποιητοῦ φυγὴν ἐκ τῆς μάχης, τὰ
ὅπλα ῥίψαντος· τῷ τὰ μὲν χρηστὰ μὴ γράψαι τὰ δ᾽ αἰσχρὰ
μὴ παραλιπεῖν μαρτυρήσας τοῖς ἀπὸ μιᾶς κακίας καὶ τὸν
φθόνον φύεσθαι καὶ τὴν ἐπιχαιρεκακίαν λέγουσι.

16 Μετὰ ταῦτα τοὺς Ἀλκμαιωνίδας, ἄνδρας γενομένους καὶ τὴν πατρίδα τῆς τυραννίδος ἐλευθερώσαντας,
εἰς αἰτίαν ἐμβαλὼν προδοσίας δέξασθαί φησι τὸν C
Πεισίστρατον ἐκ τῆς φυγῆς καὶ συγκαταγαγεῖν ἐπὶ τῷ
γάμῳ τῆς Μεγακλέους θυγατρός· τὴν δὲ παῖδα πρὸς τὴν
μητέρα φράσαι τὴν ἑαυτῆς ὅτι « ὦ μαμμίδιον, ὁρᾷς; οὐ
μίγνυταί μοι κατὰ νόμον Πεισίστρατος »· ἐπὶ τούτῳ δὲ
τοὺς Ἀλκμαιωνίδας τῷ παρανομήματι σχετλιάσαντας
ἐξελάσαι τὸν τύραννον.

17 Ἵνα τοίνυν μηδ᾽ οἱ Λακεδαιμόνιοι τῶν Ἀθηναίων
ἔλαττον ἔχωσι τῆς κακοηθείας, τὸν ἐν αὐτοῖς μάλιστα
θαυμαζόμενον καὶ τιμώμενον ὅρα πῶς διαλελύμανται, τὸν
Ὀθρυάδαν· « τὸν δὲ ἕνα, φησί, τὸν περιλειφθέντα τῶν
τριηκοσίων αἰσχυνόμενον ἀπονοστέειν ἐς Σπάρτην, τῶν D
⟨οἱ⟩ συλλοχιτέων διεφθαρμένων, αὐτοῦ μιν ἐν τῇσι
Θυρέῃσι καταχρήσασθαι ἑωυτόν. » Ἄνω μὲν γὰρ ἀμφοτέ-
ροις ἐπίδικον εἶναι τὸ νίκημά φησιν, ἐνταῦθα δὲ τῇ αἰσχύνῃ
τοῦ Ὀθρυάδου ἧτταν τῶν Λακεδαιμονίων κατεμαρτύρησεν·
ἡττηθέντα μὲν γὰρ ζῆν αἰσχρὸν ἦν, περιγενέσθαι δὲ
νικῶντα κάλλιστον.

to a duel. Pittacus responded, and flung a net over the man and killed him,
for all the fellow's strength and size. The Mytileneans offered Pittacus
large rewards: he threw his spear and asked only for the land covered by   B
its flight, land which is still called the Pittaceum. And what did Herodotus
do when he got to that point? Instead of Pittacus' exploit he described the
flight from battle of the poet Alcaeus, who threw his armour away. By
not putting in a good story and by not leaving aside a bad one he backs
up those who say that joy at others' misfortunes is born of one and the
same vice as jealousy.

16. After that he attacks (1.60.2) the Alcmeonids for treachery. The
Alcmeonids were heroes who freed their land from tyranny, but he
accuses them of taking Peisistratus in from exile and of helping to put him   C
back in power provided he married Megacles' daughter. But the girl said
to her mother (61.1/2), "O mummy, you see, Peisistratus doesn't make
love to me the normal way." For that, he says, the Alcmeonids drove out
the tyrant, in indignation at his abnormal behaviour.

17. In order that the Spartans may collect as much of his malice as the
Athenians, consider his humiliating treatment (82.8) of Othryades, a man
they particularly admired and honoured. "The sole survivor of the three
hundred", he says, "was ashamed to return to Sparta after the death of his   D
companions and killed himself at Thyreae." Earlier he says that the
victory was claimed by both sides, but here he makes the shame of
Othryades serve as evidence of Spartan defeat, because it was shameful
to live on defeated and glorious to survive as victor.

18 Ἐῶ τοίνυν ὅτι τὸν Κροῖσον ἀμαθῆ καὶ ἀλάζονα
καὶ γελοῖον φήσας ἐν πᾶσιν, ὑπὸ τούτου φησίν, αἰχμαλώτου
γενομένου, καὶ παιδαγωγεῖσθαι καὶ νουθετεῖσθαι τὸν
Κῦρον, ὃς φρονήσει καὶ ἀρετῇ καὶ μεγαλονοίᾳ πολὺ
πάντων δοκεῖ πεπρωτευκέναι τῶν βασιλέων· τῷ δὲ
Κροίσῳ μηδὲν ἄλλο καλὸν ἢ τὸ τιμῆσαι τοὺς θεοὺς ἀναθή- E
μασι πολλοῖς καὶ μεγάλοις μαρτυρήσας, αὐτὸ τοῦτο πάντων ἀσεβέστατον ἀποδείκνυσιν ἔργον. Ἀδελφὸν γὰρ
αὐτοῦ Πανταλέοντα περὶ τῆς βασιλείας [αὐτῷ] διαφέρεσθαι,
ζῶντος ἔτι τοῦ πατρός· τὸν οὖν Κροῖσον, ὡς εἰς τὴν
βασιλείαν κατέστη, τῶν ἑταίρων καὶ φίλων τοῦ Πανταλέον-
τος ἕνα τῶν γνωρίμων ἐπὶ κνάφου διαφθεῖραι καταξαινό-
μενον, ἐκ δὲ τῶν χρημάτων αὐτοῦ ποιησάμενον ἀναθήματα
τοῖς θεοῖς ἀποστεῖλαι. Δηιόκην δὲ τὸν Μῆδον ἀρετῇ καὶ
δικαιοσύνῃ κτησάμενον τὴν ἡγεμονίαν οὐ φύσει γενέσθαι
φησὶ τοιοῦτον, ἐρασθέντα δὲ τυραννίδος ἐπιθέσθαι προσ- F
ποίημά τι δικαιοσύνης.

19 Ἀλλ᾽ ἀφίημι τὰ τῶν βαρβάρων· ἀφθονίαν γὰρ
αὐτὸς ἐν τοῖς Ἑλληνικοῖς πεποίηκεν. Ἀθηναίους τοίνυν
καὶ τοὺς πολλοὺς τῶν ἄλλων Ἰώνων ἐπαισχύνεσθαι τῷ
ὀνόματι τούτῳ, μὴ βουλομένους ἀλλὰ φεύγοντας Ἴωνας
κεκλῆσθαι, τοὺς δὲ νομίζοντας αὐτῶν γενναιοτάτους
εἶναι καὶ ὁρμηθέντας ἀπὸ τοῦ πρυτανείου τῶν Ἀθηναίων
ἐκ βαρβάρων παιδοποιήσασθαι γυναικῶν, πατέρας αὐτῶν
⟨καὶ ἄνδρας⟩ καὶ παῖδας φονεύσαντας· διὸ τὰς γυναῖκας
νόμον θέσθαι ⟨καὶ⟩ ὅρκους ἐπελάσαι καὶ παραδοῦναι
ταῖς θυγατράσι, μήποτε ὁμοσιτῆσαι τοῖς ἀνδράσι μηδ᾽ ὀνο-
μαστὶ βοῆσαι τὸν ἑαυτῆς ἄνδρα, καὶ τοὺς νῦν ὄντας
Μιλησίους | ἐξ ἐκείνων γεγονέναι τῶν γυναικῶν. Ὑπειπὼν 859 A
δὲ καθαρῶς Ἴωνας γεγονέναι τοὺς Ἀπατούρια ἄγοντας
ἑορτήν, «ἄγουσι δὲ πάντες, φησί, πλὴν Ἐφεσίων καὶ
Κολοφωνίων.» Τούτους μὲν ⟨οὖν⟩ οὕτως ἐκκέκλεικε τῆς
εὐγενείας.

18. I omit the presentation of Croesus first as a prize ignoramus and braggart and fool (27; 30–33; 53–56; 71; 75) and then, after being made prisoner, as guide and counsellor of Cyrus (88–91); Cyrus seems to be far and away the first of kings for intelligence and courage and generosity. The only good thing Herodotus records of Croesus is his honouring of the E gods with plentiful and sizeable dedications (50–52; 92), yet he presents even this as an entirely ungodly action. He says (92.2–4) that Croesus' brother Pantaleon disputed the succession with him in their father's lifetime; when Croesus became king he killed one of the nobles who were friends and supporters of Pantaleon by flaying him on a carding comb, and sent the gods dedications made from the man's wealth. He says too (96.2) that Deioces the Mede won power because of the quality of his justice, but that he was not like that by nature: his justice was a pretence, adopted to satisfy his "ambition for power."   F

19. But enough of his treatment of non-Greeks: he has made abundant provision on the Greek side! He says (143.3) the Athenians and most of the other Ionians are "ashamed of the name" Ionian: they don't like to be called by it and avoid it; even those who (146.2) "thought they were of the purest blood, the ones who started from the Government House in Athens," got children by non-Greek women whose fathers, husbands and sons they had murdered. The women therefore (146.3) "established a law by oath and passed it down to their female descendants, forbidding them to sit at table with their husbands or to address them by name." The Milesians of today are descendants of those women. Having suggested 859 A (147.2) that those who celebrate the Apaturia are the pure-bred Ionians, he remarks "they all keep the festival except the men of Ephesus and Colophon." Thus he has denied these men their proper quality.

20 Πακτύην δ' ἀποστάντα Κύρου φησὶ ⟨...⟩ Κυμαίους
⟨...⟩ καὶ Μυτιληναίους ἐκδιδόναι παρασκευάζεσθαι τὸν
ἄνθρωπον «ἐπὶ μισθῷ ⟨ὅσῳ δή⟩, οὐ γὰρ ἔχω γε εἰπεῖν
ἀτρεκέως.» Εὖ τὸ μὴ διαβεβαιοῦσθαι πόσος ἦν ὁ μισθός,
τηλικοῦτο δ' Ἑλληνίδι πόλει προσβαλεῖν ὄνειδος, ὡς δὴ
σαφῶς εἰδότα ; Χίους μέντοι τὸν Πακτύην κομισθέντα
πρὸς αὐτοὺς ἐξ ἱροῦ Ἀθηναίης πολιούχου ἐκδοῦναι, καὶ B
ταῦτα ποιῆσαι τοὺς Χίους τὸν Ἀταρνέα μισθὸν λαβόντας.
Καίτοι Χάρων ὁ Λαμψακηνὸς ἀνὴρ πρεσβύτερος, ἐν τοῖς
περὶ Πακτύην λόγοις γενόμενος, τοιοῦτον οὐδὲν οὔτε
Μυτιληναίοις οὔτε Χίοις ἄγος προστέτριπται· ταυτὶ δὲ
κατὰ λέξιν γέγραφε· «Πακτύης δ' ὡς ἐπύθετο προσελαύ-
νοντα τὸν στρατὸν τὸν Περσικὸν ᾤχετο φεύγων ἄρτι μὲν
εἰς Μυτιλήνην, ἔπειτα δὲ εἰς Χίον· καὶ αὐτοῦ ἐκράτησε
Κῦρος».

21 Ἐν δὲ τῇ τρίτῃ τῶν βίβλων διηγούμενος τὴν
Λακεδαιμονίων ἐπὶ Πολυκράτη τὸν τύραννον στρατείαν
αὐτοὺς μὲν οἴεσθαί φησι καὶ λέγειν Σαμίους, ὡς χάριν
ἐκτίνοντες αὐτοῖς τῆς ἐπὶ Μεσσηνίους βοηθείας στρατεύ- C
σειαν, τούς τε φεύγοντας κατάγοντες τῶν πολιτῶν καὶ τῷ
τυράννῳ πολεμοῦντες· ἀρνεῖσθαι δὲ τὴν αἰτίαν ταύτην
Λακεδαιμονίους καὶ λέγειν ὡς οὐ βοηθοῦντες οὐδ' ἐλευθεροῦντες, ἀλλὰ τιμωρούμενοι Σαμίους στρατεύσαιντο,
κρατῆρά τινα πεμπόμενον Κροίσῳ παρ' αὐτῶν καὶ θώρακα
πάλιν παρ' Ἀμάσιδος κομιζόμενον αὐτοῖς ἀφελομένους.
Καίτοι πόλιν ἐν τοῖς τότε χρόνοις οὔτε φιλότιμον οὕτως
οὔτε μισοτύραννον ἴσμεν ὡς τὴν Λακεδαιμονίων γενομένην·
ποίου γὰρ ἕνεκα θώρακος ἢ τίνος κρατῆρος ἑτέρου D
Κυψελίδας μὲν ἐξέβαλον ἐκ Κορίνθου καὶ Ἀμβρακίας, ἐκ
δὲ Νάξου Λύγδαμιν, ἐξ Ἀθηνῶν δὲ τοὺς Πεισιστράτου
παῖδας, ἐκ δὲ Σικυῶνος Αἰσχίνην, ἐκ Θάσου δὲ Σύμμαχον,
ἐκ δὲ Φωκέων Αὖλιν, ἐκ Μιλήτου δ' Ἀριστογένη, τὴν

20. When Pactyes threw off allegiance to Cyrus, the men of Cyme <...> and the Mytileneans, he says (160.2), "were about to give him up in return for a sum of money (how much I cannot say definitely)." Bravo Herodotus for not going firm on how much the sum was; and yet he disgraces a Greek community all the same, as much as if he did know for sure! As for the Chians, he says that when Pactyes was brought to them, they handed him over from sanctuary with Athena Poliuchus, and got the   B district of Atarneus as their reward for the deed. And yet Charon of Lampsacus, an older writer, in his account of the Pactyes story, has inflicted no such disgrace on Mytilene or Chios at all; his text reads: 'When Pactyes learnt that the Persian army was riding up, he took to flight, first to Mytilene, and then to Chios, and there Cyrus got him.'

21. In the third of the books, when describing the Spartan expedition against the tyrant Polycrates, he reports (3.47.1) the declared view of the Samians that the Spartans came to restore the exiles and to fight the tyrant   C in gratitude for Samian help against the Messenians; whereas the Spartans, he says, deny this account of it, and say that they made their expedition not to help the Samians or to free them but to take vengeance on them for having stolen a mixing bowl which they (the Spartans) were sending to Croesus (1.70.2) and a corslet which Amasis was sending to them. And yet we know of no city so proud of its own good name and so hostile to tyrants as Sparta then was. What sort of a corslet, or what sort of a mixing bowl was it that made them expel the Cypselids from Corinth and   D Ambracia, Lygdamis from Naxos, the sons of Peisistratus from Athens, Aeschines from Sicyon, Symmachus from Thasos, Aulis from Phocis, Aristogenes from Miletus, and made them end the pattern of power in

δ' ἐν Θετταλοῖς δυναστείαν ἔπαυσαν, Ἀριστομήδη καὶ
Ἀγέλαον καταλύσαντες διὰ Λεωτυχίδου τοῦ βασιλέως ;
περὶ ὧν ἐν ἄλλοις ἀκριβέστερον γέγραπται· κατὰ
δ' Ἡρόδοτον οὔτε κακίας οὔτ' ἀβελτερίας ὑπερβολὴν
λελοίπασιν, εἰ τὴν καλλίστην καὶ δικαιοτάτην τῆς
στρατείας ἀρνούμενοι πρόφασιν ὡμολόγουν διὰ μνησικα- E
κίαν καὶ μικρολογίαν ἐπιτίθεσθαι δυστυχοῦσιν ἀνθρώποις
καὶ κακῶς πράττουσιν.

22 Οὐ μὴν ἀλλὰ Λακεδαιμονίους μὲν ἀμωσγέπως
ὑποπεσόντας αὐτοῦ τῷ γραφείῳ προσέχρωσε· τὴν δὲ
Κορινθίων πόλιν, ἐκτὸς δρόμου κατὰ τοῦτον οὖσαν τὸν
τόπον, ὅμως προσπεριλαβὼν ὁδοῦ, φασί, πάρεργον
ἀνέπλησεν αἰτίας δεινῆς καὶ μοχθηροτάτης διαβολῆς.
Συνεπελάβοντο γάρ, φησί, τοῦ στρατεύματος ⟨τοῦ⟩ ἐπὶ
Σάμον ὥστε γενέσθαι ⟨καὶ⟩ Κορίνθιοι προθύμως, ὕβρισμα-
τος εἰς αὐτοὺς ὑπὸ Σαμίων πρότερον ὑπάρξαντος. Ἦν δὲ
τοιοῦτο· Κερκυραίων παῖδας τριακοσίους τῶν πρώτων
Περίανδρος ὁ Κορίνθου τύραννος ἐπ' ἐκτομῇ παρ' Ἀλυάτ- F
την ἔπεμπε· τούτους ἀποβάντας εἰς τὴν νῆσον οἱ Σάμιοι
διδάξαντες ἐν ἱερῷ Ἀρτέμιδος ἱκέτας καθίζεσθαι καὶ
τρωκτὰ προτιθέντες αὐτοῖς ὁσημέραι σησάμου καὶ μέλιτος
περιεποίησαν. Τοῦθ' ὕβρισμα Σαμίων εἰς Κορινθίους
ὁ συγγραφεὺς προσαγορεύει καὶ διὰ τοῦτό φησι συμπαροξῦναι Λακεδαιμονίους κατ' αὐτῶν ἔτεσιν οὐκ ὀλίγοις
ὕστερον, ἔγκλημα ποιησαμένους ὅτι τριακοσίους παῖδας
Ἑλλήνων ἐφύλαξαν ἄνδρας. Ὁ δὲ τοῦτο Κορινθίοις προστριβόμενος τοὔνειδος ἀποφαίνει τοῦ τυράννου μοχθηρο-
τέραν τὴν πόλιν· ἐκεῖνος μὲν γὰρ τὸν υἱὸν αὐτοῦ Κερκυ-
ραίους ἀνελόντας ἡμύνατο, Κορίνθιοι δὲ τί παθόντες ἐτιμω-
ροῦντο Σαμίους ἐμποδὼν στάντας | ὠμότητι καὶ παρανομίᾳ 860 A
τοσαύτῃ, καὶ ταῦτα μετὰ τρεῖς γενεὰς ὀργὴν καὶ μνησικα-
κίαν ἀναφέροντες ὑπὲρ τυραννίδος, ἧς καταλυθείσης πᾶν

Thessaly when Aristomedes and Agelaus were put down through king Leotychides? Other writers have dealt with these events more fully. According to Herodotus, however, the Spartans plumbed the depths of evil and stupidity if they refused the excellent justification there was for their campaign and decided to make their attack upon men already in misery and distress just out of petty vindictiveness. E

22. Even so, to some extent the Spartans fell for their blacking from his pen; but Corinth was surely well out of his way for such treatment. Nevertheless, it was worth the detour, as they say: he managed a monster of an accusation against them, a most grievous slander. "The Corinthians too," he says (3.48), "were very willing to lend help in the expedition against Samos," since there was a Samian insult outstanding against them from earlier. It was as follows: Periander tyrant of Corinth had sent off to Alyattes three hundred boys belonging to the leading families in F Corcyra for castration. When they put in at Samos the people there told the boys to sit as suppliants in the temple of Artemis and they brought them food every day of sesame seed and honey and saved them. This is the insult of Samos to Corinth that our historian presents, and this is why, he says, the Corinthians egged on the Spartans against her so many years later, their complaint being that the Samians had preserved the manhood of three hundred boys of Greece! Anyone attributing such shameful behaviour to the Corinthians makes the city out to be worse than its tyrant was: when the Corcyreans murdered his son (53.7) Periander took his revenge, but what made the Corinthians seek vengeance on Samos when she had stood in the way of such savagery and lawlessness, and why do 860 A it two generations later (48.1), never relaxing their passionate resentment of a tyranny long undone, a tyranny so harsh and heavy upon them that

τε μνῆμα καὶ πᾶν ἴχνος ἐξαλείφοντες καὶ ἀφανίζοντες
οὐκ ἐπαύοντο, χαλεπῆς καὶ βαρείας αὐτοῖς γενομένης ;
Ἀλλὰ δὴ τὸ μὲν ὕβρισμα τοιοῦτον ἦν τὸ Σαμίων εἰς
Κορινθίους · τὸ δὲ τιμώρημα ποῖόν τι τὸ Κορινθίων εἰς
Σαμίους ; εἰ γὰρ ὄντως ὠργίζοντο Σαμίοις, οὐ παροξύνειν,
ἀποτρέπειν δὲ μᾶλλον αὐτοῖς ἦν προσῆκον Λακεδαιμονίους ἐπὶ Πολυκράτη στρατευομένους, ὅπως μὴ τοῦ
τυράννου καταλυθέντος ἐλεύθεροι Σάμιοι γένοιντο καὶ
παύσαιντο δουλεύοντες. Ὃ δὲ μέγιστόν ἐστι, τί δήποτε B
Κορίνθιοι Σαμίοις μὲν ὠργίζοντο βουληθεῖσι σῶσαι καὶ
μὴ δυνηθεῖσι ⟨τοὺς⟩ Κερκυραίων παῖδας, Κνιδίοις δὲ
τοῖς σώσασι καὶ ἀποδοῦσιν οὐκ ἐνεκάλουν ; καίτοι
Κερκυραῖοι Σαμίων μὲν ἐπὶ τούτῳ λόγον οὐ πολὺν ἔχουσι,
Κνιδίων δὲ μέμνηνται καὶ Κνιδίοις εἰσὶ τιμαὶ καὶ ἀτέλειαι
καὶ ψηφίσματα παρ' αὐτοῖς · οὗτοι γὰρ ἐπιπλεύσαντες
ἐξήλασαν ἐκ τοῦ ἱεροῦ τοὺς Περιάνδρου φύλακας, αὐτοὶ
δ' ἀναλαβόντες τοὺς παῖδας εἰς Κέρκυραν διεκόμισαν, ὡς
Ἀντήνωρ τε ὁ Κρητικὸς ἱστόρηκε καὶ Διονύσιος ὁ
Χαλκιδεὺς ἐν ταῖς Κτίσεσιν.   C

Ὅτι δ' οὐ τιμωρούμενοι Σαμίους ἀλλ' ἐλευθεροῦντες
ἀπὸ τοῦ τυράννου καὶ σῴζοντες ἐστράτευσαν οἱ Λακεδαιμόνιοι, Σαμίοις αὐτοῖς ἔστι χρήσασθαι μάρτυσιν. Ἀρχίᾳ
γὰρ ἀνδρὶ Σπαρτιάτῃ λαμπρῶς ἀγωνισαμένῳ τότε καὶ
πεσόντι τάφον εἶναι δημοσίᾳ κατεσκευασμένον ἐν Σάμῳ
καὶ τιμώμενον ὑπ' αὐτῶν λέγουσι · διὸ καὶ τοὺς ἀπογόνους
τοῦ ἀνδρὸς ἀεὶ διατελεῖν Σαμίοις οἰκείως καὶ φιλανθρώπως
προσφερομένους, ὡς αὐτὸς Ἡρόδοτος ταῦτα γοῦν ἀπομε-
μαρτύρηκεν.

23 Ἐν δὲ τῇ πέμπτῃ, τῶν ἀρίστων Ἀθήνησι καὶ
πρώτων ἀνδρῶν Κλεισθένη μὲν ἀναπεῖσαί φησι τὴν
Πυθίαν ψευδόμαντιν γενέσθαι, προφέρουσαν ἀεὶ Λακεδαι- D
μονίοις ἐλευθεροῦν ἀπὸ τῶν τυράννων [ἀεὶ] τὰς Ἀθήνας,

they never let up their efforts to efface and abolish every memory and every trace of it?

Suppose, however, that such was the insult of Samos to Corinth: what sort of revenge was it that the Corinthians were attempting? If they really were angry with the Samians, they should not have spurred on the Spartan expedition against Polycrates but should have tried instead to avert it, so that Polycrates would not be undone, and the Samians would not get their freedom and would carry on as his slaves. But the biggest problem is this: why on earth did the Corinthians get angry with the Samians who wanted to save the boys of Corcyra but could not, yet made no complaint against the Cnidians who did save them and who sent them back? The Samians do not figure large in Corcyra on this topic, but the Cnidians are remembered: they have honours and special privileges established by decree, because they were the ones who sailed in and drove Periander's guards away from the temple, and they picked up the boys and took them back to Corcyra, as reported both by Antenor the Cretan and by Dionysius of Chalcis in his 'Foundations.'

The Spartan expedition was in any case not one of revenge but of liberation from tyranny, as the Samians themselves bear witness: they say that Archias, a Spartiate who fought and died gloriously in the campaign (55.1), has a tomb there erected at public expense and still maintained with its honours; as a result his descendants continue to have close ties of friendship with the Samians. Herodotus himself at least bears witness of that (55.2).

23. In the fifth book, he says (5.63.1) that Cleisthenes, member of a prominent noble family at Athens, "bribed the priestess" to give a false response: she insisted to the Spartans that they should rid Athens of its

καλλίστῳ μὲν ἔργῳ καὶ δικαιοτάτῳ προσάπτων ἀσεβήματος διαβολὴν τηλικούτου καὶ ῥᾳδιουργήματος, ἀφαιρούμενος δὲ τοῦ θεοῦ μαντείαν καλὴν καὶ ἀγαθὴν καὶ τῆς λεγομένης συμπροφητεύειν Θέμιδος ἀξίαν. Ἰσαγόραν δὲ τῆς γαμετῆς ὑφίεσθαι Κλεομένει φοιτῶντι παρ' αὐτήν · ὡς δ' εἴωθε, παραμιγνὺς πίστεως ἔνεκα τοῖς ψόγοις ἐπαίνους τινάς, « Ἰσαγόρης δέ, φησίν, ὁ Τισάνδρου οἰκίης μὲν ἦν δοκίμου, ἀτὰρ τὰ ἀνέκαθεν οὐκ ἔχω φράσαι · θύουσι δὲ οἱ συγγενεῖς Ε αὐτοῦ Διὶ Καρίῳ.» Εὔρυθμός γε καὶ πολιτικὸς ὁ μυκτὴρ τοῦ συγγραφέως, εἰς Κᾶρας ὥσπερ εἰς κόρακας ἀποδιοπομπουμένου τὸν Ἰσαγόραν. Ἀριστογείτονα μέντοι οὐκέτι κύκλῳ καὶ κακῶς, ἀλλ' ἄντικρυς διὰ πυλῶν εἰς Φοινίκην ἐξελαύνει, Γεφυραῖον γεγονέναι λέγων ἀνέκαθεν · τοὺς δὲ Γεφυραίους οὐκ ἀπ' Εὐβοίας οὐδ' Ἐρετριεῖς, ὥσπερ οἴονταί τινες, ἀλλὰ Φοίνικας εἶναί φησιν, αὐτὸς οὕτω πεπυσμένος.

Ἀφελέσθαι τοίνυν Λακεδαιμονίους μὴ δυνάμενος τὴν Ἀθηναίων ἐλευθέρωσιν ἀπὸ τῶν τυράννων αἰσχίστῳ πάθει κάλλιστον ἔργον οἷός τ' ἐστὶν ἀφανίζειν καὶ καταισχύνειν. Ταχὺ γὰρ μετανοῆσαί φησιν αὐτούς, ὡς οὐ F ποιήσαντας ὀρθῶς, ὅτι κιβδήλοισι μαντηίοισιν ἐπαρθέντες ἄνδρας ξείνους ὄντας αὐτοῖσι καὶ ὑποσχομένους ὑποχειρίας παρέξειν τὰς Ἀθήνας ἐξήλασαν ἐκ τῆς πατρίδος τοὺς τυράννους καὶ δήμῳ ἀχαρίστῳ παρέδωκαν τὴν πόλιν. Εἶτα μεταπεμψαμένους Ἱππίαν ἀπὸ Σιγείου κατάγειν εἰς τὰς Ἀθήνας · ἀντιστῆναι δὲ Κορινθίους αὐτοῖς καὶ ἀποτρέψαι, Σωκλέους διελθόντος ὅσα Κύψελος καὶ Περίανδρος κακὰ τὴν Κορινθίων πόλιν εἰργάσαντο τυραννοῦντες. | Καίτοι Περιάνδρου σχετλιώτερον οὐδὲν 861 A οὐδ' ὠμότερον ἔργον ἱστορεῖται τῆς ἐκπομπῆς τῶν τριακοσίων ἐκείνων, οὓς ἐξαρπάσασι καὶ διακωλύσασι παθεῖν ταῦτα Σαμίοις ὀργίζεσθαί φησι καὶ μνησικακεῖν

tyrants. A fine and proper deed of liberation is thereby linked with a piece
of gross impiety and fraud, and the god is denied credit for an excellent
instruction, worthy indeed of Themis who is said to take part in the
responses. He says too (70.1) that Isagoras connived at Cleomenes'
"relations with his wife;" mingling, as usual, some words of praise with
his disapproval to make it convincing, he says (66.1) "Isagoras son of
Tisander was a man of reputable family, though I do not know the origin
of it; however members of his family offer sacrifice to Carian Zeus." E
What an elegant and courteous sneer on the part of our historian, dumping
Isagoras ritually among the carrion of Caria! Aristogeiton he deals with
straight: nothing roundabout or cowardly here; through the gates he goes,
to Phoenicia, declared (55) to be a Gephyrean by origin. The Gephyreans,
he says (57.1), are not from Euboea and are not Eretrians, as some people
think, but Phoenicians: he has himself "looked into the matter."

He may not be able to deny the Spartans their liberation of Athens from
its tyrants, but he can blot out and defame a fine deed by reporting a
shameful reaction. He says the Spartans soon had a change of heart, F
thinking they had "made a mistake (91.2). On the strength of certain
oracles, which proved to be a swindle, they had expelled from their
country men who were their friends, men who had promised to make
Athens dependent, the tyrants, and had put power into the hands of an
ungrateful rabble." So they sent for Hippias from Sigeum and tried to put
him back in Athens. But the Corinthians resisted and dissuaded them,
Socles describing the evils done to Corinth when Cypselus and Periander
were tyrants. And yet no wickeder or nastier deed is told of Periander 861 A
than the despatch of those three hundred. But when the Samians grabbed
them and saved them from their fate, the Corinthians, he says (3.49.2),

Κορινθίους ὥσπερ ὑβρισθέντας. Τοσαύτης ἀναπίμπλησι
ταραχῆς καὶ διαφωνίας τὸ κακόηθες αὐτοῦ τὸν λόγον,
ἐξ ἁπάσης τῇ διηγήσει προφάσεως ὑποδυόμενον.

24 Ἐν δὲ τοῖς ἐφεξῆς τὰ περὶ Σάρδεις διηγούμενος,
ὡς ἐνῆν μάλιστα διέλυσε καὶ διελυμήνατο τὴν πρᾶξιν,
ἃς μὲν Ἀθηναῖοι ναῦς ἐξέπεμψαν Ἴωσι τιμωροὺς ἀποστᾶσι
βασιλέως, ἀρχεκάκους τολμήσας προσειπεῖν ὅτι τοσαύτας B
πόλεις καὶ τηλικαύτας Ἑλληνίδας ἐλευθεροῦν ἐπεχείρησαν
ἀπὸ τῶν βαρβάρων, Ἐρετριέων δὲ κομιδῇ μνησθεὶς ἐν
παρέργῳ καὶ παρασιωπήσας μέγα κατόρθωμα καὶ ἀοίδιμον.
Ἤδη γὰρ ὡς ⟨τῶν⟩ περὶ τὴν Ἰωνίαν συγκεχυμένων καὶ
στόλου βασιλικοῦ προσπλέοντος, ἀπαντήσαντες ἔξω
Κυπρίους ἐν τῷ Παμφυλίῳ πελάγει κατεναυμάχησαν·
εἶτ' ἀναστρέψαντες ὀπίσω καὶ τὰς ναῦς ἐν Ἐφέσῳ καταλι-
πόντες ἐπέθεντο Σάρδεσι καὶ Ἀρταφέρνην ἐπολιόρκουν
εἰς τὴν ἀκρόπολιν καταφυγόντα, βουλόμενοι τὴν Μιλήτου
λῦσαι πολιορκίαν· καὶ τοῦτο μὲν ἔπραξαν καὶ τοὺς C
πολεμίους ἀνέστησαν ἐκεῖθεν, ἐν φόβῳ θαυμαστῷ γενομέ-
νους· πλήθους δ' ἐπιχυθέντος αὐτοῖς, ἀπεχώρησαν. Ταῦτα
δ' ἄλλοι τε καὶ Λυσανίας ὁ Μαλλώτης ἐν τοῖς περὶ
Ἐρετρίας εἴρηκε· καὶ καλῶς εἶχεν, εἰ καὶ διὰ μηδὲν
ἄλλο, τῇ γοῦν ἁλώσει καὶ φθορᾷ τῆς πόλεως ἐπειπεῖν τὸ
ἀνδραγάθημα τοῦτο καὶ τὴν ἀριστείαν· ὃ δὲ καὶ κρατηθέν-
τας αὐτοὺς ὑπὸ τῶν βαρβάρων φησὶν εἰς τὰς ναῦς κατα-
διωχθῆναι, μηδὲν τοιοῦτο τοῦ Λαμψακηνοῦ Χάρωνος
ἱστοροῦντος, ἀλλὰ ταυτὶ γράφοντος κατὰ λέξιν·
« Ἀθηναῖοι δ' εἴκοσι τριήρεσιν ἔπλευσαν ἐπικουρήσοντες
τοῖς Ἴωσι, καὶ εἰς Σάρδεις ἐστρατεύσαντο καὶ εἷλον τὰ D
περὶ Σάρδεις ἅπαντα χωρὶς τοῦ τείχους τοῦ βασιληίου·
ταῦτα δὲ ποιήσαντες ἐπαναχωροῦσιν εἰς Μίλητον ».

were angry, and "bore the Samians a grudge for it." Such are the confusion and contradiction which come from malice: they slip into his narrative on any excuse.

24. In the following section, describing the Sardis incident he did all in his power to destroy and demean the deed, having the nerve to say that the ships which the Athenians sent to support the Ionians in their rebellion against the king were (5.97.3) "the beginning of evil" because they attempted to free all those fine Greek cities; and the Eretrian ships he B scarcely mentions except in passing (99.1): their epic feat he passes over in silence. Since Ionia was in turmoil by now, and a royal squadron of ships was on its way, the Eretrians encountered outside and beat some Cypriots in a seafight in Pamphylian waters; then they returned, left their ships at Ephesus, attacked Sardis and besieged Artaphernes on the acropolis where he had fled, the aim being to raise the siege of Miletus. Which they achieved: they got the enemy out of the place and put them C into a remarkable panic too. They withdrew only when swamped by superior numbers. This has been recorded by several writers, notably Lysanias of Mallos in his history of Eretria.

It would have been a good thing to record so courageous and heroic an exploit, if for no other reason then at least to mark the capture and destruction of Miletus. But Herodotus says (102) the Greek forces were defeated by the Persians and were pursued to their ships, though Charon of Lampsacus has no such tale to tell at all: he writes (I quote): 'The Athenians sailed with twenty triremes to help the Ionians. They marched to Sardis and took all of it except the royal fortress. After this they D withdrew to Miletus.'

25 Ἐν δὲ τῇ ἕκτῃ διηγησάμενος περὶ Πλαταιέων
ὡς σφᾶς αὐτοὺς ἐδίδοσαν Σπαρτιάταις, οἳ δὲ μᾶλλον
ἐκέλευσαν πρὸς Ἀθηναίους τρέπεσθαι «πλησιοχώρους
ἐόντας αὐτοῖς καὶ τιμωρέειν οὐ κακούς», προστίθησιν οὐ
καθ᾽ ὑπόνοιαν οὐδὲ δόξαν, ἀλλ᾽ ὡς ἀκριβῶς ἐπιστάμενος,
ὅτι «ταῦτα συνεβούλευον οἱ Λακεδαιμόνιοι οὐ κατ᾽ εὔνοιαν
⟨οὕτω⟩ τῶν Πλαταιέων, ὡς βουλόμενοι τοὺς Ἀθηναίους
ἔχειν πόνον συνεστεῶτας Βοιωτοῖς.» Οὐκοῦν εἰ μὴ
κακοήθης Ἡρόδοτος, ἐπίβουλοι μὲν καὶ κακοήθεις Λακεδαι- E
μόνιοι, ἀναίσθητοι δ᾽ Ἀθηναῖοι παρακρουσθέντες, Πλαταιεῖς δ᾽ οὐ κατ᾽ εὔνοιαν οὐδὲ τιμήν, ἀλλὰ πολέμου
πρόφασις εἰς μέσον ἐρρίφησαν.

26 Καὶ μὴν τὴν πανσέληνον ἤδη σαφῶς ἐξελήλεγκται
Λακεδαιμονίων καταψευδόμενος, ἥν φησι περιμένοντας
αὐτοὺς εἰς Μαραθῶνα μὴ βοηθῆσαι τοῖς Ἀθηναίοις· οὐ γὰρ
μόνον ἄλλας μυρίας ἐξόδους καὶ μάχας πεποίηνται
μηνὸς ἱσταμένου, μὴ περιμείναντες τὴν πανσέληνον,
ἀλλὰ καὶ ταύτης τῆς μάχης, ἕκτῃ Βοηδρομιῶνος ἱσταμένου
γενομένης, ὀλίγον ἀπελείφθησαν, ὥστε καὶ θεάσασθαι
τοὺς νεκροὺς ἐπελθόντες ἐπὶ τὸν τόπον. Ἀλλ᾽ ὅμως F
ταῦτα περὶ τῆς πανσελήνου γέγραφεν· «Ἀδύνατα δέ
σφι ⟨ἦν⟩ τὸ παραυτίκα ποιεῖν ταῦτα, οὐ βουλομένοισι
λύειν τὸν νόμον· ἦν γὰρ ἱσταμένου τοῦ μηνὸς ⟨ἐνάτη⟩·
ἐνάτῃ δὲ οὐκ ἐξελεύσεσθαι ἔφασαν, οὐ πλήρεος ἐόντος
τοῦ κύκλου. Οὗτοι μὲν οὖν τὴν πανσέληνον ἔμενον.»
Σὺ δὲ μεταφέρεις τὴν πανσέληνον εἰς ἀρχὴν μηνὸς
⟨ἐκ⟩ διχομηνίας, καὶ τὸν οὐρανὸν ὁμοῦ καὶ τὰς ἡμέρας
καὶ πάντα πράγματα συνταράσσεις· καὶ τὰ τῆς Ἑλλάδος
ἐπαγγελλόμενος γράφειν ⟨ὡς μὴ ἀκλεᾶ γένηται⟩, | ἐσπου- 862 A
δακὼς δὲ περὶ τὰς Ἀθήνας διαφερόντως, οὐδὲ τὴν πρὸς
Ἄγρας πομπὴν ἱστόρηκας ἣν πέμπουσιν ἔτι νῦν τῇ ἕκτῃ
χαριστήρια τῆς νίκης ἑορτάζοντες. Ἀλλὰ τοῦτό γε

25. In the sixth book, in dealing with the Plataeans' offer of themselves to the Spartiates (but *they* told them to turn to Athens (6.108.3): "Athens is your neighbour and Athenian help is by no means to be despised"), he adds, not as a suspicion or even as opinion but as if he knew it for sure, "The advice did not proceed from goodwill towards to Plataea, but merely from the Spartans' desire to embroil Athens in quarrels with the Boeotians." So: if Herodotus was not malicious, then the Spartans were malicious as well as treacherous, the Athenians were fools not to see the deception, and   E the Plataeans were chucked into the ring to provoke a fight: no kindness or consideration about it!

26. Another plain instance of his capacity to misrepresent is the full moon story. He says the Spartans failed to help the Athenians at Marathon because they were waiting for the full moon. But the Spartans have gone out on thousands of other campaigns in the first half of a month and fought battles without waiting for a full moon, while this battle took place on the sixth day of Boedromion in its first half, and even so they only just missed it: when they reached the site, the dead were still there to be seen (120). In spite of which, he has written concerning the full moon (106.3–107.1):   F "They were unable to do so promptly because they did not wish to break their law. It was the ninth day of the month, and they said they could not take the field until the moon was full. So they waited for the full moon."

But you are switching the full moon to the start of the month from the middle, and muddling up the heavens and the calendar and everything else at once! You claim to be writing the history of Greece "to preserve the memory" of it (Prologue), you are particularly earnest about Athens'   862 A performance, and yet you even fail to record the procession to Agrae, which they still celebrate on 6th. Boedromion as a festival of thanksgiv-

βοηθεῖ τῷ Ἡροδότῳ πρὸς ἐκείνην τὴν διαβολὴν ἣν ἔχει
κολακεύσας τοὺς Ἀθηναίους ἀργύριον πολὺ λαβεῖν
παρ' αὐτῶν. Εἰ γὰρ ἀνέγνω ταῦτ' Ἀθηναίοις, οὐκ ἂν εἴασαν
οὐδὲ περιεῖδον ἐνάτῃ τὸν Φιλιππίδην παρακαλοῦντα
Λακεδαιμονίους ἐπὶ τὴν μάχην ἐκ τῆς μάχης γεγενημένον,
καὶ ταῦτα δευτεραῖον εἰς Σπάρτην ἐξ Ἀθηνῶν, ὡς αὐτός
φησιν, ἀφιγμένον · εἰ μὴ μετὰ τὸ νικῆσαι τοὺς πολεμίους B
Ἀθηναῖοι μετεπέμποντο τοὺς συμμάχους. Ὅτι μέντοι
δέκα τάλαντα δωρεὰν ἔλαβεν ἐξ Ἀθηνῶν Ἀνύτου τὸ
ψήφισμα γράψαντος, ἀνὴρ Ἀθηναῖος οὐ τῶν παρημελη-
μένων ἐν ἱστορίᾳ, Δίυλλος εἴρηκεν. Ἀπαγγείλας δὲ τὴν
ἐν Μαραθῶνι μάχην ὁ Ἡρόδοτος, ὡς μὲν οἱ πλεῖστοι
λέγουσι, καὶ τῶν νεκρῶν τῷ ἀριθμῷ καθεῖλε τὸ ἔργον.
Εὐξαμένους γάρ φασι τοὺς Ἀθηναίους τῇ Ἀγροτέρᾳ
θύσειν χιμάρους ὅσους ἂν τῶν βαρβάρων καταβάλωσιν,
εἶτα μετὰ τὴν μάχην ἀναρίθμου πλήθους τῶν νεκρῶν
ἀναφανέντος, παραιτεῖσθαι ψηφίσματι τὴν θεὸν ὅπως
καθ' ἕκαστον ἐνιαυτὸν ἀποθύωσι πεντακοσίας τῶν χιμάρων. C

27 Οὐ μὴν ἀλλὰ τοῦτ' ἐάσαντες ἴδωμεν ⟨τὰ⟩ μετὰ
τὴν μάχην · «Τῇσι δὲ λοιπῇσι, ⟨φησίν⟩, οἱ βάρβαροι
ἐξανακρουσάμενοι καὶ ἀναλαβόντες ἐκ τῆς νήσου ἐν τῇ
ἔλιπον τὰ ἐξ Ἐρετρίης ἀνδράποδα, περιέπλεον Σούνιον,
βουλόμενοι φθῆναι τοὺς Ἀθηναίους ἀφικόμενοι εἰς τὸ
ἄστυ · αἰτίη δ' ἔσχεν Ἀθηναίοισι ἐξ Ἀλκμεωνιδέων
μηχανῆς αὐτοὺς ταῦτα ἐπινοηθῆναι · τούτους γὰρ συνθε-
μένους τοῖσι Πέρσῃσι ἀναδεῖξαι ἀσπίδα ἐοῦσιν ἤδη ἐν τῇσι
νηυσί · οὗτοι μὲν δὴ περιέπλεον Σούνιον.» Ἐνταῦθα τὸ
μὲν τοὺς Ἐρετριέας ἀνδράποδα προσειπεῖν, οὔτε τόλμαν
Ἑλλήνων οὐδενὸς οὔτε φιλοτιμίαν ἐνδεεστέραν παρα- D
σχομένους καὶ παθόντας ἀνάξια τῆς ἀρετῆς, ἀφείσθω ·
διαβεβλημένων δὲ τῶν Ἀλκμαιωνιδῶν, ἐν οἷς οἱ μέγιστοί
τε τῶν οἴκων καὶ δοκιμώτατοι τῶν ἀνδρῶν ἦσαν, ἐλάττων

ing for their victory. At least there is something here to help Herodotus against the charge he bears of getting money from the Athenians for flattering them. If he had read them that version, they would not have let it go by: Philippides summoning the Spartans to battle on the ninth, when he had already taken part in it, since he got to Sparta the day after he left Athens, as Herodotus himself says (106.1) – unless the Athenians used to send for their allies only after beating the enemy! But it is an Athenian, B Diyllus, no negligible historian, who says Herodotus received, upon the proposal of Anytus, a prize of ten talents.

After recording the fight at Marathon, Herodotus, as most people say, has spoilt the achievement again by giving the numbers of the dead (117.1). The Athenians, they say, had vowed to Artemis Agrotera that they would sacrifice to her one goat for every enemy killed; then, after the battle, finding the corpses beyond number, they begged leave of the goddess by decree to sacrifice each year a total of five hundred goats. C 27. Never mind that; let us look at events after the battle (115). "The rest of the ships got off", he says, "and the Persians aboard them, after picking up their Eretrian slaves whom they had left on Aegilia, laid a course round Sunium for Athens, which they hoped to reach in advance of the Athenian army. In Athens the Alcmeonidae were accused of suggesting this move; they had, it was said, an understanding with the Persians, and raised a shield as a signal to them when they were already on board. So the Persian fleet was on its way round Sunium." Calling the Eretrians slaves though they had displayed as proud a determination as any Greeks and had D suffered what their courage did not deserve, we will ignore; likewise his slander of the Alcmeonids, amongst whom were some of Athens' most important families and most distinguished men: but the greatness of the

PLUTARCH

λόγος· ἀνατέτραπται δὲ τῆς νίκης τὸ μέγεθος καὶ τὸ
τέλος εἰς οὐδὲν ἥκει τοῦ περιβοήτου κατορθώματος,
οὐδ' ἀγών τις ἔοικεν οὐδ' ἔργον γεγονέναι τοσοῦτον,
ἀλλὰ πρόσκρουσμα βραχὺ τοῖς βαρβάροις ἀποβᾶσιν,
ὥσπερ οἱ διασύροντες καὶ βασκαίνοντες λέγουσιν, εἰ
μετὰ τὴν μάχην οὐ φεύγουσι κόψαντες τὰ πείσματα
τῶν νεῶν, τῷ φέροντι προσωτάτω τῆς Ἀττικῆς ἀνέμῳ Ε
παραδόντες αὐτούς· ἀλλ' αἴρεται μὲν ἀσπὶς αὐτοῖς
προδοσίας σημεῖον, ἐπιπλέουσι δὲ ταῖς Ἀθήναις ἐλπίζοντες
αἱρήσειν καὶ καθ' ἡσυχίαν Σούνιον κάμψαντες ὑπεραιωροῦν-
ται Φαλήρων, οἱ δὲ πρῶτοι καὶ δοκιμώτατοι τῶν ἀνδρῶν
⟨προδιδόασιν⟩ ἀπεγνωκότες τὴν πόλιν· καὶ γὰρ ἀπολύων
ὕστερον Ἀλκμαιωνίδας ἑτέροις τὴν προδοσίαν ἀνατίθησιν·
« ἀνεδείχθη μὲν γὰρ ἀσπίς, καὶ τοῦτο οὐκ ἔστιν ἄλλως
εἰπεῖν », φησὶν ⟨ὡς⟩ αὐτὸς ἰδών. Τοῦτο δ' ἀμήχανον
μὲν ἦν γενέσθαι, νενικηκότων κατὰ κράτος τῶν Ἀθηναίων·
γενόμενον δ' οὐκ ἂν ὑπὸ τῶν βαρβάρων συνώφθη, φυγῇ
καὶ πόνῳ πολλῷ καὶ τραύμασι καὶ βέλεσιν εἰς τὰς ναῦς
ἐλαυνομένων καὶ ἀπολιπόντων τὸ χωρίον, ὡς ἕκαστος F
τάχους εἶχεν. Ἀλλ' ὅταν γε πάλιν ὑπὲρ τῶν Ἀλκμαιωνιδῶν
ἀπολογεῖσθαι προσποιούμενος ἃ πρῶτος ἀνθρώπων ἐπενή-
νοχεν ἐγκλήματα εἴπῃ « ⟨θώυμα δέ μοι⟩ καὶ οὐκ ἐνδέχομαι
τὸν λόγον Ἀλκμεωνίδας ἄν ποτε ἀναδεῖξαι Πέρσῃσι ἐκ
συνθήματος ἀσπίδα, βουλομένους ⟨ὑπὸ βαρβάροισί⟩ τε
εἶναι Ἀθηναίους ⟨καὶ⟩ ὑπὸ Ἱππίῃ », κόμματός τινος
ἀναμιμνήσκομαι παροιμιακοῦ·

Μένε, καρκίνε, καί σε μεθήσω.

Τί γὰρ ἐσπούδακας καταλαβεῖν εἰ καταλαβὼν μεθιέναι
μέλλεις ; Καὶ σὺ κατηγορεῖς, εἶτ' ἀπολογῇ· | καὶ γράφεις 863 Α
κατ' ἐπιφανῶν ἀνδρῶν διαβολάς, ἃς πάλιν ἀναιρεῖς,
ἀπιστῶν γε σεαυτῷ δηλονότι· σεαυτοῦ γὰρ ἀκήκοας
λέγοντος Ἀλκμαιωνίδας ἀνασχεῖν ἀσπίδα νενικημένοις

victory is gone! The climax of the famous exploit has come to nothing!
No fight, no great action seems to have happened at all; just a brief clash
with the Persians after their landing, which is what jealous and disparaging critics try to say. After the battle, didn't the Persians cut their ships'
cables and flee, abandoning themselves to the wind that would take them
furthest from Attica? No: a shield is raised as a sign to them of treachery, E
and they sail for Athens expecting to take it, they double Sunium at their
ease and hover off Phalerum, while Athens' first and finest citizens
prepare to betray her in despair. He does later acquit the Alcmeonids of
treachery, but by doing so lays the charge against others (124.2): "A
shield was held up: that is a fact and cannot be denied," he says, as if he
saw it for himself! But since the Athenians had won a decisive victory,
it could not have happened; and if it did, it could not have been seen by
the foe, who were abandoning the area and tumbling into their ships amid F
flight and fuss and wounds and weapons as fast as each could manage.
But when later he pretends to defend the Alcmeonids, dropping the
charges which he himself was first to take up, and when he says (121.1):
"The tale of the Alcmeonidae treacherously signalling to the Persians
with a shield is, to me, quite extraordinary, and I cannot accept it: would
they wish to see Athens ruled by Hippias under foreign control?" I am
reminded of a piece of verse:
        'Wait, little crab, and I will let you go!'
Why such efforts to make a catch if you mean to let it go? First you
prosecute, then you defend. You bring wicked charges against famous 863 A
men, which you then withdraw, obviously from loss of confidence: you
must have heard yourself saying that the Alcmeonids raised a shield to the

καὶ φεύγουσι τοῖς βαρβάροις. Καὶ μὴν ἐν οἷς περὶ
'Αλκμαιωνιδῶν ἀπολογῇ σεαυτὸν ἀποφαίνεις συκοφάντην·
εἰ γὰρ «μᾶλλον ἢ ὁμοίως Καλλίῃ τῷ Φαινίππου,
'Ιππονίκου δὲ πατρί, φαίνονται μισοτύραννοι ἐόντες»,
ὡς ἐνταῦθα γράφεις, 'Αλκμαιωνίδαι, ποῦ θήσεις αὐτῶν
ἐκείνην τὴν συνωμοσίαν ἣν ἐν τοῖς πρώτοις γέγραφας,
ὡς ἐπιγαμίαν ποιησόμενοι Πεισιστράτῳ κατήγαγον αὐτὸν
ἀπὸ τῆς φυγῆς ἐπὶ τὴν τυραννίδα καὶ οὐκ ἂν ἐξήλασαν B
αὖθις, ἕως διεβλήθη παρανόμως τῇ γυναικὶ μιγνύμενος ;
Ταῦτα μὲν οὖν τοιαύτας ἔχει ταραχάς.

⟨Μεταξὺ δὲ⟩ τῆς 'Αλκμαιωνιδῶν διαβολῆς καὶ ὑπονοίας, τοῖς Καλλίου τοῦ Φαινίππου χρησάμενος ἐπαίνοις
καὶ προσάψας αὐτῷ τὸν υἱὸν 'Ιππόνικον, ὃς ἦν καθ᾽ 'Ηρόδο-
τον ἐν τοῖς πλουσιωτάτοις 'Αθηναίων, ὡμολόγησεν ὅτι,
μηδὲν τῶν πραγμάτων δεομένων, ἀλλὰ θεραπείᾳ καὶ
χάριτι τοῦ 'Ιππονίκου τὸν Καλλίαν παρενέβαλεν.

28 'Επεὶ δ᾽ 'Αργείους ἅπαντες ἴσασιν οὐκ ἀπει-
παμένους τοῖς "Ελλησι τὴν συμμαχίαν, ⟨ἡγεῖσθαι δὲ
κατὰ τὸ ἥμισυ πάσης τῆς συμμαχίας⟩ ἀξιώσαντας
ὡς ἂν μὴ Λακεδαιμονίοις ἐχθίστοις καὶ πολεμιωτάτοις
οὖσι ποιοῦντες ἀεὶ τὸ προστασσόμενον ἕπωνται, καὶ C
τοῦτ᾽ ἄλλως οὐκ ἦν, αἰτίαν κακοηθεστάτην ὑποβάλ-
λεται, γράφων· «'Επεὶ δέ σφεας παραλαμβάνειν τοὺς
"Ελληνας, οὕτω δὴ ἐπισταμένους ὅτι οὐ μεταδώσουσι
τῆς ἀρχῆς Λακεδαιμόνιοι, μεταιτέειν ἵν᾽ ἐπὶ προφάσεως
ἡσυχίαν ἄγωσι.» Τούτων δ᾽ ὕστερον ἀναμνῆσαί φησιν
'Αρταξέρξην ἀναβάντας εἰς Σοῦσα πρέσβεις 'Αργείων,
κἀκεῖνον εἰπεῖν ὡς «οὐδεμίαν νομίζοι πόλιν "Αργεος
φιλιωτέρην»· εἶθ᾽ ὑπείκων, ὥσπερ εἴωθε, καὶ ἀναδυό-
μενος οὐκ εἰδέναι φησὶ περὶ τούτων ἀτρεκέως, εἰδέναι
δ᾽ ὅτι πᾶσιν ἀνθρώποις ἐστὶν ἐγκλήματα καὶ «οὐκ
'Αργείοισιν αἴσχιστα πεποίηται. 'Εγὼ δὲ λέγειν ὀφείλω D

beaten, fleeing Persians! As for your defence of the Alcmeonids, that proves you a humbug: for if, as you write (121.1), they were "obviously greater tyrant-haters than even Callias, the son of Phaenippus and father of Hipponicus," how will you deal with that conspiracy of theirs which you mentioned at their first appearance (1.60.2), that they brought Peisistratus back from exile to be tyrant in order to set up a marriage link with him, and they wouldn't have driven him back into exile, until he was   B accused of abnormal sex with the girl he married? Such are the confusions of the story.

In the midst of doubting and defaming the Alcmeonids come the praises of Callias son of Phaenippus, not omitting his son Hipponicus, who in Herodotus' day was one of the richest men in Athens: so Callias gets a mention in the tale not because he had to, but to gratify Hipponicus. 28. Everybody knows that the Argives did not refuse to join the Greek alliance, but asked for a half share in the leadership of it (7.148.4), so as not to be under their bitterest enemies the Spartans, doing their bidding   C all the time. That is how it was: but Herodotus insinuates a most malicious interpretation, writing (150.3): "When the Greeks were trying to obtain their support, they did make the claim to share the command because they knew that the Spartans would refuse to grant it, and that they would thus have an excuse for taking no part in the war." Later on he says (151) that Argive ambassadors to Susa reminded Artaxerxes of this and Artaxerxes said "'There is no city which I believe to be a better friend to me than Argos.'" Then he adds, stepping back as usual (152.1), that he "cannot guarantee the story," but he does know that complaints can be made against all men (152.3): "the Argives are not the worst. My business is   D

⟨τὰ λεγόμενα, πείθεσθαί γε μὴν οὐ παντάπασι ὀφείλω,⟩ καί μοι τὸ ἔπος τοῦτο ἐχέτω ἐς πάντα τὸν λόγον. Ἐπεὶ καὶ ταῦτα λέγεται ὡς ἄρα Ἀργεῖοι ἦσαν οἱ ἐπικαλεσάμενοι τὸν Πέρσην ἐπὶ τὴν Ἑλλάδα, ἐπειδή σφι πρὸς τοὺς Λακεδαιμονίους κακῶς ἡ αἰχμὴ ἑστήκεε, ⟨πᾶν⟩ δὴ βουλόμενοι σφίσι εἶναι πρὸ τῆς παρούσης λύπης ».

Ἆρ' οὖν οὐχ, ὅπερ αὐτὸς τὸν Αἰθίοπά φησι πρὸς τὰ μύρα καὶ τὴν πορφύραν εἰπεῖν, ὡς δολερὰ μὲν τὰ χρίματα, δολερὰ δὲ τὰ εἵματα τῶν Περσέων ἐστί, τοῦτ' ἄν τις εἴποι πρὸς αὐτὸν ὡς δολερὰ μὲν τὰ ῥήματα, δολερὰ δὲ τὰ σχήματα τῶν Ἡροδότου λόγων ,   E

Ἑλικτὰ κοὐδὲν ὑγιὲς ἀλλὰ πᾶν πέριξ,

ὥσπερ οἱ ζῳγράφοι τὰ λαμπρὰ τῇ σκιᾷ τρανότερα ποιοῦσιν, οὕτω ταῖς ἀρνήσεσι τὰς διαβολὰς ἐπιτείνοντος αὐτοῦ καὶ τὰς ὑπονοίας ταῖς ἀμφιβολίαις βαθυτέρας ποιοῦντος; Ἀργεῖοι δ' ὅτι μὲν οὐ συναράμενοι τοῖς Ἕλλησιν, ἀλλὰ διὰ τὴν ἡγεμονίαν καὶ τῆς ἀρετῆς Λακεδαιμονίοις ἐκστάντες, κατήσχυναν [ἂν] τὸν Ἡρακλέα καὶ τὴν εὐγένειαν, οὐκ ἔστιν ἀντειπεῖν. ⟨Ὑπὸ⟩ Σιφνίοις γὰρ ἦν καὶ Κυθνίοις ἄμεινον ἐλευθεροῦν τοὺς Ἕλληνας ἢ Σπαρτιάταις φιλονικοῦντας ὑπὲρ ἀρχῆς ἐγκαταλιπεῖν τοσούτους καὶ τοιού- F τους ἀγῶνας. Εἰ δ' αὐτοὶ ἦσαν οἱ ἐπικαλεσάμενοι τὸν Πέρσην ἐπὶ τὴν Ἑλλάδα διὰ τὴν κακῶς ἐστῶσαν αὐτοῖς αἰχμὴν πρὸς Λακεδαιμονίους, πῶς οὐκ ἐμήδιζον ἀναφανδὸν ἥκοντος οὐδ', εἰ μὴ συστρατεύειν ἐβούλοντο βασιλεῖ, τὴν γοῦν Λακωνικὴν ὑπολειπόμενοι κακῶς ἐποίουν, ἢ Θυρέας ἥπτοντο πάλιν ἢ τρόπον ἄλλον ἀντελαμβάνοντο καὶ παρηνώχλουν Λακεδαιμονίοις, | μέγα βλάψαι δυνά- 864 A μενοι τοὺς Ἕλληνας, εἰ μὴ παρῆκαν εἰς Πλαταιὰς ἐκείνους ἐκστρατεῦσαι τοσούτοις ὁπλίταις ;

29 Ἀλλ' Ἀθηναίους γε μεγάλους ἐνταῦθα τῷ λόγῳ πεποίηκε καὶ σωτῆρας ἀνηγόρευκε τῆς Ἑλλάδος ' ὀρθῶς

to record what people say, but I am by no means bound to believe it – and that may be taken to apply to this book as a whole. There is yet another story about the Argives: it was they, according to some, who invited the Persians to invade Greece, because their war with Sparta was going badly and they felt that anything would be better than their present sufferings."

Why not adopt what Herodotus himself says (3.22) that the Ethiopian said about Persian perfume and purple clothes, that the myrrh was a pretence and the garments a pretence, and so say to him that his words are a pretence and his history a pretence, 'all twisted, nothing sound, all back E to front'? Like painters using shadow to bring out bright parts, he strengthens his attacks by denials and deepens suspicion by ambiguity. It cannot be denied that the Argives brought shame upon their noble descent from Heracles by not joining the Greek alliance and by leaving courage to the Spartans, all because of the leadership. It would have been better to free Greece under the leadership of Siphnos and Cythnos than to miss all those great battles by quarrelling about command with the Spartiates. F But if they did invite Xerxes into Greece because of their unsuccessful war with Sparta, why did they not medize openly when he came? If they did not want to join his army, why did they not ravage Laconia when they stayed behind, or seize Thyrea again, or find some other way of being a nuisance? They could have done great harm to the Greek cause if they 864 A had interfered with the Spartans' march to Plataea, with all those hoplites involved.

29. At least at this point he has done the Athenians proud – or so I shall be told – and has declared them (7.139.5) "saviours of Greece;" and quite

γε ποιῶν καὶ δικαίως, εἰ μὴ πολλὰ καὶ βλάσφημα προσῆν τοῖς ἐπαίνοις. Νῦν δὲ προδοθῆναι μὲν ἂν λέγων ὑπὸ τῶν ἄλλων Ἑλλήνων Λακεδαιμονίους, «μονωθέντας δ' ἂν καὶ ἀποδεξαμένους ἔργα μεγάλα ἀποθανεῖν γενναίως ⟨...⟩, ἢ πρὸ τούτου ὁρῶντας καὶ τοὺς ⟨ἄλλους⟩ Ἕλληνας μηδίζοντας ὁμολογίῃ ἂν χρήσασθαι πρὸς Ξέρξεα», δῆλός ἐστιν οὐ τοῦτο λέγων εἰς τὸν Ἀθηναίων ἔπαινον, ἀλλ' Ἀθηναίους ἐπαινῶν, ἵνα κακῶς εἴπῃ τοὺς ἄλλους B ἅπαντας. Τί γὰρ ἄν τις ἔτι δυσχεραίνοι Θηβαίους ἀεὶ καὶ Φωκέας πικρῶς αὐτοῦ καὶ κατακόρως ἐξονειδίζοντος, ὅπου καὶ τῶν προκινδυνευσάντων ὑπὲρ τῆς Ἑλλάδος τὴν οὐ ⟨γενομένην μέν⟩, γενομένην δ' ἄν, ὡς αὐτὸς εἰκάζει, καταψηφίζεται προδοσίαν; Αὐτοὺς δὲ Λακεδαιμονίους ἐν ἀδήλῳ θέμενος ἐπηπόρησεν εἴτ' ἔπεσον ἂν μαχόμενοι τοῖς πολεμίοις εἴτε παρέδωκαν ἑαυτούς, μικροῖς γε νὴ Δία τεκμηρίοις αὐτῶν ἀπιστήσας τοῖς περὶ Θερμοπύλας.

30 Διηγούμενος δὲ συμπεσοῦσαν ναυαγίαν ταῖς βασιλικαῖς ναυσὶ καὶ ὅτι πολλῶν χρημάτων ἐκπεσόντων Ἀμεινοκλῆς ὁ Κρητίνεω Μάγνης ἀνὴρ ὠφελήθη μεγάλως, «χρύσεα C ἄφατα [καὶ] χρήματα περιβαλόμενος», οὐδὲ τοῦτον ἄδηκτον παρῆκεν, «ἀλλ' ὁ μὲν τἆλλα, φησίν, οὐκ εὐτυχέων εὑρήμασι μέγα πλούσιος ἐγένετο· ἦν γάρ τις καὶ τοῦτον ἄχαρις συμ⟨φορὴ λυπεῦσα παιδοφόνος⟩». Τοῦτο μὲν οὖν παντὶ δῆλον ὅτι τὰ χρυσᾶ χρήματα καὶ τὰ εὑρήματα καὶ τὸν ἐκβρασσόμενον ὑπὸ τῆς θαλάσσης πλοῦτον ἐπεισήγαγε τῇ ἱστορίᾳ, χώραν καὶ τόπον ποιῶν ἐν ᾧ θήσεται τὴν Ἀμεινοκλέους παιδοφονίαν.

31 Ἀριστοφάνους δὲ τοῦ Βοιωτοῦ γράψαντος ὅτι χρήματα μὲν αἰτήσας οὐκ ἔλαβε παρὰ Θηβαίων, ἐπιχειρῶν D δὲ τοῖς νέοις διαλέγεσθαι καὶ συσχολάζειν ὑπὸ τῶν ἀρχόντων ἐκωλύθη δι' ἀγροικίαν αὐτῶν καὶ μισολογίαν,

right and proper too, except for all the defamation amid the praise. He says that the Spartans would have been betrayed by the rest of the Greeks and (139.3) "would have been left alone – to perform prodigies of valour and to die nobly, or before that, the sight of the rest of Greece submitting to Persia might have driven them to make terms with Xerxes." Plainly that was not said in order to praise Athens; he praises Athens in order to   B abuse all the others. There is little point in complaining of his constant bitter attacks on Thebes and Phocis when even those who did hazard their lives for Greece are attacked for a treachery which never happened but which he reckons would have. He leaves in doubt what the Spartans themselves would have done: would they have fallen fighting the enemy or would they have surrendered? I suppose he had no confidence in the slight indications they gave of themselves at Thermopylae!

30. When he describes the shipwreck which befell the king's ships and says (190) many objects of value were lost, and Ameinocles son of   C Cretines of Magnesia did himself a lot of good "picking up gold articles beyond counting," he didn't let even him go uncriticised: he adds "This made him a very rich man, though in other respects he proved less fortunate; for he met with a distressing disaster in the murder of his son." That makes it very obvious that Herodotus raised the topic of the objects of gold and the finds and the wealth "washed ashore" just to provide space in which to mention Ameinocles' murder of his son.

31. Aristophanes the Boeotian recorded that Herodotus asked the Thebans for money and failed to get it; when he tried to talk to their young   D men and to share their studies, he was prevented by the authorities because of their crude and anti-intellectual nature. There is no other

ἄλλο μὲν οὐδὲν ἔστι τεκμήριον· ὁ δ' Ἡρόδοτος τῷ
Ἀριστοφάνει μεμάρτυρηκε, δι' ὧν τὰ μὲν ψευδῶς, τὰ
δ' ⟨ἀδίκως⟩, τὰ δὲ ὡς μισῶν καὶ διαφερόμενος τοῖς
Θηβαίοις ἐγκέκληκε. Θεσσαλοὺς μὲν γὰρ ὑπ' ἀνάγκης ἀποφαίνεται μηδίσαι τὸ πρῶτον, ἀληθῆ λέγων· καὶ περὶ τῶν
ἄλλων Ἑλλήνων μαντευόμενος ὡς προδόντων ἂν Λακεδαιμονίους, ὑπεῖπεν ὡς «οὐκ ἐκόντων ἀλλ' ὑπ' ἀνάγκης
ἁλισκομένων κατὰ πόλεις.» Θηβαίοις δὲ τῆς αὐτῆς E
ἀνάγκης οὐ δίδωσι τὴν αὐτὴν συγγνώμην. Καίτοι
πεντακοσίους μὲν εἰς τὰ Τέμπη καὶ Μναμίαν στρατηγὸν
ἔπεμψαν, εἰς δὲ Θερμοπύλας ὅσους ἤτησε Λεωνίδας·
οἳ καὶ μόνοι σὺν Θεσπιεῦσι παρέμειναν αὐτῷ, τῶν ἄλλων
ἀπολιπόντων μετὰ τὴν κύκλωσιν· ἐπεὶ δὲ τῶν παρόδων
κρατήσας ὁ βάρβαρος ἐν τοῖς ὅροις ἦν καὶ Δημάρατος ὁ
Σπαρτιάτης διὰ ξενίας εὔνους ὢν Ἀτταγίνῳ τῷ προεστῶτι
τῆς ὀλιγαρχίας διεπράξατο φίλον βασιλέως γενέσθαι καὶ
ξένον, οἱ δ' Ἕλληνες ἐν ταῖς ναυσὶν ἦσαν, πεζῇ δ' οὐδεὶς
προσήλαυνεν, οὕτω προσεδέξαντο τὰς διαλύσεις ὑπὸ F
τῆς μεγάλης ἀνάγκης ἐγκαταληφθέντες. Οὔτε γὰρ θάλασσα
καὶ νῆες αὐτοῖς παρῆσαν ὡς Ἀθηναίοις, οὔτ' ἀπωτάτω
κατῴκουν ὡς Σπαρτιᾶται τῆς Ἑλλάδος ἐν μυχῷ, μιᾶς δ'
ἡμέρας ὁδὸν καὶ ἡμισείας ἀπέχοντι τῷ Μήδῳ συστάντες
ἐπὶ τῶν στενῶν καὶ διαγωνισάμενοι μετὰ μόνων Σπαρτιατῶν
καὶ Θεσπιέων ἠτύχησαν. | Ὁ δὲ συγγραφεὺς οὕτως ἐστὶ 865 A
δίκαιος ὥστε Λακεδαιμονίους μὲν μονωθέντας καὶ γενομένους συμμάχων ἐρήμους τυχὸν ἄν φησιν ὁμολογίῃ χρήσασθαι πρὸς Ξέρξεα. Θηβαίοις δὲ τὸ αὐτὸ διὰ τὴν αὐτὴν
ἀνάγκην παθοῦσι λοιδορεῖται. Τὸ δὲ μέγιστον καὶ κάλλιστον ἔργον ἀνελεῖν μὴ δυνηθεὶς ὡς οὐ πραχθὲν αὐτοῖς, αἰτίᾳ
φαύλῃ καὶ ὑπονοίᾳ διαλυμαινόμενος ταῦτ' ἔγραφεν· «Οἱ
μέν νυν ξύμμαχοι ⟨οἱ⟩ ἀποπεμπόμενοι ᾤχοντό τε ἀπιόντες
καὶ ἐπείθοντο Λεωνίδῃ, Θεσπιέες δὲ καὶ Θηβαῖοι κατέμειναν

evidence for this episode, except that Herodotus bears it out by his own attacks on the Thebans, part false, part unfair, part made in hatred and part in antipathy. He says (172.1) "the Thessalians medized at first under compulsion," and that is true; when he makes his guess that the rest of the Greeks would have betrayed the Spartans, he added (139.3) "not that they would have wished to desert them, but they could not have helped doing so, falling victims one by one." The Thebans don't get the same E understanding from him, though they faced the same pressures. And yet they sent five hundred hoplites to Tempe under Mnamias, and as many to Thermopylae as Leonidas asked for; and these alone, together with the Thespians, stayed with Leonidas when the rest deserted after the Persian outflanking movement.

Not till after Xerxes had control of their passes and was on their borders, and Demaratus the Spartiate who enjoyed a guest-friendship with Attaginus the leader of the Theban oligarchy had arranged for him to be on similar terms with the king, and the Greeks were in their ships, and no reinforcement was coming by land, not till then did they submit F to dire necessity and accept the king's terms. They had no sea and ships like Athens, nor did they live miles away in a far corner of Greece like the Spartiates. Xerxes was a day and a half away when they stood firm in the pass and fought it out with only the Spartiates and the Thespians, and failed. Our historian has the fairness to say (139.4) that it is possible the 865 A Spartans, left alone and bereft of allies, might have "made terms with Xerxes." But when the Thebans had the same experience, and for the same reason, he abuses them. He could not obliterate their great and glorious deed and claim they never did it, but he diminished it by casting doubt on its motive, by saying (222) "Thus it was that the confederate troops, by Leonidas' orders, abandoned their posts and left the pass, all

μοῦνοι παρὰ Λακεδαιμονίοισι. Τούτων δὲ Θηβαῖοι μὲν ἀέκοντες ἔμενον καὶ οὐ βουλόμενοι — κατεῖχε γάρ σφεας Λεωνίδης ἐν ὁμήρων λόγῳ ποιεύμενος —, Θεσπιέες δὲ ἑκόντες μάλιστα, οἳ οὐδαμὰ ἔφασαν ἀπολιπόντες Λεωνίδην Β καὶ τοὺς μετὰ τούτου ἀπαλλάξεσθαι.»

Εἶτ' οὐ δῆλός ἐστιν ἰδίαν τινὰ πρὸς Θηβαίους ἔχων ὀργὴν καὶ δυσμένειαν, ὑφ' ἧς οὐ μόνον διέβαλε ψευδῶς καὶ ἀδίκως τὴν πόλιν, ἀλλ' οὐδὲ τοῦ πιθανοῦ τῆς διαβολῆς ἐφρόντισεν, οὐδ' ὅπως αὐτὸς ἑαυτῷ τὰ ἐναντία λέγων ⟨πᾶσι⟩ παρ' ὀλίγους ἀνθρώποις οὐ φανεῖται συνειδώς ; Προειπὼν γὰρ ὡς ὁ Λεωνίδης, « ἐπεί τ' ᾔσθετο τοὺς συμμάχους ἐόντας ἀπροθύμους καὶ οὐκ ἐθέλοντας συγκινδυνεύειν, κελεύσαι σφέας ἀπαλλάττεσθαι », πάλιν μετ' ὀλίγον λέγει τοὺς Θηβαίους ἄκοντας αὐτὸν κατασχεῖν, οὓς C εἰκὸς ἦν ἀπελάσαι καὶ [μὴ] βουλομένους παραμένειν, εἰ μηδίζειν αἰτίαν εἶχον. Ὅπου γὰρ οὐκ ἐδεῖτο τῶν μὴ προθύμων, τί χρήσιμον ἦν ἀναμεμῖχθαι μαχομένοις ἀνθρώπους ὑπόπτους ; Οὐ γὰρ δὴ φρένας εἶχε τοιαύτας ὁ τῶν Σπαρτιατῶν βασιλεὺς καὶ τῆς Ἑλλάδος ἡγεμών, ὥστε « κατέχειν ἐν ὁμήρων λόγῳ » τοῖς τριακοσίοις τοὺς τετρακοσίους ὅπλ' ἔχοντας καὶ προσκειμένων ἔμπροσθεν ἤδη καὶ ὄπισθεν ἅμα τῶν πολεμίων· καὶ γὰρ εἰ πρότερον ἐν ὁμήρων λόγῳ ποιούμενος ἦγεν αὐτούς, ἔν γε τοῖς ἐσχάτοις εἰκὸς ἦν καιροῖς ἐκείνους τε Λεωνίδα μηδὲν φροντίσαντας ἀπαλλαγῆναι καὶ Λεωνίδαν δεῖσαι D τὴν ὑπ' ἐκείνων μᾶλλον ἢ τῶν βαρβάρων κύκλωσιν. Ἄνευ δὲ τούτων, πῶς οὐ γελοῖος ὁ Λεωνίδας, τοὺς μὲν ἄλλους Ἕλληνας ἀπιέναι κελεύων ὡς αὐτίκα μάλα τεθνηξομένους, Θηβαίους δὲ κωλύων ὡς ὑπ' αὐτοῦ φυλάττοιντο τοῖς Ἕλλησιν ἀποθνήσκειν μέλλοντος ; Εἰ γὰρ ὡς ἀληθῶς ἐν ὁμήρων λόγῳ, μᾶλλον δ' ἀνδραπόδων, περιῆγε τοὺς ἄνδρας, οὐ κατέχειν ὤφειλεν αὐτοὺς μετὰ τῶν ἀπολουμένων, ἀλλὰ παραδοῦναι τοῖς ἀπιοῦσι τῶν Ἑλλή-

except the Thespians and the Thebans who remained with the Spartans. The Thebans were detained by Leonidas as hostages very much against their will; but the Thespians of their own accord refused to desert B Leonidas and his men."

That makes quite plain Herodotus' personal and private animosity towards Thebes. Because of it he not only defamed its people on a false and unjust basis but even neglected to make his attack convincing, not to mention the fact that the self-contradiction of it will be clear to virtually everyone. He says first (220.2) Leonidas "dismissed the allies when he realised that they had no heart for the fight and were unwilling to take their share of the danger," and a little further on (222) that he kept the Thebans C "against their will," when it was sensible, if they were thought likely to medize, to drive them away even if they wanted to stay. Where there was no place for reluctant hearts, what was the use of suspect men alongside the fighters? The king of the Spartiates and leader of the Greeks was not quite so stupid as to "detain as hostages" four hundred armed men beside his own three hundred, when the enemy were already bearing down upon them before and behind. Even if he had taken them along earlier in events as hostages, at the end they were likely to abandon Leonidas regardless, D and he would have more to fear from them behind him than from the enemy behind him.

All that apart, it was ridiculous of Leonidas to order away the other Greeks because of their imminent death but to prevent the Thebans going so that he could keep an eye on them for Greece while facing his own death. If he really was dragging them around as hostages, or rather as slaves, he ought not to have kept them with the doomed but handed them

νων. Ὁ δὲ λοιπὸν ἦν τῶν αἰτίων εἰπεῖν, ὅτι ὡς ἀπολου-
μένους κατεῖχε, καὶ τοῦτ᾽ ἀνῄρηκεν ὁ συγγραφεύς, οἷς Ε
περὶ τῆς φιλοτιμίας τοῦ Λεωνίδου κατὰ λέξιν ⟨εἴρηκε⟩·
«Ταῦτα δὲ δὴ ἐπιλεγόμενον Λεωνίδην καὶ βουλόμενον
καταθέσθαι κλέος μούνων Σπαρτιητέων ἀποπέμψαι τοὺς
συμμάχους μᾶλλον ἢ τῇσι γνώμῃσι διενεχθέντας.»
Ὑπερβολὴ γὰρ εὐηθείας ἦν, ἧς ἀπήλαυνε δόξης τοὺς
συμμάχους κατέχειν μεθέξοντας τοὺς πολεμίους. Ὅτι
τοίνυν οὐ διεβέβλητο τοῖς Θηβαίοις ὁ Λεωνίδας, ἀλλὰ
καὶ φίλους ἐνόμιζε βεβαίους, ἐκ τῶν πεπραγμένων δῆλόν
ἐστι. Καὶ γὰρ παρῆλθεν εἰς Θήβας ἄγων τὸ στράτευμα καὶ
δεηθεὶς ἔτυχεν οὗ μηδὲ εἷς ἄλλος, ἐν τῷ ἱερῷ κατακοιμηθῆ-
ναι τοῦ Ἡρακλέους, καὶ τὴν ὄψιν ἣν εἶδεν ὄναρ ἐξήγγειλε Ζ
τοῖς Θηβαίοις· ἔδοξε γὰρ ἐν θαλάσσῃ πολὺν ἐχούσῃ
καὶ τραχὺν κλύδωνα τὰς ἐπιφανεστάτας καὶ μεγίστας
πόλεις τῆς Ἑλλάδος ἀνωμάλως διαφέρεσθαι καὶ σαλεύειν,
τὴν δὲ Θηβαίων ὑπερέχειν τε πασῶν καὶ μετέωρον ἀρθῆναι
πρὸς τὸν οὐρανὸν εἶτ᾽ ἐξαίφνης ἀφανῆ γενέσθαι· καὶ
ταῦτα μὲν ἦν ὅμοια τοῖς ὕστερον χρόνῳ πολλῷ συμπεσοῦσι
περὶ τὴν πόλιν. |

32 Ὁ δ᾽ Ἡρόδοτος ἐν τῇ διηγήσει τῆς μάχης καὶ 866 Α
τοῦ Λεωνίδου τὴν μεγίστην ἠμαύρωκε πρᾶξιν, αὐτοῦ
πεσεῖν πάντας εἰπὼν ἐν τοῖς στενοῖς περὶ τὸν Κολωνόν·
ἐπράχθη δ᾽ ἄλλως. Ἐπεὶ γὰρ ἐπύθοντο νύκτωρ τὴν
περίοδον τῶν πολεμίων, ἀναστάντες ἐβάδιζον ἐπὶ τὸ
στρατόπεδον καὶ τὴν σκηνὴν [ὀλίγου δεῖν] βασιλέως,
ὡς ἐκεῖνον αὐτὸν ἀποκτενοῦντες καὶ περὶ ἐκείνῳ τεθνηξό-
μενοι· μέχρι μὲν οὖν τῆς σκηνῆς ἀεὶ τὸν ἐμποδὼν φονεύον-
τες, τοὺς δ᾽ ἄλλους τρεπόμενοι προῆλθον· ἐπεὶ δ᾽ οὐχ
ηὑρίσκετο Ξέρξης, ζητοῦντες ἐν μεγάλῳ καὶ ἀχανεῖ
στρατεύματι καὶ πλανώμενοι μόλις ὑπὸ τῶν βαρβάρων Β
πανταχόθεν περιχυθέντων διεφθάρησαν. Ὅσα δ᾽ ἄλλα

over to the departing Greeks. As for the last possibility, that he kept them
so that they would be killed, our historian has destroyed that too in what   E
he has said about Leonidas' ambition (220.4); I quote: "It was the thought
of this oracle, combined with his wish to lay up for the Spartiates a
treasure of fame in which no other city should share, that made Leonidas
dismiss those troops, not a difference of opinions." It would be an excess
of folly to have his enemies share in the glory from which he was
expelling his allies. Leonidas was not at odds with Thebes; he considered
them sound friends indeed, and that is clear from what had happened. He
had taken his army into Thebes and had asked for a thing which no one
had asked for before, to sleep in the temple of Heracles, and he told the   F
Thebans what he had seen as he dreamt: it seemed there was a rough and
stormy sea, and the most famous and important cities of Greece were
reeling and rolling upon it; Thebes out-topped them all and was raised on
high to the sky, and suddenly was lost to sight. That was similar to what
much later did happen to the city.

32. In his description of the battle, Herodotus has also painted Leonidas'   866A
heroic deed in dark colours. He says (225.2/3) that they all fell in the
narrowest part by the hill. The truth is different. When they learnt in the
night of the enemy's journey round behind them, they arose and set out
for the Persian camp and the tent of the king, intending to kill him and
willing to die in the attempt. Forward they went, right to the tent, killing
anyone in their way and routing the rest; when they failed to find Xerxes,
they started hunting for him throughout his huge and sprawling army, and
as they roamed around they were hemmed in by the enemy on every side
and at last with difficulty were slain.   B

πρὸς τούτῳ τολμήματα καὶ ῥήματα τῶν Σπαρτιατῶν καταλέλοιπεν, ἐν τῷ Λεωνίδου βίῳ γραφήσεται· μικρὰ δ' οὐ χεῖρόν ἐστι καὶ νῦν διελθεῖν. Ἀγῶνα μὲν γὰρ ἐπιτάφιον αὐτῶν ἠγωνίσαντο πρὸ τῆς ἐξόδου καὶ τοῦτον ἐθεῶντο πατέρες αὐτῶν καὶ μητέρες· αὐτὸς δ' ὁ Λεωνίδας πρὸς μὲν τὸν εἰπόντα παντελῶς ὀλίγους ἐξάγειν αὐτὸν ἐπὶ τὴν μάχην «πολλοὺς μέν, ἔφη, τεθνηξομένους»· πρὸς δὲ τὴν γυναῖκα, πυνθανομένην ἐξιόντος εἴ τι λέγοι, μεταστραφεὶς εἶπεν «ἀγαθοῖς γαμεῖσθαι καὶ ἀγαθὰ τίκτειν». Ἐν δὲ Θερμοπύλαις μετὰ τὴν κύκλωσιν δύο C τῶν ἀπὸ γένους ὑπεξελέσθαι βουλόμενος ἐπιστολὴν ἐδίδου ⟨τῷ⟩ ἑτέρῳ καὶ ἔπεμπεν· ὁ δ' οὐκ ἐδέξατο φήσας μετ' ὀργῆς· «μαχατάς τοι, οὐκ ἀγγελιαφόρος, εἱπόμαν»· τὸν δ' ἕτερον ἐκέλευεν εἰπεῖν τι πρὸς τὰ τέλη τῶν Σπαρτιατῶν· ὁ δ' ἀπεκρίνατο· ⟨«κρείσσων ἐγὼ μένων καὶ κρεῖσσον' ἐμοῦ μένοντος⟩ τὰ πράγματα», καὶ τὴν ἀσπίδα λαβὼν εἰς τάξιν κατέστη. Ταῦτ' οὐκ ἄν τις ἐπετίμησεν, ἄλλου παραλιπόντος· ὁ δὲ τὴν Ἀμάσιδος ἀποψόφησιν καὶ τὴν τῶν ὄνων τοῦ κλέπτου προσέλασιν καὶ τὴν τῶν ἀσκῶν ἐπίδοσιν καὶ πολλὰ τοιαῦτα συναγαγὼν καὶ διαμνημονεύων, οὐκ ἀμελείᾳ δόξειεν ἂν καὶ ὑπεροψίᾳ D προΐεσθαι καλὰ μὲν ἔργα καλὰς δὲ φωνάς, ἀλλ' οὐκ εὐμενὴς ὢν πρὸς ἐνίους οὐδὲ δίκαιος.

33 Τοὺς δὲ Θηβαίους πρῶτον μέν φησι «μετὰ τῶν Ἑλλήνων ἐόντας μάχεσθαι ὑπ' ἀνάγκης ἐχομένους·» οὐ γὰρ μόνον Ξέρξης, ὡς ἔοικεν, ἀλλὰ καὶ Λεωνίδας μαστιγοφόρους εἶχεν ἑπομένους, ὑφ' ὧν οἱ Θηβαῖοι παρὰ γνώμην ἠναγκάζοντο μαστιγούμενοι μάχεσθαι. Καὶ τίς ἂν ὠμότερος τούτου γένοιτο συκοφάντης, ὃς μάχεσθαι μὲν ὑπ' ἀνάγκης φησὶ τοὺς ἀπελθεῖν καὶ φεύγειν δυναμένους, μηδίσαι δ' ἑκόντας, οἷς οὐδεὶς παρῆν βοηθῶν; Ἑξῆς δὲ τούτοις γέγραφεν ὅτι «τῶν ἄλλων ἐπειγομένων ἐπὶ

The other surviving deeds and sayings of the Spartiates I shall record in my life of Leonidas; there is no harm in reporting a few now. Before marching out from Sparta they celebrated their own funeral games, and their fathers and mothers attended. When Leonidas was told that he was taking very few to fight, he said, 'Plenty enough to die.' When his wife asked him if he had a special word as he left, he turned and said, 'Marry heroes and bear them.' At Thermopylae, after the encirclement, when he wanted to save two men of good family, he tried to give one a letter and so send him away. But the fellow refused and said angrily, 'I came with you as a soldier, not as an errand-boy.' The other man was told to report to the Spartiate authorities but replied, <'I'm better here, and if I am then so are> things,' and he picked up his shield and took his place. There would be no objection to these omissions in another author, but this is Herodotus, who gave us Amasis' rude retort to Apries (2.162.3), the thief and his donkeys and the wineskin (121), and lots of other such stuff, so that one can hardly think he omits noble deeds and noble sayings from carelessness and oversight: to certain people he is neither friendly nor fair.

33. He says of the Thebans (7.233.1) that first they "remained with the army and were compelled to make some show of resistance." So men with whips were available not only to Xerxes but also to Leonidas, were they, and they whipped the Thebans on and forced them to fight against their will! What piece of slander could be nastier than that? It says that men with the power to run away and escape fought because they had no choice, and men with no one coming to their aid opted to medize. Next he has written (233.1/2) that when the rest "made their hurried retreat to

τὸν Κολωνὸν ἀποσχισθέντες οἱ Θηβαῖοι χεῖράς τε προέτειναν καὶ ἦισαν ἄσσον τῶν βαρβάρων, λέγοντες τὸν ἀλη- E
θέστατον τῶν λόγων ὡς μηδίσειαν καὶ γῆν τε καὶ ὕδωρ ⟨...⟩
ἔδοσαν βασιλεῖ, ὑπὸ δ' ἀνάγκης ἐχόμενοι εἰς Θερμοπύλας
ἀπικοίατο καὶ ἀναίτιοι εἶεν τοῦ τρώματος τοῦ γενομένου
βασιλεῖ· ταῦτα λέγοντες περιεγένοντο· εἶχον γὰρ καὶ
Θεσσαλοὺς τούτων τῶν λόγων μάρτυρας.» Ὅρα διὰ
τοσούτων ἐν βαρβάροις κραυγαῖς καὶ παμμιγέσι θορύβοις
καὶ φυγαῖς καὶ διώξεσιν ἀκουομένην δικαιολογίαν καὶ
μαρτύρων ἀνάκρισιν καὶ Θετταλοὺς μεταξὺ τῶν φονευο-
μένων καὶ πατουμένων ὑπ' ἀλλήλων παρὰ τὰ στενὰ Θηβαίοις συνδικοῦντας, ὅτι τῆς Ἑλλάδος αὐτοὺς κρατοῦντας
ἄχρι Θεσπιῶν ἔναγχος ἐξήλασαν μάχῃ περιγενόμενοι F
καὶ τὸν ἄρχοντα Λατταμύαν ἀποκτείναντες. Ταῦτα γὰρ
ὑπῆρχε Βοιωτοῖς τότε καὶ Θετταλοῖς πρὸς ἀλλήλους,
ἐπιεικὲς δὲ καὶ φιλάνθρωπον οὐδέν. Ἀλλὰ δὴ τῶν Θετταλῶν
μαρτυρούντων, πῶς περιεγένοντο Θηβαῖοι; «τοὺς μὲν
αὐτῶν ἀπέκτειναν οἱ βάρβαροι προσιόντας», ὡς αὐτὸς
εἴρηκε, «τοὺς δὲ [τι] πλεῦνας, κελεύσαντος Ξέρξεω,
ἔστιξαν στίγματα βασιλήια, ἀρξάμενοι ἀπὸ τοῦ στρατηγοῦ
Λεοντιάδεω». | ⟨Ἀλλ'⟩ οὔτε Λεοντιάδης ἐν Θερμοπύλαις 867 A
ἦν στρατηγός, ἀλλ' Ἀνάξανδρος, ὡς Ἀριστοφάνης ἐκ
τῶν κατ' ἄρχοντας ὑπομνημάτων ἱστόρησε καὶ Νίκανδρος
ὁ Κολοφώνιος· οὔτε γιγνώσκει τις ἀνθρώπων πρὸ
Ἡροδότου στιχθέντας ὑπὸ Ξέρξου Θηβαίους. Ἐπεὶ
μέγιστον ἦν ἀπολόγημα τῆς διαβολῆς καὶ καλῶς εἶχε τὴν
πόλιν ἀγάλλεσθαι τοῖς στίγμασιν ἐκείνοις, ὡς Ξέρξου
δικάσαντος ἐχθίστοις χρήσασθαι Λεωνίδῃ καὶ Λεοντιάδῃ·
τοῦ μὲν γὰρ ᾐκίσατο πεπτωκότος τὸ σῶμα, τοῦ δὲ ζῶντος
ἔστιξεν. Ὁ δὲ τὴν μὲν εἰς Λεωνίδαν ὠμότητα δήλωμα ποιούμενος ὅτι μάλιστα δὴ ἀνδρῶν ὁ βάρβαρος ἐθυμώθη ζῶντι B
Λεωνίδῃ, Θηβαίους δὲ καὶ μηδίζοντας λέγων ἐν Θερμοπύ-

the little hill, the Thebans detached themselves and approached the enemy with outstretched hands, crying out that in their zeal for the Persian E interest they had given earth and water to the king, and had no share in the responsibility for the injury done him, because they had come to Thermopylae against their will. It was all too true – and, when it was backed up by the evidence of the Thessalians, it saved their lives."

Can you imagine that plea being heard, and the examination of the evidence for it, in the midst of all that, among the alien yells and the babel of noise and men fleeing and men pursuing, and then the Thessalians, in the middle of the killing and the trampling, bearing witness for the Thebans on the spot: 'Greece as far as Thespiae was recently in our F power, but they fought us and won and drove us out, killing our leader Lattamyas'? That was the situation between Boeotia and Thessaly in those days; no moderation or friendliness at all. But suppose the Thessalians did bear witness: in what way did the Thebans survive even so? "A few were killed by the Persians on their first approach," as he has said (233.2), "but the majority were branded by Xerxes' orders with the royal mark, beginning with Leontiades their commander." First: 867 A Leontiades was not in command at Thermopylae; Anaxander was, as Aristophanes recorded from the Magistrates' Register, and Nicander of Colophon agrees. Second: before Herodotus there is no knowledge at all of Thebans branded by Xerxes. It would have been a fine defence for the city against the slander, and there could well have been pride in those marks of branding, if Xerxes had adjudged Leonidas and Leontiades enemies of equal rank: Leonidas' dead body he mutilated, and Leontiades' living body he branded. But Herodotus treats Xerxes' savagery towards Leonidas as proof that the Persian was more furious with him than with B anyone else on earth, whereas he says the Thebans were branded at

λαις στιχθῆναι καὶ στιχθέντας αὖθις ἐν Πλαταιαῖς μηδίζειν προθύμως δοκεῖ μοι, καθάπερ Ἱπποκλείδης ὁ τοῖς σκέλεσι χειρονομῶν ἐπὶ τῆς τραπέζης, εἰπεῖν ἂν ἐξορχούμενος τὴν ἀλήθειαν · «οὐ φροντὶς Ἡροδότῳ.»

34 Ἐν δὲ τῇ ὀγδόῃ τοὺς Ἕλληνάς φησι καταδειλιάσαντας ἀπὸ τοῦ Ἀρτεμισίου δρησμὸν βουλεύεσθαι ἔσω εἰς τὴν Ἑλλάδα, καὶ τῶν Εὐβοέων δεομένων ὀλίγον ἐπιμεῖναι χρόνον, ὅπως ὑπεκθοῖντο γενεὰς καὶ τὸ οἰκετικόν, ὀλιγωρεῖν, ἄχρι οὗ Θεμιστοκλῆς ἀργύριον λαβὼν Εὐρυβιάδῃ τε μετέδωκε καὶ Ἀδειμάντῳ τῷ Κορινθίων στρατηγῷ · C τότε δὲ μεῖναι καὶ διαναυμαχῆσαι πρὸς τοὺς βαρβάρους. Ὁ μὲν Πίνδαρος, οὐκ ὢν συμμάχου πόλεως ἀλλὰ μηδίζειν αἰτίαν ἐχούσης, ὅμως τοῦ Ἀρτεμισίου μνησθεὶς ἐπιπεφώνηκεν ·

Ὅθι παῖδες Ἀθαναίων ἐβάλοντο φαεννὰν
κρηπῖδ' ἐλευθερίας.

Ἡρόδοτος δέ, ὑφ' οὗ κεκοσμῆσθαί τινες ἀξιοῦσι τὴν Ἑλλάδα, δωροδοκίας καὶ κλοπῆς ἔργον ἀποφαίνει τὴν νίκην ἐκείνην γενομένην καὶ τοὺς Ἕλληνας ἀκουσίως ἀγωνισαμένους, ὑπὸ τῶν στρατηγῶν ἐξαπατηθέντας ἀργύριον λαβόντων. Καὶ τοῦτο πέρας οὐ γέγονεν αὐτῷ τῆς κακοηθείας · ἀλλὰ πάντες μὲν ἄνθρωποι σχεδὸν ὁμολογοῦσι ταῖς ναυμαχίαις αὐτόθι κρατοῦντας τοὺς Ἕλληνας D ὅμως ὑφέσθαι τοῦ Ἀρτεμισίου τοῖς βαρβάροις, τὰ περὶ Θερμοπύλας ἀκούσαντας · οὐδὲ γὰρ ἦν ὄφελος ἐνταῦθα καθημένους φρουρεῖν τὴν θάλασσαν, ἐντὸς Πυλῶν τοῦ πολέμου γεγονότος καὶ Ξέρξου τῶν παρόδων κρατοῦντος. Ἡρόδοτος δέ, πρὶν ἀπαγγελῆναι τὸν Λεωνίδου θάνατον, ἤδη ποιεῖ τοὺς Ἕλληνας βουλευομένους ἀποδιδράσκειν · λέγει δ' οὕτω · «Τρηχέως δὲ περιεφθέντες, καὶ οὐκ ἥκιστα Ἀθηναῖοι, τῶν αἱ ἡμίσειαι τῶν νεῶν τετρωμέναι

Thermopylae though they were medizing, and, having been branded, were still medizing enthusiastically at Plataea! I'm reminded of Hippocleides (6.129), who danced with his legs on the table: Herodotus seems to be dancing away the truth, and saying "I could hardly care less." 34. In the eighth book he says (8.4/5) that the Greeks "turned coward, and began to consider abandoning Artemisium and making their escape to the inner parts of Greece;" the Euboeans begged them to wait a little while so that they could get out their families and slaves, but were ignored, until they paid money to Themistocles and he gave part to Eurybiades and part to Adeimantus the Corinthian commander: then they stayed and fought C it out at sea with the Persians. The poet Pindar, from a city not in the alliance but accused of medism, has nevertheless spoken in memory of Artemisium 'where the children of the Athenians laid a bright foundation stone of freedom.' Some people think Herodotus is the one who glorified Greece, but he makes out that the victory at Artemisium was the product of bribery and theft, and the Greeks fought not of their own free will but tricked into it by their silver-guilty commanders.

Not that that is the limit of his malice. Almost everyone agrees that D in the seafights at Artemisium the Greeks won, but yielded the position to the enemy when they heard about Thermopylae: there was no point in sitting there guarding the sea when the war had passed beyond the Gates and Xerxes held the passes. But Herodotus has the Greeks already planning to run away before the news of Leonidas' death, saying as follows (18): "they had been so roughly handled – especially the Athenians, half of whose ships were damaged – that they determined to quit

ἦσαν, δρησμὸν ἐβούλευον ⟨...⟩ εἰς τὴν Ἑλλάδα.» Καίτοι
τὴν πρὸ τοῦ ἀγῶνος ἀναχώρησιν οὕτως ὀνομάσαι μᾶλλον E
δ' ὀνειδίσαι δεδόσθω· ὁ δὲ καὶ πρότερον δρασμὸν εἶπε
καὶ νῦν δρασμὸν ὀνομάζει καὶ μετ' ὀλίγον πάλιν ἐρεῖ δρασ-
μόν (οὕτω πικρῶς τῷ ῥήματι προσπέφυκε)· «Τοῖσι δὲ
βαρβάροισι αὐτίκα μετὰ ταῦτα πλοίῳ ἦλθε ἀνὴρ Ἑστιαιεύς,
ἀγγέλλων τὸν δρησμὸν τὸν ⟨ἀπ'⟩ Ἀρτεμισίου τὸν τῶν
Ἑλλήνων· οἱ δὲ ὑπὸ ἀπιστίης τὸν μὲν ἀγγέλλοντα
εἶχον ἐν φυλακῇ, νέας δὲ ταχείας ἀπέστειλαν προκατοψο-
μένας.»

Τί σὺ λέγεις; ἀποδιδράσκειν ὡς κεκρατημένους,
οὓς οἱ πολέμιοι μετὰ τὴν μάχην ἀπιστοῦσι φεύγειν ὡς
πολὺ κρατοῦντας; Εἶτα πιστεύειν ἄξιον τούτῳ γράφοντι
περὶ ἀνδρὸς ἢ πόλεως μιᾶς, ὃς ἑνὶ ῥήματι τὸ νίκημα τῆς F
Ἑλλάδος ἀφαιρεῖται καὶ τὸ τρόπαιον καθαιρεῖ καὶ τὰς
ἐπιγραφὰς ἃς ἔθεντο παρὰ τῇ Ἀρτέμιδι τῇ Προσ⟨ηῴα⟩
κόμπον ἀποφαίνει καὶ ἀλαζονείαν; ἔχει δ' οὕτω τὸ
ἐπίγραμμα·

Παντοδαπῶν ἀνδρῶν γενεὰς Ἀσίας ἀπὸ χώρας
    παῖδες Ἀθηναίων τῷδέ ποτ' ἐν πελάγει
ναυμαχίᾳ δαμάσαντες, ἐπεὶ στρατὸς ὤλετο Μήδων, |
    σήματα ταῦτ' ἔθεσαν παρθένῳ Ἀρτέμιδι.   868 A

Ἐν μὲν οὖν ταῖς μάχαις οὐκ ἔταξε τοὺς Ἕλληνας οὐδ' ἐδή-
λωσεν ἣν ἑκάστη πόλις ἔχουσα χώραν ἐναυμάχησε,
κατὰ δὲ τὸν ἀπόπλουν, ὃν αὐτὸς δρασμὸν προσαγορεύει,
πρώτους φησὶ Κορινθίους πλεῖν ὑστάτους δ' Ἀθηναίους.

35 Ἔδει μὲν οὖν μηδὲ τοῖς μηδίσασιν Ἑλλήνων
ἄγαν ἐπεμβαίνειν, καὶ ταῦτα Θούριον μὲν ὑπὸ τῶν ἄλλων
νομιζόμενον, αὐτὸν δὲ Ἁλικαρνασσέων περιεχόμενον, οἳ
Δωριεῖς ὄντες μετὰ τῆς γυναικωνίτιδος ἐπὶ τοὺς Ἕλληνας
ἐστράτευσαν· ὁ δὲ τοσοῦτον ἀποδεῖ τοῦ πραότερον

and withdraw further south." Now, granted, he can call, or rather miscall, E withdrawal before battle quitting: but he spoke earlier of quitting, and he says quitting now, and he will say it again in a while, so bitterly he clings to the word (23.1): "Immediately after this a native of Hestiaea sailed to Aphetae with the news that the Greeks had quitted Artemisium. The Persians refused to believe it; they put the man under guard and sent off a party of some fast ships to see for themselves."

What are you saying? They are running away defeated after a battle in which the enemy believe them victorious and cannot credit their flight? Can we believe what he writes of any single man or state when he wipes F out a whole Greek victory in a word, throwing down its memorial and making vain boast out of the verses inscribed to Artemis Proseoa, which go (Campbell XXIV):

> 'The sons of Athens fighting from this shore
> > once overcame a motley host arrayed
> from Asiatic lands: after the war
> > they raised this stone to Artemis the Maid'?   868 A

In the fights he failed to give the Greek dispositions or show what station each city fought from, and in the withdrawal (which he calls quitting) he says (21.2) "the Corinthians led, the Athenians bringing up the rear."

35. He ought not to come down so fiercely even on the Greeks who medized; after all, he's only a Thurian, according to the usual account, though his own attachment is to Halicarnassus, whose people are Dorians: they joined the expedition to Greece with their harem in tow! Yet he is

ὀνομάζειν τὰς τῶν μηδισάντων ἀνάγκας, ὥστε περὶ
Θετταλῶν διηγησάμενος ὅτι Φωκεῦσιν, ἐχθροῖς καὶ B
πολεμίοις οὖσι, προσέπεμψαν, ἐπαγγελλόμενοι τὴν χώραν
αὐτῶν ἀβλαβῆ διαφυλάξειν, εἰ πεντήκοντα τάλαντα
μισθὸν λάβοιεν, ταῦτα περὶ Φωκέων γέγραφεν αὐτοῖς
ὀνόμασιν· «Οἱ γὰρ Φωκεῖς μοῦνοι τῶν ταύτῃ ἀνθρώπων
οὐκ ἐμήδιζον, ⟨κατ᾽ ἄλλο μὲν οὐδέν, ὡς⟩ ἐγὼ συμβαλλόμενος εὑρίσκω, κατὰ δὲ τὸ ἔχθος τὸ Θεσσαλῶν· εἰ δὲ
Θεσσαλοὶ τὰ Ἑλλήνων ηὖξον, ὡς ἐμοὶ δοκεῖ, ἐμήδιζον
ἂν οἱ Φωκεῖς.» Καίτοι μετὰ μικρὸν αὐτὸς ἐρεῖ τρισκαίδεκα
πόλεις τῶν Φωκέων ὑπὸ τοῦ βαρβάρου κατακεκαῦσθαι,
διεφθάρθαι τὴν χώραν, ἐμπεπρῆσθαι τὸ ἐν Ἄβαις ἱερόν, C
ἄνδρας ἀπολωλέναι καὶ γυναῖκας, ὅσοι μὴ διαφυγόντες
ἔφθησαν εἰς τὸν Παρνασόν. Ἀλλ᾽ ὅμως τοὺς τὰ ἔσχατα
παθεῖν ἐπὶ τῷ μὴ προέσθαι τὸ καλὸν ὑπομείναντας εἰς
τὴν αὐτὴν ἔθετο κακίαν τοῖς προθυμότατα μηδίσασι·
καὶ τὰ ἔργα τῶν ἀνδρῶν ψέξαι μὴ δυνηθεὶς αἰτίας ἐκάθητο
φαύλας καὶ ὑπονοίας ἐπὶ τοῦ γραφείου συντιθεὶς κατ᾽ αὐτῶν
καὶ κελεύων οὐκ ἀφ᾽ ὧν ἔπραξαν, ⟨ἀλλ᾽ ἀφ᾽ ὧν ἔπραξαν
ἄν⟩, εἰ μὴ ταῦτα Θετταλοῖς ἔδοξε, κρίνεσθαι τὴν διάνοιαν
αὐτῶν, ὥσπερ χώρας ἀντειλημμένης ὑφ᾽ ἑτέρων τῆς προδοσίας ἀπολειφθέντων. Εἰ τοίνυν Θετταλούς τις ἐπεχείρει
τοῦ μηδισμοῦ παραιτεῖσθαι, λέγων ὡς οὐ ταῦτ᾽ ἐβούλοντο, D
τῇ δὲ πρὸς Φωκέας διαφορᾷ τοῖς Ἕλλησι προστιθεμένους
ὁρῶντες αὐτοὶ παρὰ γνώμην ἐμήδισαν, ἆρ᾽ οὐκ ἂν αἴσχιστα
κολακεύειν ἔδοξε καὶ πρὸς ἑτέρων χάριν αἰτίας χρηστὰς
ἐπὶ πράγμασι φαύλοις πορίζων διαστρέφειν τὴν ἀλήθειαν ;
Ἐγὼ μὲν οἶμαι. Πῶς οὖν οὐ περιφανέστατα δόξει συκο-
φαντεῖν ὁ μὴ δι᾽ ἀρετὴν τὰ βέλτιστα Φωκεῖς ἑλομένους
ἀποφαινόμενος, ἀλλ᾽ ὅτι τἀναντία Θετταλοὺς ἔγνωσαν
φρονοῦντας ; Οὐδὲ γὰρ εἰς ἑτέρους, ὥσπερ εἴωθεν, ἀνάγει
τὴν διαβολὴν ἀκηκοέναι λέγων, ἀλλ᾽ αὐτὸς εὑρίσκειν

a long way from polite vocabulary about the pressures on the medizers: when the Phocians received a message from their bitter enemies the B Thessalians, that for fifty talents their land could be kept unscathed, he writes of the Thessalians as follows (30), and I quote: "The Phocians were the only people in this part of Greece who had not gone over to the Persians, and in my considered opinion their motive was simply and solely their hatred of Thessaly. If Thessaly had remained loyal, no doubt the Phocians would have deserted to Persia." And yet in a short while (32–33) he will be speaking of thirteen Phocian towns burnt to the ground, their land laid waste, the shrine at Abae burnt down, and all the C men and women who didn't escape to Parnassus killed. They endured the worst they could suffer simply not to betray their honour, but nevertheless Herodotus put them in the same class for cowardice as the keenest of medizers.

He could not find fault with their heroic deeds, but he sat at his desk constructing a cheap motivation for them, mere suspicious conjecture, telling us to estimate their intentions not from what they did do but from what they would have done if the Thessalians had not done what *they* decided to do – as if the Phocians failed to be traitors because that space was occupied by others. Suppose one tried to excuse Thessalian medism D by saying they did not plan to medize, but did so against their will, thanks to their quarrel with the Phocians, when they saw that the Phocians were joining the Greeks: surely that would be a despicable piece of flattery, to destroy the truth by providing good reasons for bad deeds just to please one side? I reckon it would. So how can anyone not appear the plainest hypocrite who represents the Phocians choosing the path of heroism not because they were heroes but because they found the Thessalians had picked the other path? Herodotus doesn't, as he often does, put the blame on other people by saying "I heard;" he says "in my considered opinion."

συμβαλλόμενος. Εἰπεῖν οὖν ἔδει τὰ τεκμήρια δι' ὧν Ε
ἐπείσθη τοὺς ὅμοια πράττοντας τοῖς ἀρίστοις τὰ αὐτὰ τοῖς
φαυλοτάτοις διανοηθῆναι· τὸ γὰρ τῆς ἔχθρας γελοῖόν
ἐστιν· οὔτε γὰρ Αἰγινήτας ἐκώλυσεν ἡ πρὸς Ἀθηναίους
διαφορὰ καὶ Χαλκιδεῖς ἡ πρὸς Ἐρετριέας καὶ Κορινθίους
ἡ πρὸς Μεγαρέας τῇ Ἑλλάδι συμμαχεῖν· οὐδ' αὖ πάλιν
Θετταλοὺς μηδίζοντες οἱ πολεμιώτατοι Μακεδόνες τῆς
πρὸς τὸν βάρβαρον φιλίας ἀπέστρεψαν· τὰς γὰρ ἰδίας
ἀπεχθείας ὁ κοινὸς ἀπέκρυψε κίνδυνος, ὥστε τῶν ἄλλων
παθῶν ἐκπεσόντας ἢ τῷ καλῷ δι' ἀρετὴν ἢ τῷ συμφέροντι
δι' ἀνάγκην προστίθεσθαι τὴν γνώμην. Οὐ μὴν ἀλλὰ
καὶ μετὰ τὴν ἀνάγκην ἐκείνην ᾗ κατελήφθησαν ὑπὸ F
Μήδοις γενέσθαι, πάλιν μετεβάλοντο πρὸς τοὺς Ἕλληνας
οἱ ἄνδρες, καὶ Λακράτης μὲν αὐτοῖς ὁ Σπαρτιάτης
ἄντικρυς ἐμαρτύρησεν· αὐτὸς δ' ὁ Ἡρόδοτος ὥσπερ
ἐκβιασθεὶς ἐν τοῖς Πλαταιικοῖς ὁμολογεῖ καὶ Φωκέας
παραγενέσθαι τοῖς Ἕλλησιν.

36 Οὐ δεῖ δὲ θαυμάζειν εἰ τοῖς ἀτυχήσασιν ἔγκειται
πικρῶς, ὅπου καὶ τοὺς παραγενομένους καὶ συγκινδυνεύ-
σαντας |εἰς τὴν τῶν πολεμίων μερίδα καὶ προδοτῶν 869 A
μετατίθησι· «Νάξιοι γὰρ τρεῖς ἔπεμψαν τριήρεις συμμάχους τοῖς βαρβάροις, εἷς δὲ τῶν τριηράρχων Δημόκριτος
ἔπεισε τοὺς ἄλλους ἑλέσθαι τὰ τῶν Ἑλλήνων.» Οὕτως
οὐδ' ἐπαινεῖν ἄνευ τοῦ ψέγειν οἶδεν, ἀλλ' ἵν' εἷς ἀνὴρ
ἐγκωμιασθῇ, πόλιν ὅλην δεῖ κακῶς ἀκοῦσαι καὶ δῆμον.
Μαρτυρεῖ δ' αὐτοῖς τῶν μὲν πρεσβυτέρων Ἑλλάνικος, τῶν
δὲ νεωτέρων Ἔφορος, ὁ μὲν ἕξ, ὁ δὲ πέντε ναυσὶν αὐτοὺς
[Ναξίους] ἐλθεῖν τοῖς Ἕλλησι βοηθοῦντας ἱστορήσας.
Αὐτὸς δὲ καὶ παντάπασιν ἑαυτὸν ὁ Ἡρόδοτος ἐξελέγχει
ταῦτα πλαττόμενον. Οἱ μὲν γὰρ Ναξίων ὡρογράφοι
λέγουσι καὶ πρότερον Μεγαβάτην ἀπώσασθαι ναυσὶ B
διακοσίαις ἐπιπλεύσαντα τῇ νήσῳ, καὶ Δᾶτιν αὖθις

He should have declared what evidence persuaded him that men who E
successfully produced the deeds of heroes had intended the deeds of
cowards.

This business of mutual enmity is ridiculous. Aegina was not kept
back by her difference with Athens, nor Chalcis by hers with Eretria, nor
Corinth by hers with Megara, from joining the fight for Greece. The
Thessalians were not diverted from making friends with Persia because
their bitter enemies the Macedonians medized. Private quarrels are
buried by a common peril; other feelings go by the board; men plan for
the good because of honour, or for advantage because of need. After the
Phocians had endured the necessity that forced them under Persian
control, they then changed back to the Greek side. Lacrates the Spartiate F
bore direct witness of that, and Herodotus himself agrees, perforce
apparently, that at Plataea there were Phocians on the Greek side (9.31.5).

36. But there is no need for surprise at his harsh treatment of the luckless,
when even those who stood firm and shared the peril are classed with 869 A
enemies and traitors. Naxos sent three triremes to join the Persians, but
one of the trierarchs, Democritus, persuaded the rest to side with the
Greeks (8.46.3). He simply does not know how to offer praise without
blame in it: one individual gets the praise, but to achieve it a whole city
and its people get a bad name. But there are people to speak for Naxos:
Hellanicus amongst older writers, and Ephorus among later ones.
Hellanicus reports that the Naxians came to the help of the Greeks with
six ships, and Ephorus says five. Herodotus (5.33–34) actually convicts
himself of his own fabrication, since the Naxian chroniclers say that when B
Megabates earlier attacked the island with two hundred ships, he was
driven off, and later the general Datis was repulsed after burning <...> to
do harm. But if, as Herodotus has said elsewhere (6.96), the Persians did

τὸν στρατηγὸν ἐξελάσαι καταπρήσαντα ⟨...⟩ ποιῆσαι
κακόν. Εἰ δέ, ὡς Ἡρόδοτος εἴρηκεν ἀλλαχόθι, τὴν μὲν
πόλιν αὐτῶν ἐμπρήσαντες διέφθειραν, οἱ δ' ἄνθρωποι
καταφυγόντες εἰς τὰ ὄρη διεσώθησαν, ἦ που καλὴν
αἰτίαν εἶχον τοῖς ἀπολέσασι τὴν πατρίδα πέμπειν
βοήθειαν, ἀλλὰ μὴ τοῖς ἀμυνομένοις ὑπὲρ τῆς κοινῆς ἐλευθερίας ἀμύνειν. Ὅτι δ' οὐκ ἐπαινέσαι βουληθεὶς Δημόκρι-
τον, ἀλλ' ἐπ' αἰσχύνῃ Ναξίων συνέθηκε τὸ ψεῦδος,
δῆλός ἐστι τῷ παραλιπεῖν ὅλως καὶ παρασιωπῆσαι τὸ C
Δημοκρίτου κατόρθωμα καὶ τὴν ἀριστείαν ἣν ἐπιγράμματι
Σιμωνίδης ἐδήλωσε·

Δημόκριτος τρίτος ἦρξε μάχης, ὅτε πὰρ Σαλαμῖνα
Ἕλληνες Μήδοις σύμβαλον ἐν πελάγει·
πέντε δὲ νῆας ἕλεν δηίων, ἕκτην δ' ὑπὸ χειρὸς
ῥύσατο βαρβαρικῆς Δωρίδ' ἁλισκομένην.

37   Ἀλλὰ τί ἄν τις ἀγανακτοίη περὶ Ναξίων; εἰ γὰρ
εἰσὶν ἀντίποδες ἡμῶν, ὥσπερ ἔνιοι λέγουσι, τῆς γῆς τὰ
κάτω περιοικοῦντες, οἶμαι μηδ' ἐκείνους ἀνηκόους εἶναι
Θεμιστοκλέους καὶ τοῦ Θεμιστοκλέους βουλεύματος,
ὃ βουλεύσας τῇ Ἑλλάδι ναυμαχῆσαι πρὸ τῆς Σαλαμῖνος D
ἱδρύσατο ναὸν ⟨Ἀριστο⟩βούλης Ἀρτέμιδος ἐν Μελίτῃ,
τοῦ βαρβάρου καταπολεμηθέντος. Τοῦτο μὲν τοῦ Θεμιστοκλέους ὁ χαρίεις συγγραφεὺς ὅσον ἐφ' ἑαυτῷ παραιρού-
μενος καὶ τὴν δόξαν εἰς ἕτερον μεταφέρων ταῦτα γράφει
κατὰ λέξιν· «Ἐνταῦθα δὲ Θεμιστοκλέα ἀφικόμενον ἐπὶ
τὴν νέα εἴρετο Μνησίφιλος ἀνὴρ Ἀθηναῖος ὅ τι σφιν
εἴη βεβουλευμένον· πυθόμενος δὲ πρὸς αὐτοῦ ὡς εἴη
δεδογμένον ἀνάγειν τὰς νέας πρὸς τὸν Ἰσθμὸν καὶ πρὸ τῆς
Πελοποννήσου ναυμαχέειν, ⟨εἶπε⟩· «Οὐκ ἄρα, ἢν ἀπαί-
ρωσι τὰς νέας ἀπὸ Σαλαμῖνος, οὐδὲ περὶ μιῆς ἔτι πατρίδος
ναυμαχήσεις· κατὰ γὰρ πόλεις ἕκαστοι τρέψονται.» Καὶ E

burn the city and destroy Naxos and the people fled to the hills for safety, then what a fine cause they had to be sending aid to their own destroyers and not to be helping those who were fighting for freedom for all! Herodotus constructed his fiction not to praise Democritus but to disgrace Naxos, and that is plain from his complete omission and suppression of Democritus' real piece of heroism, displayed instead in Simonides' poem   C (Campbell XIX):

> 'Democritus was third man in to fight
> > at Salamis where Greek and Persian met.
> Five ships he took, and rescued from her plight
> > a Dorian sixth, by pressing foes beset.'

37. But why get cross about Naxos? If there are people on the other side of the earth, as some say, living on the underside of the world, even they, I'm sure, have not failed to hear of Themistocles and Themistocles' battle-plan, the one he constructed for Greece, to fight at sea off Salamis;   D and after the total defeat of Xerxes he built at Melite a temple of Artemis of Best Counsel. Our charming historian does his best to steal Themistocles' achievement from him and to give the glory to another by saying, and I quote (8.57/8): "When Themistocles arrived at his ship an Athenian named Mnesiphilus asked him what plan it had been decided to adopt. On learning that they had resolved to sail to the Isthmus and to fight there in defence of the Peloponnese, 'No, no,' he exclaimed; 'once the fleet leaves Salamis, it will no longer be one country that you'll be fighting for. Everyone will go home.'" And a little later: "'Try, if you   E

μετ' ὀλίγον · « ἀλλὰ εἴ τις ἔστι μηχανή, ἴθι τε καὶ πειρῶ
διαχέαι τὰ βεβουλευμένα, ἤν κως δύνῃ ἀναγνῶσαι
Εὐρυβιάδεα μεταβουλεύσασθαι ὥστε αὐτοῦ μενεῖν ».
Εἶθ' ὑπειπὼν ὅτι « κάρτα τῷ Θεμιστοκλεῖ ἤρεσε ἡ ὑποθήκη,
καὶ οὐδὲν πρὸς ταῦτα ἀμειψάμενος » ἀφίκετο πρὸς τὸν
Εὐρυβιάδην, πάλιν αὐταῖς λέξεσι γέγραφεν · « Ἐνταῦθα
δὲ Θεμιστοκλῆς παριζόμενός ⟨οἱ⟩ καταλέγει κεῖνά τε πάντα
ἃ ἤκουσε Μνησιφίλου ἑωυτοῦ ποιεύμενος, καὶ ἄλλα
⟨πολλὰ⟩ προστιθείς ». Ὁρᾷς ὅτι κακοηθείας προστρί-
βεται τῷ ἀνδρὶ δόξαν, ἴδιον αὐτοῦ βούλευμα ποιεῖσθαι τὸ
τοῦ Μνησιφίλου λέγων.

38 Ἔτι δὲ μᾶλλον τῶν Ἑλλήνων καταγελῶν, Θεμιστο- F
κλέα μὲν οὔτε φησὶ φρονῆσαι τὸ συμφέρον ἀλλὰ παριδεῖν,
ὃς Ὀδυσσεὺς ἐπωνομάσθη διὰ τὴν φρόνησιν · Ἀρτεμισίαν
δὲ τὴν Ἡροδότου πολῖτιν, μηδενὸς διδάξαντος, αὐτὴν
ἀφ' ἑαυτῆς ἐπινοήσασαν Ξέρξῃ προειπεῖν ὡς « οὐχ οἷοί
τε πολλὸν χρόνον ἔσονταί τοι ἀντέχειν οἱ Ἕλληνες, ἀλλά
σφεας διασκεδᾷς, κατὰ πόλεις δὲ ἕκαστοι φεύξονται ⟨…⟩ · |
καὶ οὐκ εἰκὸς αὐτούς, ἤν σὺ ἐπὶ τὴν Πελοπόννησον 870 A
ἐλαύνῃς τὸν πεζὸν στρατόν, ἀτρεμήσειν, οὐδέ σφιν
μελήσειν πρὸ τῶν Ἀθηναίων ναυμαχέειν · ἤν δὲ αὐτίκα
ἐπειχθῇς ναυμαχῆσαι, δειμαίνω μὴ ὁ ναυτικὸς στρατὸς
κακωθεὶς καὶ τὸν ⟨πεζὸν⟩ προσδηλήσηται. » Ταῦτα μὲν
οὖν μέτρων ἐνδεῖ τῷ Ἡροδότῳ Σίβυλλαν ἀποφῆναι
τὴν Ἀρτεμισίαν τὰ μέλλοντα προθεσπίζουσαν οὕτως
ἀκριβῶς. Διὸ καὶ Ξέρξης αὐτῇ παρέδωκε τοὺς ἑαυτοῦ
παῖδας ἀπάγειν εἰς Ἔφεσον · ἐπελέληστο γὰρ ἐκ Σούσων,
ὡς ἔοικεν, ἄγειν γυναῖκας, εἰ γυναικείας ἐδέοντο παραπομ-
πῆς οἱ παῖδες.

possibly can, to upset the plan of the conference – it may be that you will be able to persuade Eurybiades to change his mind and remain at Salamis.'" Then, adding "Themistocles highly approved of this suggestion, and without saying a word he went to Eurybiades;" (again I quote) "Themistocles, taking a seat beside him, repeated Mnesiphilus' arguments as if they were his own, with many new ones added." You can see how he stamps a name for malice on the man, by saying he made Mnesiphilus' plan out to be his own.

38. He has yet more contempt of the Greeks to express. He says that **F** Themistocles couldn't see what was needed and overlooked it, even though he was nicknamed Odysseus for his intelligence, while Artemisia, Herodotus' own compatriot, without anybody's prompting could say to Xerxes out of her own considered judgement (68 β/γ): "'The Greeks will not be able to hold out against you for long; you will soon cause their forces to disperse – they will soon break up and go home. If you march **870 A** with your army towards the Peloponnese, those men are not likely to be very easy in their minds – they will hardly like the idea of fighting in defence of the Athenians. If, on the other hand, you rush into a naval action, my fear is that the defeat of your fleet may involve the army too.'" Herodotus should have used verse for that, to present Artemisia as a Sibyl predicting the future so accurately! As reward for the advice, Xerxes gave her his children to take back to Ephesus (103): presumably he had forgotten to bring women from Susa, if it was female escort the children needed.

82 PLUTARCH

39 Ἀλλ' ὧν μὲν ἔψευσται, λόγος ἡμῖν οὐδείς · ἃ δέ B
γε κατέψευσται μόνον ἐξετάζομεν. Φησὶ τοίνυν Ἀθηναίους
λέγειν ὡς Ἀδείμαντος ὁ Κορινθίων στρατηγός, ἐν χερσὶ
τῶν πολεμίων γενομένων, ὑπερεκπλαγεὶς καὶ καταδείσας
ἔφευγεν, οὐ πρύμναν κρουσάμενος οὐδὲ διαδὺς ἀτρέμα
διὰ τῶν μαχομένων, ἀλλὰ λαμπρῶς ἐπαράμενος τὰ ἱστία
καὶ τὰς ναῦς ἁπάσας ἀποστρέψας · εἶτα μέντοι κέλης
ἐλαυνόμενος αὐτῷ συνέτυχε περὶ τὰ λήγοντα τῆς Σαλα-
μινίας, ἐκ δὲ τοῦ κέλητος ἐφθέγξατό τις · «Σὺ μέν, ὦ
Ἀδείμαντε, φεύγεις καταπροδοὺς τοὺς Ἕλληνας · οἳ
δὲ καὶ δὴ νικῶσι, καθάπερ ἠρῶντο ἐπικρατῆσαι τῶν
ἐχθρῶν.» Ὁ δὲ κέλης οὗτος ἦν, ὡς ἔοικεν, οὐρανοπετής · C
τί γὰρ ἔδει φείδεσθαι μηχανῆς τραγικῆς, ἐν πᾶσι τοῖς
ἄλλοις ὑπερπαίοντα τοὺς τραγῳδοὺς ἀλαζονείᾳ ; Πιστεύ-
σας οὖν ὁ Ἀδείμαντος ἐπανῆλθεν εἰς τὸ στρατόπεδον
ἐπ' ἐξειργασμένοις · «αὕτη φάτις ἔχει ὑπὸ Ἀθηναίων ·
οὐ μέντοι Κορίνθιοι ὁμολογέουσιν, ἀλλὰ ἐν πρώτοισι
σφέας αὐτοὺς τῆς ναυμαχίης νομίζουσι γενέσθαι · μαρτυρεῖ δέ σφι καὶ ἡ ἄλλη Ἑλλάς». Τοιοῦτός ἐστιν ἐν πολλοῖς
ὁ ἄνθρωπος · ἑτέρας καθ' ἑτέρων διαβολὰς καὶ κατηγορίας
κατατίθησιν, ὥστε μὴ διαμαρτεῖν τοῦ φανῆναί τινα
πάντως πονηρόν · ὥσπερ ἐνταῦθα περίεστιν αὐτῷ, πιστευο- D
μένης μὲν τῆς διαβολῆς Κορινθίους ἀδοξεῖν, ἀπιστουμένους
⟨δ'⟩ Ἀθηναίους · ἣν οἶμαι μηδὲ Κορινθίων Ἀθηναίους,
ἀλλὰ τοῦτον ἀμφοτέρων ὁμοῦ καταψεύδεσθαι. Θουκυδίδης
γοῦν ἀντιλέγοντα ποιῶν τῷ Κορινθίῳ τὸν Ἀθηναῖον ἐν
Λακεδαίμονι καὶ πολλὰ περὶ τῶν Μηδικῶν λαμπρυνόμενον
ἔργων καὶ περὶ τῆς ἐν Σαλαμῖνι ναυμαχίας οὐδεμίαν
αἰτίαν προδοσίας ἢ λιποταξίας ἐπενήνοχε Κορινθίοις ·
οὐδὲ γὰρ εἰκὸς ἦν Ἀθηναίους ταῦτα βλασφημεῖν περὶ
τῆς Κορινθίων πόλεως, ἣν τρίτην μὲν ἑώρων μετὰ
Λακεδαιμονίους καὶ μεθ' αὐτοὺς ἐγχαραττομένην τοῖς ἀπὸ

39. But I am not bothered about his mere falsehoods: it is his malicious B
falsehoods that we are examining. He says (94) that the Athenians have
a story that Adeimantus the Corinthian commander fled in terror and
panic when the enemy came to grips: he didn't back water or slip quietly
through the ranks as they engaged, but brazenly raised his sails and turned
all his ships; but then a little boat making speed met him near the top end
of Salamis and a voice cried out from the boat, 'So you have betrayed the
Greeks, Adeimantus, and are running away: but the prayers of the Greeks
are being answered, and they are victorious over their enemies.' The little C
boat was heaven-sent, it seems: since Herodotus outdoes the tragic poets
in all other sorts of nonsense, why should he refrain from a *deus ex machina?*
Anyway, Adeimantus believed and (94.4) "rejoined the fleet after the
action was over. This, as I said, is an Athenian story, and the Corinthians
do not admit the truth of it: on the contrary, they believe that their ships
played a most distinguished part in the battle – and the rest of Greece gives
evidence in their favour."

That is typical of the fellow: he makes a variety of attacks and
accusations against different people, and that way cannot fail to put
someone in the wrong. Here his gain is that the Corinthians will be in the D
wrong if the tale against them is credited, and the Athenians will be if they
are not. I think it is not the Athenians perjuring themselves against the
Corinthians but Herodotus perjuring himself against both of them together.
At least Thucydides has brought no charge of treachery or desertion
against the Corinthians into the reply of the Athenians at Sparta, when the
Athenian boasts at length of Athens' prowess in the Persian wars and
particularly at the battle of Salamis: it would not be sensible for Athenians
to make that attack on Corinth when they could see its name engraved on

τῶν βαρβάρων ἀναθήμασιν· ἐν δὲ Σαλαμῖνι παρὰ τὴν E
πόλιν ἔδωκαν αὐτοῖς θάψαι τε τοὺς ἀποθανόντας, ὡς
ἄνδρας ἀγαθοὺς γενομένους, ⟨καὶ⟩ ἐπιγράψαι τόδε τὸ
ἐλεγεῖον·

Ὦ ξεῖν', εὔυδρόν ποτ' ἐναίομεν ἄστυ Κορίνθου,
νῦν δ' ἅμ' Αἴαντος νᾶσος ἔχει Σαλαμίς.
ἐνθάδε Φοινίσσας νῆας καὶ Πέρσας ἑλόντες
καὶ Μήδους, ἱερὰν Ἑλλάδα ῥυσάμεθα.

Τὸ δ' ἐν Ἰσθμῷ κενοτάφιον ἐπιγραφὴν ἔχει ταύτην·

Ἀκμᾶς ἑστακυῖαν ἐπὶ ξυροῦ Ἑλλάδα πᾶσαν
ταῖς αὐτῶν ψυχαῖς κείμεθα ῥυσάμενοι.

Διοδώρου δέ τινος τῶν Κορινθίων τριηράρχων ἐν ἱερῷ F
Λητοῦς ἀναθήμασι κειμένοις καὶ τοῦτ' ἐπεγέγραπτο·

Ταῦτ' ἀπὸ δυσμενέων Μήδων ναῦται Διοδώρου
ὅπλ' ἀνέθεν Λατοῖ, μνάματα ναυμαχίας.

Αὐτός γε μὴν ὁ Ἀδείμαντος, ᾧ πλεῖστα λοιδορούμενος
Ἡρόδοτος διατελεῖ καὶ λέγων «μοῦνον ἀσπαίρειν τῶν
στρατηγῶν, ὡς φευξόμενον ἀπ' Ἀρτεμισίου καὶ μὴ
περιμενοῦντα», σκόπει τίνα δόξαν εἶχεν·

Οὗτος Ἀδειμάντου κείνου τάφος, ὃν διὰ πᾶσα
Ἑλλὰς ἐλευθερίας ἀμφέθετο στέφανον. |

Οὔτε γὰρ τελευτήσαντι τοιαύτην εἰκὸς ἦν ἀνδρὶ δειλῷ 871 A
καὶ προδότῃ γενέσθαι τιμήν, οὔτ' ἂν ἐτόλμησε τῶν
θυγατέρων ὄνομα θέσθαι τῇ μὲν Ναυσινίκην, τῇ δ' Ἀκροθί-
νιον, τῇ δ' Ἀλεξιβίαν, Ἀριστέα δὲ καλέσαι τὸν υἱόν,
εἰ μή τις ἦν ἐπιφάνεια καὶ λαμπρότης περὶ αὐτὸν ἀπὸ
τῶν ἔργων ἐκείνων. Καὶ μὴν ὅτι μόναι τῶν Ἑλληνίδων
αἱ Κορίνθιαι γυναῖκες εὔξαντο τὴν καλὴν ἐκείνην καὶ
δαιμόνιον εὐχήν, ἔρωτα τοῖς ἀνδράσι τῆς πρὸς τοὺς

the war memorial in third place after Sparta and themselves. Moreover, E
he Athenians granted the Corinthians burial for their dead on Salamis by
the town, as heroes, with the inscription of the following elegy (Campbell
XI):

> 'Sir, once our home was Corinth's spring-fed town;
> now Ajax' isle of Salamis keeps our peace.
> Here Medes and Persians and Phoenicians down
> we sent, and so protected holy Greece.'

The cenotaph at the Isthmus bears the following inscription (Campbell
XII):

> 'Balanced upon the razor's edge was Greece:
> we saved her with our lives and so find peace.'

There is the inscription in the temple of Leto on the offerings made by F
Diodorus, one of the Corinthian captains (Campbell XIII):

> 'These weapons Diodorus' sailors brought
> to Leto, marking how the Persians fought.'

As for Adeimantus himself, so plentifully and persistently abused by
Herodotus (when for instance he observes (8.5.1) that he was the only one
of the generals still trying to wriggle out of it, so as to escape Artemisium
and not wait), consider the reputation he had (Campbell X):

> 'This grave is Adeimantus', thanks to whom
> all Greece put on the garland of freedom.'

Such an honour is unlikely to be granted to a dead man who was a coward 871 A
and a traitor, nor would he have dared name his daughters Nausinice,
Acrothinium and Alexibia and his son Aristeus unless he had derived
some notable glory from his exploits.

Then there is the fact that the women of Corinth, alone in Greece, made
that splendid and inspired prayer, that the goddess should make their men

βαρβάρους μάχης ἐμβαλεῖν τὴν θεόν, οὐχ ὅπως ⟨τοὺς⟩ περὶ τὸν Ἡρόδοτον ἀγνοῆσαι πιθανὸν ἦν, ἀλλ' οὐδὲ τὸν ἔσχατον Καρῶν· διεβοήθη γὰρ τὸ πρᾶγμα καὶ Σιμωνίδης B ἐποίησεν ἐπίγραμμα, χαλκῶν εἰκόνων ἀνασταθεισῶν ἐν τῷ ναῷ τῆς Ἀφροδίτης ὃν ἱδρύσασθαι Μήδειαν λέγουσιν, οἱ μὲν αὐτὴν παυσαμένην ⟨ἐρῶσαν⟩ τοῦ ἀνδρός, οἱ δ' ἐπὶ τῷ τὸν Ἰάσονα τῆς Θέτιδος ἐρῶντα παῦσαι τὴν θεόν. Τὸ δ' ἐπίγραμμα τοῦτ' ἔστιν·

Αἵδ' ὑπὲρ Ἑλλάνων τε καὶ ἰθυμάχων πολιητᾶν
ἐστάθεν εὐξάμεναι Κύπριδι δαιμονίᾳ.
Οὐ γὰρ τοξοφόροισιν ἐμήδετο δῖ' Ἀφροδίτα
Μήδοισ' Ἑλλάνων ἀκρόπολιν προδόμεν.

ταῦτ' ἔδει γράφειν καὶ τούτων μεμνῆσθαι, μᾶλλον ἢ τὴν Ἀμεινοκλέους ἐμβαλεῖν ⟨συμφορὰν καὶ⟩ παιδο- C φονίαν.

40 Τῶν τοίνυν αἰτιῶν τῶν κατὰ Θεμιστοκλέους ἀνέδην ἐμφορηθεὶς ἐν οἷς κλέπτοντα καὶ πλεονεκτοῦντα λάθρα τῶν ἄλλων στρατηγῶν οὔ φησι παύσασθαι περὶ τὰς νήσους, τέλος αὐτῶν Ἀθηναίων τὸν στέφανον ἀφελόμενος Αἰγινήταις ἐπιτίθησι, γράφων ταῦτα· «πέμψαντες ἀκροθίνια οἱ Ἕλληνες εἰς Δελφοὺς ἐπηρώτων τὸν θεὸν κοινῇ εἰ λελάβηκε πλήρεα καὶ ἀρεστὰ ⟨τὰ⟩ ἀκροθίνια· ὁ δὲ παρ' Ἑλλήνων μὲν τῶν ἄλλων ἔφησε ἔχειν, παρ' Αἰγινητέων δὲ οὔ· ἀλλ' ἀπῄτεε αὐτοὺς τὰ ἀριστεῖα τῆς ἐν Σαλαμῖνι ναυμαχίας». Οὐκέτι Σκύθαις οὐδὲ Πέρσαις οὐδ' Αἰγυπτίοις τοὺς ἑαυτοῦ λόγους ἀνατίθησι πλάττων, ὥσπερ Αἴσωπος D κόραξι καὶ πιθήκοις, ἀλλὰ τῷ τοῦ Πυθίου προσώπῳ χρώμενος, ἀπωθεῖ τῶν ⟨ἐν⟩ Σαλαμῖνι πρωτείων τὰς Ἀθήνας, Θεμιστοκλεῖ δὲ τῶν δευτερείων ἐν Ἰσθμῷ γενομένων διὰ τὸ τῶν στρατηγῶν ἕκαστον αὐτῷ μὲν τὸ πρωτεῖον ἐκείνῳ δὲ τὸ δευτερεῖον ἀποδοῦναι, καὶ τέλος τῆς

fall in love with fighting the Persians: never mind the ignorance of Herodotus and his contemporaries, even the remotest Carian must have known of it, for the tale was told all over the place and Simonides wrote B an epigram when the bronze statues were dedicated in the temple of Aphrodite (the temple which they say Medea built, either for falling out of love with her husband or for the goddess stopping Jason loving Thetis), as follows (Campbell XIV):

> 'Here stand the women who in prayer appealed
>> to Cypris for the men of Greece so bold.
> Bright Aphrodite had no mind to yield
>> to Persians bearing bows our Greek stronghold.'

That was worth writing down, that was worth recording, rather than drag in Ameinocles' misfortune of killing his son.   C

40. When Herodotus has gorged himself on his accusations against Themistocles, saying (112) he went round and round the islands enriching himself by thefts and exactions unknown to the other leaders, he finally takes the victors' crown away from the Athenians and bestows it upon Aegina, writing (122): "After the despatch of the thank-offerings to Delphi, the Greeks asked the god, in the name of the country generally, if he felt he had received his full share and was satisfied. His answer was that he was satisfied with what everyone had given, except the Aeginetans: from them he demanded the prize for valour won at Salamis." No more fictions now, in which Scythians and Persians and Egyptians are made D to speak as Aesop uses crows and monkeys: he uses the Pythian god himself to put down Athens from pride of place at Salamis. Then (123) when Themistocles won second personal prize at the Isthmus (because each of the commanders awarded himself the first prize but they all

κρίσεως μὴ λαβούσης, δέον αἰτιάσασθαι τὴν φιλοτιμίαν τῶν στρατηγῶν, πάντας ἀποπλεῦσαί φησι τοὺς Ἕλληνας ὑπὸ φθόνου μὴ βουληθέντας ἀναγορεῦσαι τὸν ἄνδρα πρῶτον.

41 Ἐν δὲ τῇ ἐνάτῃ καὶ τελευταίᾳ τῶν βίβλων, ὅσον ἦν ὑπόλοιπον ἔτι τῆς πρὸς Λακεδαιμονίους αὐτῷ δυσμενείας ἐκχέαι σπεύδων, τὸ παρ' αὐτὸν ἀφείλετο τὴν ἀοίδιμον νίκην καὶ τὸ περιβόητον Πλαταιᾶσι κατόρθωμα E τῆς πόλεως· γέγραφε γὰρ ὡς πρότερον μὲν ὡρρώδουν τοὺς Ἀθηναίους μὴ πεισθέντες ὑπὸ Μαρδονίου τοὺς Ἕλληνας ἐγκαταλίπωσι· τοῦ δ' Ἰσθμοῦ τειχισθέντος ἐν ἀσφαλεῖ θέμενοι τὴν Πελοπόννησον ἠμέλουν ἤδη τῶν ἄλλων καὶ περιεώρων, ἑορτάζοντες οἴκοι καὶ τοὺς πρέσβεις τῶν Ἀθηναίων κατειρωνευόμενοι καὶ διατρίβοντες. Πῶς οὖν ἐξῆλθον εἰς Πλαταιὰς πεντακισχίλιοι Σπαρτιᾶται, περὶ αὐτὸν ἔχων ἀνὴρ ἕκαστος ἑπτὰ εἵλωτας; ἢ πῶς κίνδυνον ἀράμενοι τοσοῦτον ἐκράτησαν καὶ κατέβαλον μυριάδας τοσαύτας; Ἄκουσον αἰτίας πιθανῆς· Ἔτυχε, φησίν, F ἐν Σπάρτῃ παρεπιδημῶν ἐκ Τεγέας ἀνὴρ ὄνομα Χείλεως, ᾧ φίλοι τινὲς καὶ ξένοι τῶν ἐφόρων ἦσαν· οὗτος οὖν ἔπεισεν αὐτοὺς ἐκπέμψαι τὸ στράτευμα, λέγων ὅτι τοῦ διατειχίσματος οὐδὲν ὄφελός ἐστι Πελοποννησίοις, ἂν Ἀθηναῖοι Μαρδονίῳ προσγένωνται. Τοῦτο Παυσανίαν ἐξήγαγεν εἰς Πλαταιὰς μετὰ τῆς δυνάμεως· | εἰ δέ τι 872 A κατέσχεν οἰκεῖον ἐν Τεγέᾳ πρᾶγμα τὸν Χείλεων ἐκεῖνον, οὐκ ἂν ἡ Ἑλλὰς περιεγένετο.

42 Πάλιν δὲ τοῖς Ἀθηναίοις οὐκ ἔχων ὅ τι χρήσαιτο, ⟨ποτὲ μὲν αἴρει⟩ ποτὲ δὲ καταβάλλει τὴν πόλιν ἄνω καὶ κάτω μεταφέρων, οὓς Τεγεάταις μὲν εἰς ἀγῶνα λέγει περὶ τῶν δευτερείων καταστάντας Ἡρακλειδῶν τε μεμνῆσθαι καὶ τὰ πρὸς Ἀμαζόνας πραχθέντα προφέρειν ταφάς

awarded him second prize, and so the awarding failed to work), Herodotus
ought to have established a case against the self-esteem of the commanders, whereas he says simply (124.1) they all sailed away, being unwilling
to declare Themistocles first out of envy.

41. In the ninth and last book he was in haste to vent his remaining anti-
Spartan animosity, and as far as he could he played down that epic victory
at Plataea which was their crowning achievement. He has written (9.6– E
8) that they were scared at first of the Athenians listening to Mardonius
and abandoning the Greek cause; but when the Isthmus was fortified and
they had made the Peloponnese safe, then they stopped bothering about
anyone else and held festivals in Sparta and wasted the time of the
Athenian delegation by prevaricating. How come then that five thousand
Spartiates marched out to Plataea, each one attended by seven helots?
How come they accepted the great danger, and overcame and slew so
many thousands? Try this for a convincing explanation! He says (9):
there happened to be living temporarily in Sparta a man from Tegea F
named Cheileos, and some of the ephors were close friends of his. He it
was who persuaded them to send out the army, saying that if the
Athenians joined Mardonius, the wall was no use to the Peloponnesians.
So that is what drew Pausanias to Plataea with his army; if that Cheileos 872 A
fellow had been kept in Tegea by some personal business, Greece would
not have survived!

42. As for the Athenians, he cannot decide how to handle them.
Sometimes he praises them, sometimes the opposite, for ever shifting his
treatment. He says (26–27) they quarrelled with the Tegeans about the
right to second-best position in the line: in their pride and in their longing
to win the leadership of the left wing, they recalled the Heracleidae
episode and put forward what they themselves had done to the Amazons

τε Πελοποννησίων τῶν ὑπὸ τῇ Καδμείᾳ πεσόντων· καὶ
τέλος εἰς τὸν Μαραθῶνα καταβαίνειν τῷ λόγῳ φιλοτι-
μουμένους καὶ ἀγαπῶντας ἡγεμονίας τυχεῖν τοῦ ἀριστεροῦ
κέρως· ὀλίγον δ' ὕστερον αὐτοῖς Παυσανίαν καὶ Σπαρτιά- B
τας τῆς ἡγεμονίας ὑφίεσθαι καὶ παρακαλεῖν ὅπως κατὰ
Πέρσας ἀντιταχθῶσι τὸ δεξιὸν κέρας παραλαβόντες,
αὐτοῖς δὲ παραδόντες τὸ εὐώνυμον, ὡς ἀηθείᾳ τὴν πρὸς
τοὺς βαρβάρους μάχην ἀπολεγομένοις. Καίτοι γελοῖον,
εἰ μὴ συνήθεις εἶεν οἱ πολέμιοι, μάχεσθαι μὴ θέλειν.
Ἀλλὰ τούς γ' ἄλλους Ἕλληνας εἰς ἕτερον ὑπὸ τῶν
στρατηγῶν ἀγομένους στρατόπεδον, «ὡς ἐκινήθησαν,
φησὶ φεύγειν ἀσμένως τὴν ἵππον πρὸς τὴν τῶν Πλαταιέων
πόλιν, φεύγοντας δ' ἀφικέσθαι πρὸς τὸ Ἡραῖον»· ἐν ᾧ καὶ
ἀπείθειαν καὶ λιποταξίαν καὶ προδοσίαν ὁμοῦ τι πάντων
κατηγόρησε. Τέλος δὲ μόνους φησὶ τοῖς μὲν βαρβάροις C
Λακεδαιμονίους καὶ Τεγεάτας, τοῖς δὲ Θηβαίοις Ἀθηναίους
συμπεσόντας διαγωνίσασθαι, τὰς δ' ἄλλας πόλεις ὁμαλῶς
ἁπάσας τοῦ κατορθώματος ἀπεστέρηκεν· οὐδένα ⟨...⟩
συνεφάψασθαι τοῦ ἀγῶνος, ἀλλὰ καθημένους πάντας
ἐπὶ τῶν ὅπλων ἐγγὺς καταλιπεῖν καὶ προδοῦναι τοὺς
ὑπὲρ αὐτῶν μαχομένους· ὀψὲ δὲ Φλιασίους καὶ Μεγαρέας
πυθομένους νικῶντα Παυσανίαν, προσφερομένους καὶ
ἐμπεσόντας εἰς τὸ Θηβαίων ἱππικόν, οὐδενὶ λόγῳ διαφθα-
ρῆναι· Κορινθίους δὲ τῇ μὲν μάχῃ παραγενέσθαι, μετὰ *
δὲ τὴν νίκην ἐπειγομένους διὰ τῶν λόφων, μὴ περι-|
πεσεῖν τοῖς ἱππεῦσι τῶν Θηβαίων· οἱ γὰρ Θηβαῖοι, D
τῆς τροπῆς γενομένης, προϊππεύοντες τῶν βαρβάρων
προθύμως παρεβοήθουν φεύγουσιν αὐτοῖς, δηλονότι
τῶν ἐν Θερμοπύλαις στιγμάτων χάριν ἀποδιδόντες.
Ἀλλὰ Κορινθίους γε καὶ τάξιν ᾗ ἐμάχοντο τοῖς βαρβάροις,
καὶ τέλος ἡλίκον ὑπῆρξεν αὐτοῖς ἀπὸ τοῦ Πλαταιᾶσιν
ἀγῶνος ἔξεστι Σιμωνίδου πυθέσθαι γράφοντος ἐπὶ τούτοις·

* See note.

and their burial of the Peloponnesians who fell at the foot of the Cadmeia, and finally in the recital of their achievements came down to Marathon. But a little later he says (46) Pausanias and the Spartiates conceded their **B** own position of command to the Athenians and invited them to take the right wing and draw up opposite the Persians, giving themselves the left wing, on the grounds that they had no practice in fighting Persians. But it is ridiculous to refuse to fight unless your enemy are familiar!

As for the rest of the Greeks, he says (52) they were being directed by their generals to a new base camp, but "once they were on the move, they fled to Plataea, only too thankful to escape the Persian cavalry. Here they came to a halt in front of the temple of Hera." Disobedience, desertion and treachery are the combined accusation in that passage. Finally he says (59.1) the Persians were met and attacked only by the Spartans and **C** Tegeans, and (67) the Thebans only by the Athenians; all the other cities he has deprived of their glory alike. None of them took a hand in the struggle, after all; they sat by, beside their weapons, and abandoned and deserted their fellows who were fighting for them. Late in the day the Phliasians and Megarians heard that Pausanias was winning (69), and they advanced and fell upon the Theban cavalry, and were simply destroyed; the Corinthians were not in the battle, but after it was won pressed through the hills and avoided contact with the Theban cavalry. **D** Once the battle turned, the Thebans rode in protection of the Persians, giving them vigorous aid as they fled (68) – obviously their thank you for being branded after Thermopylae! But as for the Corinthians and the position they held in the fight and the glory they won from the battle of Plataea, you can learn about that from what Simonides wrote upon them

Μέσσοι δ' οἵ τ' Ἔφυραν πολυπίδακα ναιετάοντες,
παντοίης ἀρετῆς ἴδριες ἐν πολέμῳ,
οἵ τε πόλιν Γλαύκοιο, Κορίνθιον ἄστυ, νέμοντες,
οἵ ⟨καὶ⟩ κάλλιστον μάρτυν ἔθεντο πόνων   E
χρυσοῦ τιμήεντος ἐν αἰθέρι· καί σφιν ἀέξει
αὐτῶν τ' εὐρεῖαν κληδόνα καὶ πατέρων.

Ταῦτα γὰρ οὐ χορὸν ἐν Κορίνθῳ διδάσκων οὐδ' ᾆσμα
ποιῶν εἰς τὴν πόλιν, ἄλλως δὲ τὰς πράξεις ἐκείνας ἐλεγεῖα
γράφων ἱστόρηκεν. Ὁ δὲ προλαμβάνων τὸν ἔλεγχον
τοῦ ψεύσματος τῶν ἐρησομένων «πόθεν οὖν πολυάνδρια
καὶ θῆκαι τοσαῦται καὶ μνήματα νεκρῶν, [ἐν] οἷς ἐναγί-
ζουσιν ἄχρι νῦν Πλαταιεῖς τῶν Ἑλλήνων συμπαρόντων ;»
⟨ὄνειδος⟩ αἴσχιον, ὡς οἶμαι, τῆς προδοσίας τῶν γενεῶν
κατηγόρηκεν ἐν τούτοις· «τῶν δὲ ἄλλων ὅσοι καὶ φαίνον- F
ται ἐν Πλαταιῇσι ἐόντες τάφοι, τούτους δέ, ὡς ἐγὼ
πυνθάνομαι, αἰσχυνομένους τῇ ἀπε⟨στοῖ⟩ τῆς μάχης
ἑκάστους χώματα χῶσαι κεινὰ τῶν ἐπιγινομένων εἴνεκ'
ἀνθρώπων». Ταύτην ⟨τὴν⟩ ἀπε⟨στὼ⟩ τῆς μάχης προδοσίαν οὖσαν Ἡρόδοτος ἀνθρώπων μόνος ἁπάντων ἤκουσε,
Παυσανίαν δὲ καὶ Ἀριστείδην καὶ Λακεδαιμονίους καὶ
Ἀθηναίους ἔλαθον οἱ Ἕλληνες ἐγκαταλιπόντες τὸν
κίνδυνον· | καὶ οὔτ' Αἰγινήτας Ἀθηναῖοι διαφόρους 873 A
ὄντας εἶρξαν τῆς ἐπιγραφῆς, οὔτε Κορινθίους ἤλεγξαν
οὓς πρότερον εἶπον φεύγειν ἀπὸ Σαλαμῖνος, ἀντιμαρτυ-
ρούσης αὐτοῖς τῆς Ἑλλάδος. Καίτοι Κλεάδας μὲν ὁ
Πλαταιεύς, ⟨ὕστερον⟩ ἔτεσι δέκα τῶν Μηδικῶν, Αἰγινήταις
χαριζόμενος, ὥς φησιν Ἡρόδοτος, ἐπώνυμον ἔχωσεν
αὐτῶν πολυάνδριον· Ἀθηναῖοι δὲ καὶ Λακεδαιμόνιοι τί
παθόντες εὐθὺς τότε πρὸς μὲν ἀλλήλους ὀλίγον ἐδέησαν
εἰς χεῖρας ἐλθεῖν περὶ τοῦ τροπαίου τῆς ἀναστάσεως,
τοὺς δ' Ἕλληνας ἀποδειλιάσαντας καὶ ἀποδράντας
οὐκ ἀπήλαυνον τῶν ἀριστείων, ἀλλ' ἐνέγραφον τοῖς

(Campbell eleg. 10 & 11):

> 'Ephyra's springs despatched the battle's core,
>> men expert in all bravery of war,
> the men of Corinth born in Glaucus' town,
>> who chose for fine witness of their renown   E
> the honoured gold on high, which magnifies
>> their fathers' and their own great enterprise.'

Simonides did not write that for a choir in Corinth nor as an ode for the city: he simply set in elegiacs the deeds he discovered.

Herodotus was expecting people to put his deceit to the test; they would ask 'Then what about the common graves, and all the burials and memorials, where the people of Plataea still make offerings in the presence of the Greeks?' He has produced a slur by way of accusation much worse, in my view, than the charge of treachery against their fellows was (85.3): "All the other funeral mounds which are to be seen F at Plataea were, so far as my information goes, erected merely for show: they are empty, and were put up to impress posterity by the various states who were ashamed of having taken no part in the battle." This treachery of missing the battle is information unique to Herodotus: these Greeks who dodged the danger were unknown to Pausanias and Aristeides and the Spartans and Athenians. Athens didn't keep Aegina's name off the 873 A inscription because of their old quarrel, nor did she challenge Corinth's place there despite the earlier charge that they ran away at Salamis (though all Greece bears witness against that). And yet, says Herodotus (85.3), it was Cleadas of Plataea, ten years after the war, who did Aegina a favour by raising a grave mound for them. Straight after the battle the Athenians and Spartans could hardly keep from scrapping with each other about the erection of a trophy: how come they didn't keep these cowardly, runaway Greeks out of the honours, but wrote their names too on the

τρίποσι καὶ τοῖς κολοσσοῖς καὶ μετεδίδοσαν τῶν λαφύρων, B
τέλος δὲ τῷ βωμῷ τὸ ἐπίγραμμα τοῦτο γράφοντες ἐνεχά-
ραξαν·

  Τόνδε ποθ᾽ Ἕλληνες Νίκης κράτει, ἔργῳ Ἄρηος,
  ⟨εὐτόλμῳ ψυχῆς λήματι πειθόμενοι,⟩
  Πέρσας ἐξελάσαντες, ἐλευθέρᾳ Ἑλλάδι κοινὸν
  ἱδρύσαντο Διὸς βωμὸν Ἐλευθερίου ;

Μὴ καὶ τοῦτο Κλεάδας ἤ τις ἄλλος, ὦ Ἡρόδοτε, κολακεύων
τὰς πόλεις ἐπέγραψε ; Τί οὖν ἐδέοντο τὴν γῆν ὀρύσσοντες
διακενῆς ἔχειν [τὰ] πράγματα καὶ ῥᾳδιουργεῖν χώματα
καὶ μνήματα τῶν ἐπιγιγνομένων ἕνεκ᾽ ἀνθρώπων κατα-
σκευάζοντες, ἐν τοῖς ἐπιφανεστάτοις καὶ μεγίστοις C
ἀναθήμασι τὴν δόξαν αὐτῶν καθιερωμένην ὁρῶντες ; Καὶ
μὴν Παυσανίας, ὡς λέγουσιν, ἤδη τυραννικὰ φρονῶν
ἐπέγραψεν ἐν Δελφοῖς·

  Ἑλλήνων ἀρχηγὸς ἐπεὶ στρατὸν ὤλεσε Μήδων
  Παυσανίας, Φοίβῳ μνῆμ᾽ ἀνέθηκε τόδε,

κοινούμενος ἀμωσγέπως τοῖς Ἕλλησι τὴν δόξαν ὧν
ἑαυτὸν ἀνηγόρευσεν ἡγεμόνα· τῶν δ᾽ Ἑλλήνων οὐκ
ἀνασχομένων ἀλλ᾽ ἐγκαλούντων, πέμψαντες εἰς Δελφοὺς
Λακεδαιμόνιοι τοῦτο μὲν ἐξεκόλαψαν, τὰ δ᾽ ὀνόματα τῶν
πόλεων, ὥσπερ ἦν δίκαιον, ἐνεχάραξαν. Καίτοι πῶς εἰκός D
ἐστιν ἢ τοὺς Ἕλληνας ἀγανακτεῖν τῆς ἐπιγραφῆς μὴ
μετασχόντας, εἰ συνῄδεισαν ἑαυτοῖς τὴν ἀπε⟨στὼ⟩ τῆς
μάχης, ἢ Λακεδαιμονίους τὸν ἡγεμόνα καὶ στρατηγὸν
ἐκχαράξαντας ἐπιγράψαι τοὺς ἐγκαταλιπόντας καὶ περι-
ιδόντας τὸν κίνδυνον ; Ὡς δεινότατόν ἐστιν, εἰ Σωχάρης
μὲν καὶ Ἀείμνηστος καὶ πάντες οἱ διαπρεπῶς ἀγωνισάμενοι
τὴν μάχην ἐκείνην οὐδὲ Κυθνίων ἐπιγραφομένων τοῖς
τροπαίοις οὐδὲ Μηλίων ἠχθέσθησαν· Ἡρόδοτος δὲ
τρισὶ μόναις πόλεσιν ἀναθεὶς τὸν ἀγῶνα τὰς ἄλλας
πάσας ἐκχαράττει τῶν τροπαίων καὶ τῶν ἱερῶν.

tripods and the statues, and gave them too a share of the spoils? Finally, B
they inscribed these verses on the altar (Campbell XV):

> 'The Greeks by Nike's force and Ares' blade
> <trusting the courage in their hearts to dare>
> drove out the Persians, and this altar made
>   to Zeus of Freedom for free Greece to share.'

Perhaps, Herodotus, Cleadas did that too, or someone else did, flattering
the cities with epigrams! What need was there for the wasted work of
excavating the earth and making empty mounds and raising monuments C
for posterity when they could see their own glory consecrated on
memorials of conspicuous magnificence? Pausanias, so they say, with
megalomania already in his mind, had inscribed at Delphi (Campbell
XVII):

> 'Pausanias commander of the Greeks
>   made this remembrance of the Medes he slew.'

In naming himself commander of the Greeks he does to some extent share
his glory with them; but the Greeks could not take it. They complained,
and the Spartans sent to Delphi and erased his words and engraved instead
the names of the allied states, as was right. And yet it is not plausible: D
either the Greeks who did not take part should not complain, if they were
aware of their own absence, or the Spartans should not erase their own
general and leader's name and substitute the names of people who stood
around watching the contest and shirking it. It is very odd if Sochares and
Aeimnestus and all the others who fought with distinction in the battle
weren't even cross at the Cythnians and the Melians being put on the
trophies, when Herodotus ascribes the victory to three cities only and
scratches out the rest from the trophies and the holy places.

43 Τεσσάρων δ' ἀγώνων τότε πρὸς τοὺς βαρβάρους E γενομένων, ἐκ μὲν 'Αρτεμισίου τοὺς Ἕλληνας ἀποδρᾶναί φησιν· ἐν δὲ Θερμοπύλαις, τοῦ στρατηγοῦ καὶ βασιλέως προκινδυνεύοντος, οἰκουρεῖν καὶ ἀμελεῖν 'Ολύμπια καὶ Κάρνεια πανηγυρίζοντας· τὰ δ' ἐν Σαλαμῖνι διηγούμενος τοσούτους περὶ 'Αρτεμισίας λόγους γέγραφεν ὅσοις ὅλην τὴν ναυμαχίαν οὐκ ἀπήγγελκε· τέλος δέ, **καθημένους ἐν Πλαταιαῖς ἀγνοῆσαι μέχρι τέλους τὸν ἀγῶνα τοὺς Ἕλληνας, ὥσπερ βατραχομυομαχίας γινομένης, ⟨ἢν⟩ Πίγρης ὁ 'Αρτεμισίας ἐν ἔπεσι παίζων καὶ φλυαρῶν ἔγραψε, σιωπῇ διαγωνίσασθαι συνθεμένων, ἵνα λάθωσι τοὺς ἄλλους, αὐτοὺς δὲ Λακεδαιμονίους ἀνδρείᾳ μὲν οὐδὲν κρείττονας γενέσθαι τῶν βαρβάρων, ἀνόπλοις δὲ** F **καὶ γυμνοῖς μαχομένους κρατῆσαι.** | Ξέρξου μὲν γὰρ 874 A αὐτοῦ παρόντος, ὑπὸ μαστίγων μόλις ὄπισθεν ὠθούμενοι προσεφέροντο τοῖς Ἕλλησιν, ἐν δὲ Πλαταιαῖς, ὡς ἔοικεν, ἑτέρας ψυχὰς μεταλαβόντες «λήματι μὲν καὶ ῥώμῃ οὐκ ἥσσονες ἦσαν· ἡ δὲ ἐσθής, ἔρημος ἐοῦσα ὅπλων, πλεῖστον ἐδηλήσατό σφεας· πρὸς γὰρ ὁπλίτας ἐόντες γυμνῆτες ἀγῶνα ἐποιέοντο». Τί οὖν περίεστιν ἔνδοξον ἢ μέγα τοῖς Ἕλλησιν ἀπ' ἐκείνων τῶν ἀγώνων, εἰ Λακεδαιμόνιοι μὲν ἀνόπλοις ἐμάχοντο, τοὺς δ' ἄλλους ἡ μάχη παρόντας ἔλαθε, κενὰ δὲ πολυάνδρια τιμώμενα τοῖς ἑκάστου, ψευστῶν δὲ γραμμάτων μεστοὶ τρίποδες ἑστᾶσι καὶ βωμοὶ παρὰ τοῖς θεοῖς, μόνος δὲ τἀληθὲς Ἡρόδοτος ἔγνω, τοὺς δ' ἄλλους ἅπαντας ἀνθρώπους ὅσοι λόγον Ἑλλήνων B ἔχουσιν ἐξηπάτηκεν ἡ φήμη τῶν τότε κατορθωμάτων, ὡς ὑπερφυῶν γενομένων; Τί δῆτα; Γραφικὸς ἀνήρ, καὶ ἡδὺς ὁ λόγος, καὶ χάρις ἔπεστι καὶ δεινότης καὶ ὥρα τοῖς διηγήμασι· «μῦθον δ' ὡς ὅτ' ἀοιδός, ἐπισταμένως» μὲν οὔ, λιγυρῶς δὲ καὶ γλαφυρῶς ἠγόρευκεν. 'Αμέλει ταῦτα καὶ κηλεῖ καὶ προσάγεται πάντας, ἀλλ' ὥσπερ

43. Four battles were fought against the Persians in that period. Herodotus E says that at Artemisium the Greeks ran away (8.18); at Thermopylae while their royal commander bore the brunt they stayed happily at home celebrating the Olympic and Carneian festivals (7.206); in his description of Salamis he has written more on queen Artemisia (8.87/8) than on the rest of the fighting put together; finally at Plataea they sat by ignorant of the battle till its end (9.69–70.1), as if it were a frog-mice fight such as Pigres, Artemisia's son, composed in idle jest, and they had agreed to fight in silence to prevent the rest knowing. He says the Spartans were no braver than the Persians, and won because they were fighting against F men naked and unarmed. When Xerxes was there, the Persians joined the 874 A battle only when driven from behind with whips, but at Plataea, it seems, they had taken new heart (62.3): "in courage and strength they were as good" but (63.2) "the chief cause of their discomfiture was their lack of armour, fighting without it against heavily armed infantry."

What then have the Greeks got left that is great or glorious in those battles, if the Spartans fought an unarmed foe, if the rest failed to notice the fight in spite of being at it, if the grave mounds are empty that each man's descendants honour, if the tripods and altars that stand before the gods are full of lies, if only Herodotus found out the truth, and if everyone B else with a tale of the Greeks to tell is deceived by a tradition of achievements quite overblown? Herodotus is an artist, and his tale reads well; there is grace and force and freshness in the narrative. He tells his tale like a Homer, not with a good understanding, but with delicacy and fluency. Quite simply, that is what beguiles everyone and draws them on;

ἐν ῥόδοις δεῖ κανθαρίδα φυλάττεσθαι τὴν βλασφημίαν αὐτοῦ καὶ κακολογίαν, λείοις καὶ ἁπαλοῖς σχήμασιν ὑποδεδυκυῖαν, ἵνα μὴ λάθωμεν ἀτόπους καὶ ψευδεῖς περὶ τῶν ἀρίστων καὶ μεγίστων τῆς Ἑλλάδος πόλεων C καὶ ἀνδρῶν δόξας λαβόντες.

but as in roses we must watch out for the rose-beetle, so in Herodotus we must watch for the mean and partisan attacks that are disguised by a smooth and soft appearance. Otherwise we shall accept all unawares opinions which are false and out of place about the best and greatest of C Greek cities and Greek heroes.

Apparatus Criticus

The entries below aim to include the points at which Hansen, Häsler, Lachenaud and Pearson do not offer the same text, except in trivial matters such as punctuation. For full detail the reader is referred particularly to Hansen and Lachenaud. N indicates a note in the Commentary.

854E   τοῦ ῾Αλικαρνασσέως Hansen: lac. c. 11 litt. EB; τοῦ ῾Ηροδότου post ᾽Αλέξανδρε Pearson Ι ἐπειδὴ δὲ κακοηθείᾳ Turnebus: inter εἶναι et μάλιστα lac. 3/4 lin. (c. 160 litt.) EB; suppl. ex. gr. Pearson ὅπερ φιλεῖ ποιεῖν ἐν τοῖς μάλιστα ὁ ῾Ηρόδοτος, τοῖς μὲν αἰσχίστῃ κολακείᾳ χαριζόμενος, τοὺς δὲ διαβάλλων καὶ συκοφαντῶν. νῦν δ᾽ οὐδεὶς τετόλμηκεν αὐτοῦ τὴν ψευδολογίαν ἐξελέγχειν, ᾗ; alii alia

F   ἀμύνεσθαι Lachenaud: ἀμυνομένοις EB Ι βιβλίων EB: βυβλίων Hansen, idemque alibi

855A   δοκεῖ δὴ Ε: δοκεῖ δὲ Β, η super ε scripta

B   σοφῶς EB: σαφῶς Bernardakis Ι ὅτῳ EB: εἴ τῳ Häsler

C   ἀτύχημά τινος EB: τινος ἀτύχημ᾽ Benseler

F   αὐτὰς add. Reiske

856B   ἐν add. Reiske

D   οὕτω Β: οὕτως Ε Ι προαποτίθεται EB: προϋποτίθεται Abresch

E   τὴν ᾽Ιοῦν suppl. Stephanus: lac. 8 litt. EB

N   ἐβούλοντο Basil.: ἐβουλέατο Β; ἐβουλεύοντο Ε

857A   θειότητα EB: ὁσιότητα Cobet

B   ἔντομά σφεα Wesseling: ἐντομὰς + lac. c. 5 litt. EB Ι νηυσὶν ἰθὺ Β: νηυσὶ νήειν Ε; τῇσι νηυσὶν Pearson Ι παισὶ add. Basil.

C   Δήμητραν EB: Δήμητρα Stephanus Ι ὃν δ᾽ add. Pearson (vel ὃν δὲ θεὸν); τίνας δ᾽ Dübner; alii alia; lac. c. 6 litt. EB

D   σέβονται et οὓς add. Reiske; ἀποφαίνων Lachenaud: ἀποφαίνονται EB; ante ῾Ηρακλέα obelum Hubert (v. Häsler XIV)

E   ἀπὸ add. Meziriacus ex Hdt.

F   ἔσχον λόγον EB: λόγον ἔσχον Benseler Ι προσώπῳ Cobet: προσωπείῳ EB

858A   πέρι post πραγμάτων Pearson ex Hdt.; ἀνθρωπηίων πράγματα Ε

N   Μυτιληναίων Bernardakis: Μιτυληναίων EB itemque alibi

B   Πιττακοῦ ἀριστείας EB: ἀριστείας Πιττακοῦ Benseler

N   ᾽Αλκμαιωνίδας EB: ᾽Αλκμεωνίδας Herwerden

D   οἱ add. Bernardakis ex Hdt. Ι ἥτταν τῶν Λακ. EB: τὴν ante ἥτταν add. Benseler; τῶν Λακ. ἥτταν Lahmeyer

E αὐτοῦ (priore loco) Herwerden: αὐτῷ EB Ι αὐτῷ del. Basil.
Ι ἐπὶ κνάφου Salmasius: ἐπινάφου E; ἐπὶ νάφου B, γ
super ν scripta; ἐπὶ γνάφου Hansen

N F προσποίημά τι Abresch: προσποιήματι EB
Ι καὶ ἄνδρας add. Reiske Ι καὶ add. Bernardakis

859A οὖν add. Bernardakis

N lac. post φησὶ Bernardakis; post Κυμαίους Dübner: nul. lac.
EB Ι ὅσῳ δὴ add. Reiske; lac. c. 4 litt. E, nullam B

C Μεσσηνίους Xylander: Μεσσήνης EB

E τοῦ ἐπὶ Σάμον Reiske: ἐπὶ Σάμῳ EB Ι καὶ add.
Stephanus Ι γὰρ Meziriacus: γε EB

860B τοὺς add. Stephanus Ι τε ὁ Κρητικὸς EB: post Κρητικὸς
add. συγγραφεὺς Schwarz; ἐν τοῖς Κρητικοῖς Kaltwasser

D ἀεὶ del. Stephanus Ι εἴωθε Hude: εἰώθει EB

E καὶ κακῶς E: κακῶς B: neutra accepta alii alia

F τοὺς τυράννους del. Cobet Ι ἀποτρέψαι Cobet:
ἀποστρέψαι EB

861A ἐκπομπῆς EB: ἐκτομῆς Leonicus

N B ἤδη .. κατεναυμάχησαν inter obelos Hansen
Ι τῶν add. Wyttenbach: lac. c. 4 litt. EB

D οὕτω add. Xylander ex Hdt. Ι καὶ κακοήθεις Λακ. B: Λακ.
καὶ κακοήθεις E

F ἦν add. Lachenaud ex Hdt. Ι ἐνάτη add. Xylander Ι ἐκ
add. Wyttenbach: alii aliter Ι ὡς μὴ ἀκλεᾶ γένηται add.
Pearson ex Hdt.: lac. c. 20 litt. EB

862A ἕκτη Valcknaer: Ἑκάτη EB

B post Ἡρόδοτος lac. pos. Pearson

C τὰ add. Turnebus Ι φησίν add. Bernardakis Ι ἔσχεν
Turnebus: ἔσχον EB: ἔσχε ἐν Cobet

E προδιδόασιν add. Amyot: lac. c. 10 litt. EB Ι ὡς add.
Wyttenbach

F προσποιούμενος Stephanus: προσποιώμεθα EB:
προσποιῆται μεθεὶς Pearson (cum καὶ εἴπῃ vel εἴπῃ δὲ
pro εἴπῃ Ι θώϋμα δέ μοι (θῶμα Häsler) add. Turnebus ex
Hdt.: lac. c. 10 litt. EB Ι ὑπὸ βαρβάροισι et καὶ add.
Turnebus ex Hdt.

863B μεταξὺ δὲ suppl. Xylander: lac. c. 12 litt. E, c. 8 litt. post
Ἀλκμαιωνιδῶν B; ἐν μέσῳ γὰρ Pearson Ι ἡγεῖσθαι ...
συμμαχίας add. Reiske ex Hdt.

C ὑπείκων Emperius: ὑπειπὼν EB

D τὰ ... ὀφείλω add. Stephanus ex Hdt. Ι ἑστήκεε, πᾶν
Stephanus: ἕστηκεν εἰ + lac. c. 4 litt. EB; ἑστήκει, πᾶν
Hansen Ι εἶναι πρὸ Turnebus: προσεῖναι EB; προεῖναι
Wyttenbach

E κοὐδὲν Dübner: καὶ οὐδὲν EB Ι ἄν del. Muret Ι ὑπὸ add.
Wyttenbach: σὺν Muret

864A post γενναίως lac. pos. Xylander Ι ἄλλους add. Xylander ex
Hdt.

B γενομένην μέν add. Lachenaud: eadem ante οὐ Pearson; γεγεινημένην μέν Meziriacus

C καὶ del. Pohlenz | -φορὴ λυπεῦσα παιδοφόνος add. Stephanus ex Hdt.: lac. c. 16 litt. EB

D ἀδίκως suppl. Lachenaud: τὰ δὲ διὰ + lac. c. 7 litt. EB; alii alia

865A αἰτίᾳ Wyttenbach: αἰτίῃ EB | οἱ add. Reiske

B πᾶσι παρ' ὀλίγους ἀνθρώποις Herwerden: παρ' ὀλίγους ἀνθρώπους EB; alii alia, quorum Häsler inter obelos ἀνθρώπους habet

C μὴ del. Basil.

D τεθνηξομένους EB: τεθνηξόμενος Leonicus | ὅτι ὡς Turnebus: ἴσως δὲ EB

E εἴρηκε suppl. Xylander: lac. c. 8 litt. EB | ταῦτα δὲ δὴ EB: ταὐτά τε δὴ Reiske ex Hdt.

N Λεωνίδην Dübner: Λεωνίδεα EB; v. Rosén XIX/XX

866A ὀλίγου δεῖν del. Reiske

B αὐτῶν (post ἐπιτάφιον) Leonicus: αὐτῷ EB; αὐτῶν Russell

C τῷ add. Wyttenbach: θατέρῳ Reiske

N κρεῖσσον ... μένοντος add. Pearson

D μαστιγούμενοι EB: del. Cobet

E post ὕδωρ Hdt. ἐν πρώτοισι habet

N ἀπικοίατο Turnebus ex Hdt.: ἀπικέατο EB | Θετταλοὺς Hansen (q. v. 42): Θεσσαλοὺς EB

F τι del. Reiske

867A ἀλλ' add. Reiske | δικάσαντος EB: δικαιώσαντος Reiske

C πέρας B: τὸ πέρας E

D post ἐβούλευον add. ἔσω Herwerden ex Hdt.

E ἀπ' add. Turnebus ex Hdt.

868B κατ' ἄλλο ... ὡς suppl. Turnebus ex Hdt.: lac. c. 18 litt. EB

C ἀλλ' ... ἄν add. Meziriacus | ἐπεχείρει Kronenberg: ἐπιχειρεῖ EB

869A ἵν' Turnebus: εἰ EB | μαρτυρεῖ EB: ἀντιμαρτυρεῖ Xylander | αὐτοῖς Reiske: αὐτῷ EB | αὐτοὺς Ναξίους EB: αὐτοὺς aut τοὺς Ναξίους Reiske

N B καταπρήσαντα ποιῆσαι κακόν EB: aut lac. post καταπρήσαντα edd. aut aliter emendaverunt

C χειρὸς ... βαρβαρικῆς Turnebus: χεῖρα ... βαρβαρικὴν EB

D 'Αριστοβούλης Xylander: βουλῆς EB | ἐνταῦθα δὲ EB: ἐνταῦθα δὴ Bernardakis ex Hdt. | εἶπε add. Turnebus ex Hdt.

E post Θεμιστοκλῆς lac. 8 litt. + ζόμενος EB: παριζόμενός οἱ Turnebus ex Hdt.; οἱ παριζόμενος Hansen | πολλὰ add. Lachenaud ex Hdt. | αὐτοῦ Bernardakis: αὑτοῦ EB

F οὔτε EB: οὐ Russell | post φεύξονται lac. susp. Turnebus

870A 'Αθηναίων EB: 'Αθηνέων Bernardakis | πεζὸν add. Leonicus ex Hdt.

B   ἀλλ' ὧν Xylander: ἄλλω EB; ἀλλ' ὧν μὲν ἄλλων Pohlenz; alii alia | ἃ δέ γε κατέψευσται Turnebus: α δε τ + lac. 3 litt. + ψευσται EB; ἃ δὲ κατέψευσται Hansen; ἃ δὲ τραγικῶς ἔψευσται Pohlenz; alii alia | ἐπαράμενος Kronenberg ex Hdt.: ἐπαιρόμενος EB

C   φείδεσθαι Emperius: τίθεσθαι EB; τίθεσθαι πλὴν Pohlenz; alii alia

D   post πιστευομένης Stephanus μὲν: δὲ EB; del. Hubert | δ' add. Lachenaud: pro ἀπιστουμένους (EB) ἀπιστουμένης Leonicus; ἀπιστουμένης δ' Stephanus | ἦν οἶμαι Wyttenbach: οἱ E; ἢ οἱ B; οἶμαι δὲ μήτ' Ἀθηναίων αὐτὸν ἀκοῦσαι κακιζόντων Κορινθίους μήτε Pearson | τοῦτον Turnebus: τούτων EB | Ἀθηναίους Reiske: Ἀθηναίοις EB; Ἀθηναῖον Pearson | ἑώρων Xylander: ἑώρα EB | μεθ' αὐτοὺς Lachenaud: μετ' αὐτοὺς Turnebus; μετ' αὐτῶν E; μετ' αὐτοὺς B, ὧν super οὓς scripto

E   καὶ add. Leonicus | ξεῖν' Brunck: ξένε EB | ῥυσάμεθα Pletho: ῥυόμεθα EB | αὐτῶν EB: αὐτῶν schol. Aristid. III 126.4 Dindorf

871A   τοὺς add. Turnebus

B   ἐρῶσαν add. Kaltwasser | δαιμονίᾳ Wilamowitz: δαιμόνιαι EB

C   συμφορὰν καὶ suppl. Pearson: lac. c. 12 litt. EB | τὰ add. Bernardakis ex Hdt.

D   ἐν add. Wyttenbach

872A   ποτὲ μὲν αἴρει add. Reiske

B   ἀπολεγομένοις Fuhrmann: ἀπολογουμένους EB fere; ἀπολεγομένους Wyttenbach

C   post οὐδένα Wyttenbach γὰρ, Reiske λέγων; nul. lac. EB

N   παραγενέσθαι: μὴ παραγενέσθαι EB

D   ᾗ Wyttenbach: ἦν EB; ἦν ἔχοντας Reiske | ἐπὶ τούτοις Fuhrmann: ἐν τούτοις EB

N   τ' Ἔφυραν Xylander: γέφυραν E, γ' Ἔφυραν B; τ' Ἐφύρην Schneidewin | post πολέμῳ lac. pos. Simonidis edd.

E   καὶ add. Ursinus: τῶν Turnebus | κάλλιστον EB· καλλίστων Turnebus | ἄλλως EB: ἁπλῶς Bernardakis | ἐλεγεῖα EB: ἐν ἐλεγείᾳ Wilamowitz | οἷς E: ἐν οἷς B | ὄνειδος suppl. Reiske: lac. c. 8 litt. EB: πρᾶγμα Pearson | γενεῶν inter obelos Hässler

F   ἀπεστοῖ Turnebus ex Hdt.: ἀπο + lac. 5 litt. EB | τὴν add. Reiske | ἀπεστῶ Turnebus ex Hdt.: ἀπο + lac. 4 litt. E, 8 B

873A   εἶπον Turnebus: νικῶντες EB; alii aliter | μὲν Hubert: ἦν EB; del. Stephanus | ὕστερον add. Stephanus: post ἔτεσιν Hansen, post δέκα Hässler | post Ἡρόδοτος add. ὃς Pearson (qui ἦν sup. legit)

N   B   εὐτόλμῳ ... πειθόμενοι add. Xylander e Pal. Anth. VI 50 |
               τὰ del. Dübner

        C   καθιερωμένην Emperius: καθιερουμένην EB | τὰ δ' B: τὰ
               E; ante τὰ obelum Häsler, sed lac. suspic. Pearson ἀπὸ τοῦ
               τρίποδος τὸ ἐλεγεῖον, πασῶν δ' ἀντεπέγραψαν suppl.
               ante τὰ | ἐνεχάραξαν B: non habet E

        D   ἀπεστὼ Manton: ἀπο + lac. 4 litt. E; ἀπόλειψιν B

        E   βατραχομυομαχίας Stephanus: βατραχομαχίας EB | ἦν
               add. Wyttenbach

     874A   ἐοῦσα Bernardakis ex Hdt.: οὖσα EB | γυμνῆτες
               Bernardakis ex Hdt.: γυμνῆται EB | ἀνόπλοις Lachenaud:
               ἀόπλοις EB

        B   κακολογίαν E: μικρολογίαν B

Commentary

a) *H. = Herodotus and P. = Plutarch throughout;*
b) *all dates henceforward are B.C. unless indicated;*
c) *references to the Introduction are by paragraph numbers.*

Malice there is no one English word which quite translates the Greek κακοήθεια. 'Prejudice' catches a large part of it but lacks the connotation of spite. Aristotle *(Rhet. 1389b20)* defines κακοήθεια as 'assuming the worse interpretation': τὸ ἐπὶ χεῖρον ὑπολαμβάνειν ἅπαντα. In P.'s view such a thing would be done only by someone temperamentally disposed to do so; for him the word marks a moral characteristic.

854E – 874C: the numbers are the page numbers of the edition of the Moralia published by A. Wechel in Frankfurt in 1599. The letters mark the subdivisions.

1.

854E **Alexander:** about a quarter of P.'s essays in the *Moralia* have addressees. Some are known figures, Greek or Roman, but not this one. The lack of definition in the address may suggest, however, that he was familiar to P., and there is an Alexander the Epicurean who takes part in the discussion in *Table Talk* II.3 'Whether the hen or the egg came first' (635E – 638A): P. describes him as 'a man of taste and some scholar' (χαρίεις καὶ φιλόλογος ἐπιεικῶς); in that discussion a couple of words of H. are quoted (H. 2.171.1: see 13/857C). P. could only have discussed the Malice of H. with a man who knew his H.; it is reasonable to think that the two Alexanders are one. A.E. Raubitschek, 'Phaidros and his Roman pupils', *Hesperia* 18 (1949) 99f. discusses two inscriptions from the Athenian agora which may well refer to this man. See also Teodorsson 213 and 222 (but he misses the quotation of H. 2.171.1 in this work).
deceived by the style: P.'s description of H.'s style here and his comparison of H. with Homer in 43/874B show how easily he could fit H.'s achievement into the Platonic frame of reference for poets and their deceptiveness; see F.S. Halliwell, *Plato Republic 10*, Warminster 1988, 3–7. P. studied the topic at length in 'How to read the poets' (14D–37B).
the man himself: P. says 'his personal disposition' (τὸ ἦθος), and the word draws attention to the theme of malice (κακοήθεια). The noun and its adjective (κακοηθής) are used nine times in the prefatory chapters and eight times in the subsequent text.
As Plato remarks: the quotation, virtually a commonplace, comes from *Rep.* 2.361A. P. cites Plato some seven hundred times; only Homer is cited more often.
Since ... malice: the MSS indicate a gap of over three lines, the longest in the work. The supplement here is enough to make sense merely. Pearson offers a full supplement *exempli gratia.*
F **the Boeotians and ... the Corinthians:** P. claimed Boeotian ancestry as a citizen of Chaeronea; he comes to their rescue in 31 and 33. His claim to rescue the Corinthians is less obvious, but probably H.'s treatment of Adeimantus seemed worse than that of anybody else, and so more worth redress (see 39, and also 22 and 42). In practice the Athenians and the Spartans are more frequently mentioned (see 17/858Cn), but not with the same passion.
my duty: P. uses the plural, 'our duty'. Elsewhere the first person plural includes the reader by implication (e.g. 39/870B); but Alexander the addressee, if rightly identified by Raubitschek (see above), came from Phalerum in Attica. P. is probably being 'editorial'.

fictions and fabrications: Burn (1972) 29 draws an important distinction between fanciful tales and deliberate lies. The Greek word translated 'fictions' carries both senses. P.'s failure to discriminate is understandable.

'Persuasion's face ... behold': the quotation is not from a surviving play. P. returns neatly to his starting point.

855A   Philip of Macedon: Philip V ruled from 221 to 179. At the battle of Cynoscephalae in 197 Roman forces liberated the southern Greek cities from his control; Titus Quinctius Flamininus the victor declared them free at the Isthmian games the next year. In *Life of Flamininus* 10 P. attributes the remark quoted here to the Aetolians, in slightly different form. The collar was a punishment for slaves, especially runaways.

Theopompus: a historian. Born in Chios c.378 he died c.305. He lived much in Athens and also travelled much. He wrote two major works, of which only fragments survive, the one (*Hellenica*) a continuation of Thucydides going down to 394 and the other (*Philippica*) a much longer treatment of events from 360 to 336. P. cites him some 25 times, but with caution; the man was learned but cantankerous. See *HCT* I 46–9, and 27/862Dn.

like winds ... open: the simile here is matched by that of the rose-beetle in the closing paragraph.

Best procedure: see Intro. 14, and 10/856D.

2.

B   Nicias ... Cleon: both are best known to us from Thucydides' *History of the Peloponnesian War*; the words quoted as soft ones are his, on Nicias in 7.50.4 and on Cleon in 4.28.5. Nicias is treated by Thucydides with, on the whole, respect and sympathy, more than perhaps he deserves, but our picture of Cleon is distorted by the animosity shown towards him in both Thucydides and Aristophanes. See Hornblower (1987) 166f. Evidence of Cleon's financial acumen has come from inscriptions discovered in Athens this century.

3.

C   no clear account: the events at Sphacteria and Amphipolis are reported in considerable detail, and the details of Amphipolis are enough to damn Cleon as a soldier. P. misrepresents Thucydides to suit his purpose.

Hyperbolus: Athenian politician of uncertain worth; he was ostracised in the last ever ostracism, held in 417 or 416, and was assassinated on Samos in 411. Thucydides does not elsewhere use μοχθηρός, 'wretched', and he says rather more against the man than P. allows: see Thuc. 8.73.3 and *HCT* V *ad loc*.

Philistus ... Dionysius: soon after the triumph over the Athenians in 413 the Syracusan democracy collapsed, and Sicily was invaded and ravaged by the Carthaginians. Power in Greek Sicily was eventually seized by Dionysius in 405; he ruled as tyrant in Syracuse and held things together as ruthlessly as necessary till his death in 367. Philistus his contemporary and supporter was sent into exile by him, but returned after Dionysius' death to take part in affairs again. In exile he had written a history of Sicily, taking a basically favourable view of the tyrant. A few scraps survive.

Digressions and diversions: H. declares himself on the subject in 4.30. "I need not apologize for the digression (on mule-breeding in Elis) – it has been my plan throughout this work." The relationship between digressions and tales of the distant past which P. proposes here may be seen in Thucydides: Hornblower (1987) 66–8 gives examples and considers it. Thucydides and H. differ over it largely because Thucydides' topic was contemporary and H.'s was not. Yet the nearer H. gets to his own times, the fewer the digressions and diversions, and P. in *Life of Theseus* 1 recognises the need for stories when sounder material is lacking. See also *Life of Pericles* 24.12 for a simpler view of digressions. Here P. may have in mind the tale of Ameinocles, which offends both of P.'s proposed contexts for such things: see 30, and 39 for a further disapproving mention.

D **the curse of tragedy:** author unknown. P. quotes the line whole in 520B. Here the first word of the line, ὄλοιο, 'Damn you', is left out.

4.

omission of good things: the tale of Pittacus, which P. tells in 15/859AB, may have been in his mind.

Cold praise: this is not the same thing as omission, but P. sees it as next door to omission.

5.

E **Professors of rhetoric:** P.'s word is σοφισταί: see 15/857Fn for his objection to H.'s use of it for the Seven Sages. But between that use of it and this over 500 years had gone by, and even in H.'s day the word was gathering connotations of disapproval, which Aristophanes in *Clouds* helped to fix. The translation here, for which see *LSJ s.v.*, represents a qualified return to respect. P. may have tried to join the profession himself: see Russell 7.

a better account should be preferred: Russell makes P.'s view at least intelligible: see ch 3, especially the second half.

Themistocles, Ephorus: P. recounts the affair in *Life of Themistocles* 23, but without mentioning his source. Ephorus, born in Cyme *c.*405, was (like Theopompus) a pupil of Isocrates; he lived in Athens and died in 330. He wrote the first universal history of Greece, from the return of the Heracleidae down to 341. The narrative was organised by topics; the scope compelled some simplification. He set the form and style of much later history. Only fragments of his work survive. Macan's comment (II 27) sums him up: 'Ephorus probably did as much as any one man ever did to corrupt history in the name of history'. The length and accuracy of P.'s quotation cannot be judged; it may well not last beyond the word 'persuaded'.

F **Thucydides ... condemning it:** the argument from silence is not sound here. Either the incident occurred but was not known to Thucydides or, more likely, it did not even occur. More interesting is Thucydides' decision to take up the stories of Pausanias and Themistocles: they form a digression (1.128.3–138) of a thoroughly Herodotean nature!

6.

the comic poets: complete plays of the fifth century comedians survive to us only from Aristophanes, but, thanks partly to P. himself (see *Lives of Pericles, Nicias* and *Alcibiades*), we know the names of several of Aristophanes' fellows and even have some scraps of what they wrote. P. did not find Aristophanes congenial (see 711F–712A and 853A–854D), but he recognised the importance of the plays for history. Aspasia, Pericles' common-law wife, is attacked for causing the war in *Acharnians* (524ff) and Pheidias, master craftsman in charge of the Acropolis building programme, in *Peace* (605ff).

856A **to squash ... the Spartans nothing:** the second phrase in effect repeats the first; P.'s rhetorical energy is being expressed. For the origins of the Peloponnesian war, see especially de Ste. Croix, who mounts a powerful attack on the traditional view that Pericles provoked it. For P.'s view, see *Life of Pericles* 31.1.

Thebe ... Alexander: Alexander, ruler of Pherae in south Thessaly, was killed by his wife Thebe *c.*359. P. recounts the event in *Life of Pelopidas* 28 and 35, and refers to it twice elsewhere (256A and, slightly differently, 768F). Xenophon, a contemporary of the event, says Thebe's brothers did the murder, compelled by her (*Hell.* 6.4.35–7).

Cato: Cato, Roman senator and stubborn constitutionalist, committed suicide after the battle of Utica in 46 rather than survive in a world dominated by one man. He became the example of republican, that is, oligarchic, ideals. P. in *Life of Cato* (Minor) 52 reckons that Caesar would have spared him.

7.

B   **Philip:** king of Macedon 359 – 336. He prided himself on his diplomacy; though successful on the battlefield, he was happy to gain his ends by money.

Alexander: the Great, Philip's son, king 336 – 323, conqueror of Persia and its empire.

Timotheus: Athenian general in the 370s and 360s, of varying fortunes; he was fined 100 talents in 356. P. records the story referred to here in 187BC and, with minor variation, in *Life of Sulla* 6.3–4.

drawing pictures: we seem to have here the equivalent of modern political cartoons. Virtually all that P. uses in evidence is literary, and no doubt the information about the pictures came to him not in the form of the cartoons themselves but in a record of them. It is worth gathering together his references in this work to evidence of non-literary origin: in 12/857B he mentions honours still being paid to Helen and Menelaus in Egypt (he might have seen what was done on his visit); in 26/862A he mentions the continuing Athenian commemoration of Marathon by procession to Agrae; in 37/869D he mentions Themistocles' temple of Artemis; in 39/870D (but see note) he refers to the names of the allies engraved on the war-memorial. The epigrams of Simonides he may have seen *in situ* (see 34/867Fn for one), but he would probably know them first as literature. As for the Corcyrean decrees mentioned in 22/860B, they too would be part of his reading, though autopsy is not impossible. For his understanding of this sort of evidence, see *Life of Nicias* 1.5.

8.

C   **who then turn in their tracks:** P. may have in mind H.'s narrative of Adeimantus' behaviour at Salamis, but he leaves the point without example. Adeimantus is vindicated in 39.

9.

Aristoxenus: born in Tarentum, he was influenced by the Pythagoreans; later he came to Athens and studied under Aristotle. He wrote principally on music (work survives) but also on philosophy, including lives of philosophers.

10.

D   **A list ... could go on:** P. seems to have forgotten that in 1 he proposed only an outline, not a total analysis, of malice; but the sentence here is in any case a rhetorical flourish, with which to conclude the preface.

11.

Io ... worship ... straits ... royal families: for Io's story see Griffith 189. Her worship has similarities with that of Isis in Egypt and Astarte in Syria. The Ionian sea bears her name still, and both the Thracian and the Crimean Bosporus (literally, Cowford) appear to commemorate her metamorphosis. Aegyptus and Danaus, kings of Egypt and Argos respectively, claimed descent from her by way of her son by Zeus, Epaphus. See 14/857En.

E   **Our excellent author says:** H. in fact says that he is giving the Phoenician version, and P. admits as much in his next sentence. Both H. and P. quote sources a good deal, and it is a little surprising that P. is not more careful to note when H. does and does not say that he is reporting the stories of others. P.'s view is that what H. reports he endorses, and if he chooses to report contradictory things, then he is endorsing at least one fib.

he falsely alleges: P. offers no evidence for his assertion. He simply does not wish to accept the story about Io, and so denounces it, with no aim of rescuing the Phoenicians from misrepresentation by H.

a worthless woman: so says Helen in *Iliad* vi 344ff; so says Aeschylus in *Agamemnon* 445–51. H. is in good company!

F **it is plain, he says ... wish to be:** H.'s sentence is memorable; in P.'s first quotation of it two small variations (in effect normalisations) suggest that it is being quoted from memory: for δῆλον γάρ and ἐβούλοντο ('it is plain' and 'they wished') H.'s MSS show δῆλα γὰρ δή and ἐβουλέατο (NB Hude prints ἐβούλοντο in contradiction of the MSS evidence; Rosén accepts ἐβουλέατο). Five lines later P. repeats the quotation, but appears to have checked the text in the interim (he would not have to unroll the papyrus far): now he gets δῆλα γὰρ δή and (here I do not accept Lachenaud's ἐβουλοντο[1]) ἐβουλέατο right, but, with concentration fading, changes the last word ἡρπάζοντο (be abducted) into ὑβρίζοντο (be raped). See Intro. 18 and 19. A small further point: when H. says "It is obvious, etc." he is still reporting the Persian version; the word (not expressed) meaning 'it is' would be the infinitive εἶναι, not the indicative ἐστί. P. could be forgiven for overlooking so small a point were he not so bent on blaming H.

the gods too were acting in folly: P.'s argument at this stage is as follows: since the gods are right to be angry at rape, so the Greeks were right to be angry at Helen's rape. But his own rhetorical question starts to distort the sequence of thought; it seems as if he is arguing for the behaviour of men and gods to be treated on the same level.

daughters of Leuctrus: the name Leuctrus may be derived from the place, Leuctra in Boeotia. There in 371 the Spartan army was so heavily defeated that Sparta never recovered her previous power in Greece. The rape story, which is not datable and may well be fiction, provides an αἰτία, an account, for the defeat. Xenophon records the story but without giving the father's name (*Hell.* 6.4.7); P., telling it in 773B–774D, says the father's name was Scedasus; so too Pausanias (9.13.5–6).

Ajax ... Cassandra: the story belongs to the sack of Troy, and was in the lost epic poem of that title. The villain is the lesser Ajax, son of Oileus. Vergil refers to the story in the *Aeneid*: i 41, ii 403ff and vi 840.

Aristomenes: P.'s argument jumps from women being carried off to men being carried off, to show that even sturdy resistance may fail.

H. tells no tale of Aristomenes at all. Such a story would belong to the original subjugation of Messenia (see 21/859C and note), but any facts which survived from then became confused with the liberation of Messenia after the battle of Leuctra. Pausanias has the tale of Aristomenes at some length (4.17 and 4.18.4–7) but it is probably untrue: see L. Pearson, 'The Pseudo-History of Messenia and its Authors' *Historia* 11 (1962) 397–426, and Forrest 70.

Philopoemen the Achaeans' general: the Achaean league, a federation of small north Peloponnesian communities, had developed in the fourth century; Alexander the Great suppressed it, but it revived in 280 and for over a hundred years had much political and military influence in the affairs of Greece. Philopoemen, born in 252, was one of its most notable leaders: he fought many battles and died in his seventieth year a prisoner of war. The story referred to here is in P.'s *Life of Philopoemen* 18. Polybius is the primary source for the man, and when Polybius fails, Livy. See R.M. Errington, *Philopoemen*, Oxford 1969.

857A **Regulus:** Marcus Atilius Regulus, consul of Rome in 256, won a victory at sea over the Carthaginians and landed in Africa, but was captured the next year. In

---

[1] ἐβούλοντο has been accepted by editors since the Basel edition of 1542; but of the two MSS, B has ἐβουλέατο, and E has ἐβουλεύοντο, more probably in correction of an original ἐβουλέατο than in error for or correction of ἐβούοντο. See Hansen 8.

249 he was sent on parole to Rome to negotiate a settlement; instead he urged his fellow Romans to fight on. The tale that he then duly returned to Carthage and to death is memorably told by Horace, *Odes* 3.5. See also Kipling, *Stalky and Co.*, *Regulus*.

leopards and tigers: P. has in mind the hunting expeditions which supplied Roman arenas with animals for the games. His argument has now strayed far from its starting point of Io and Helen.

12.

barbarophile: I have coined the word to match P.'s coinage. The quality which P. objects to in H. has several roots: one is H.'s own origins, on the fringe of the Greek world (see Intro. 12 and 23/860En); another is his refugee life (see 35/868An); a third is his cultural relationship with broad-minded Homer (see M.S. Silk, *Homer the Iliad*, Cambridge 1987, 98/9); a fourth is his sophist's sense of ethical relativity (see, for instance, the famous passage in 3.38 about what to do with fathers' corpses). Roughly half of H.'s history is devoted to the Persians and their empire; not only was he fascinated himself by what he found, but he plainly also wished his Greek audience to have a good understanding of the old enemy. In terms of the historical and narrative balance of the whole, however, he may have said too much about Egypt: see Lloyd I 154/5.

Busiris: H. mentions the place Busiris in 2.59 and 61; Busiris as a person's name is a piece of Greek misunderstanding, which H. avoided. The story of the attempted murder of Heracles was probably known to and rejected by Hecataeus before H. (see Burn (1972) 27). For all its nonsense it was popular with Greek vase-painters; some representations antedate Hecataeus.

pollution ... upon the Greeks: in *Life of Theseus* 11 P. says that Heracles killed Busiris!

B **what Egyptian produced this tale:** it may look as if P. now discriminates between x the source of the story and H. its reporter, but for P. the real blame rests on H. for giving the story circulation; the Egyptian is tossed in for mere contempt, with the implication that H. should not have heeded such a source.

many honours ... still go on: P. visited Egypt; he may have had authority for this assertion. See 7/856Bn.

13.

"sexual intercourse with boys": see K.J. Dover, *Greek Homosexuality*, London 1978. By P.'s time customs had changed, and he had strong views himself about the superiority of heterosexual love in marriage, eloquently expressed in his dialogue *Amatorius*, 748E–771E. The link P. makes with castration is tenuous. In H., the chief merit of eunuchs is loyalty (8.105), but that is perhaps a consequence of castration; for defeat in war and good looks as causes of castration see 6.9.4 and 6.32. P. objects because he thinks that H. dishonours the Greeks by saying they gave a lead in such a thing.

C **"processions ... festivals" ... twelve gods ... Dionysus:** P. does not substantiate his protests. The absence of Dionysus from the twelve gods of the Greeks (which were Zeus, Hera, Poseidon, Demeter, Ares, Apollo, Artemis, Aphrodite, Athena, Hermes, Hephaestus and Hestia) is worth noting: H. was essentially right to date him later, as he did Heracles and Pan. By his own account, official worship of Pan in Athens did not begin till after Marathon (6.105.3).

Melampus: seer and sage, he was traditionally dated to the generation before Nestor of Pylos. Melampus means Blackfoot, which is said to be a word for Egyptians: the implication might be that he went 'native' and so deserved contempt.

"I will say no more": see 1/854En; P. also quotes the phrase in 417C and 607C. He should have approved of H.'s reticence. There were rituals in Greek religious practice which were not for disclosure; H. mentions specifically the Thesmophoria in honour of Demeter, and implies that the Egyptian Mysteries deserved the same respect.

D **Heracles ... second set:** H. was impressed by the great antiquity of Egyptian civilisation. In relating things Greek to things Egyptian (partly to make things Egyptian intelligible to his Greek audience) he mostly adopted the diffusionist theory of civilisation: what comes later and is similar to something earlier is derived from it. In the matter of Heracles, H.'s researches convinced him that in fact there were two distinct gods, one Egyptian and one Greek (2.43/4), and P. overlooks this vindication of the independence of the Greek Heracles. See Lloyd I 148 and II notes *ad loc.*

14.

E **Heracles' ancestry ... the Persians:** by bringing together what H. separates, P. obscures the issue. For Heracles' descent in the thirteenth generation from Io, see Griffith 225. For P., presumably, since Io is Greek, so is Heracles: H. should not have even considered anything else; see G.L. Huxley, *Herodotus and the Epic*, Athens 1989. In H. 7.150 the Persian ambassadors to Argos accept the Greek tradition, no doubt diplomatically.

"genuine Egyptians": the word translated 'genuine', ἰθαγενής (variant forms occur), is recorded three times before H. uses it here; once in Homer (*Odyssey* xiv 203), once in Aeschylus (*Persians* 306), and in H. himself, 2.17.6. Aeschylus' use of it seems straightforward; but for H. 2.17.6 see Lloyd II *ad loc.*: 'the entire section is a polemic against Ionians, in particular Hecataeus'. Homer uses the word in the speech that deceives the faithful Eumaeus: Odysseus says that though born of a concubine he counted as 'equal with the legitimate sons', ἴσον ἰθαγενέεσσιν. When H. uses it in 6.53.2, discussing family trees, he perhaps has the same ironic smile on his face as in 1.147.1 (see 19/859Fn) when discussing the Ionians' racial purity. The position of the word in H.'s sentence is also to be noted; it comes last, like παιδοφόνος in 7.190 (see 30/864Cn). P. has missed the irony both of the smile and of the timing.

Epaphus ... Io ... Iasus ... Argus: for Epaphus and Io see 11/856Dn; Iasus is in some versions of the myth Io's father, and Argus in some versions Iasus' father. P. is concentrating on the Greekness of the line.

Homer ... Pindar: P. is using the argument from silence again (see 5/855Fn). Homer, Hesiod, Archilochus and Pindar are all mentioned by H., Homer and Pindar being quoted. Alcman belongs to the late seventh century; he wrote in Sparta, and some of his poetry has survived. So too for Stesichorus, who came from Himera in Sicily and wrote in the first part of the sixth century. Peisander may come in between in time; he came from Cameirus on Rhodes, and wrote an epic on Heracles which has not survived.

F **of Boeotia and Argos:** Heracles is Boeotian because he was conceived and born in Thebes, and Argive because his mother Alcmena's father was Electryon king of Mycenae in the Argolid.

15.

the Seven Sages: the Seven Sages flourished in the late seventh and the first half of the sixth centuries. The list varies: four seem to be constant, Thales of Miletus, Solon of Athens, Pittacus of Mytilene and Bias of Priene, and two more are frequent, Cleobulus of Lindos and Chilon the ephor of Sparta. What they share is a reputation for practical and political skills. Hence the original inclusion of Periander tyrant of Corinth rather than the most shadowy of them all, Myson of Chen. They are first listed in Plato *Protagoras* 343A, Plato necessarily substituting Myson for Periander. See Burn (1960) 207–9, and for their sayings W. Radice and B. Reynolds, *The Translator's Art*, Harmondsworth 1987, 241–53.

"sophists": the word at first meant no more than men of skill, especially men of intellectual skill; but it became a word of abuse when their ideas made other people uncomfortable. This had begun to happen in H.'s day. P.'s objection may be derived from Plato, who tried to rescue Socrates from being labelled a sophist; but H. appears to be using the word in its original sense, appropriately for the men who first earned it. He was no small sophist himself.

Thales ... a Phoenician: Thales was Milesian; the Milesians claimed descent from Cadmus, founder of Thebes in Boeotia; Cadmus was said to come from Phoenicia. On this basis P. could almost be called a Phoenician himself!

Solon: what P. quotes of the reply to Croesus (a more accurate translation would be "'Croesus, your question to me about the fortunes of man is put to one who knows that the godhead is a wholly jealous and confounding thing.") contains nothing to surprise a Greek of H.'s day; it was a commonplace of Greek thought and occurs frequently in tragedy. Solon set out his thinking and his plans for Athens in poems which P. knew well: he quotes them extensively in his *Life of Solon*. There (27) he acknowledges that an interview between Croesus and Solon was chronologically unlikely. See C.C. Chiasson, 'The Herodotean Solon', *GRBS* 27 (1986) 249–62.

858A **Pittacus:** he was elected ruler of Mytilene in 589, and served ten years. H. is uncertain whether the story he tells in 1.27.2 (it is his only mention of Pittacus: P.'s talk of trifles in the plural is a mere flourish) belonged to Pittacus or to Bias. He mentions Bias again in 1.170, but the story there belongs to the period after 546, which would be late for one of the Sages. P. gives no source for his story about Pittacus: it might come from Hellanicus (see 30/869An), also a man of Lesbos.

Mytilene: the MSS spell it Mitylene, and P. may well have done so himself; see Hansen's *apparatus criticus*, 12/13. The confusion was helped by the approximation in sound of υ to ι; in Attic Greek υ had moved from back rounded vowel to front rounded by the sixth century, eventually becoming fully fronted. See Allen 65–9.

at war over Sigeum: Sigeum in the Troad was first settled by Greeks from Lesbos in the seventh century. It was seized by the Athenians c.600 (the period of Pittacus' exploit). Eventually Periander was invited to arbitrate between the Athenians and the original settlers (H. 5.95), which he did in favour of the Athenians. In the time of Peisistratus, however, they needed to seize it again (5.94). Its capture marks the beginning of serious Athenian interest in the route to the Black Sea. Soon after 479 (see *ATL* III 206n55) it began paying tribute to the league, but its assessment was low: 1000 drachmas a year, which is about 0.2% of the total for the Hellespontine region. Possibly it contributed something by way of docks. After 300 it faded rapidly, when Alexandria Troas was founded further south, with an artificial harbour. By P.'s time it was a mere name.

H. mentions Sigeum, which it is quite likely he visited, five times, twice simply (5.94 and 95) but the first three times with definition. In 4.38 he describes it as in the Troad, using the town as a geographical marker of the north-west corner of Asia Minor. In 5.65 he speaks of Sigeum-upon-Scamander. In 5.90 he calls it Sigeum-upon-Hellespont. The site of the town has been a puzzle, but J.M. Cook (*The Troad*, Oxford 1973, ch 5) convincingly places it on the coastal ridge which shuts off the Trojan plain from the Aegean. The ridge, running north, drops close to sea level a few hundred yards south of Kum Kale, the Turkish fort which H. would now use as his marker. The fort stands on a spit of dunes which has developed since classical times. The ridge itself is of soft rock and is being steadily eroded on its west side by the waves of the Aegean. Most of old Sigeum has now gone, and any on the Aegean side went first. See G. Rapp and J.A. Gifford edd. *Archaeological Geology*, New Haven 1985 75–78.

Boats can be beached on the Aegean side, but they cannot lie comfortably at anchor except in very calm conditions: a current runs south of at least two knots (see *Mediterranean Pilot* IV 11.3.7). The place for a harbour is behind the headland, out of the current, as in the Golden Horn at Byzantium, and that is what H.'s labels point to. There is no water there for ships now: the bay of Troy has silted up over the centuries, Sigeum suffering in its turn, like Ephesus and Miletus further south (see J.C. Kraft, I. Kayan and O. Erol in *Troy: the archaeological geology*, supplementary monograph 4, Princeton 1982, 11–43; W. Leake's map after 272 in *Tour of Asia Minor*, London 1824, shows that he realised what had happened); but the prevailing wind and current have not changed (V. McGeehan Livritzis, *Journal of Nautical Archaeology* 17 (1988) 238), and modern ancient mariners face the same problems entering the Hellespont: see Tim Severin, *The Jason Voyage*, London 1985, 111–13 and 132–40, and *The Ulysees Voyage*, London 1987, 34–38.

B   **Alcaeus:** if H. had to choose between Pittacus' courage and Alcaeus' cowardice, in terms of later fame he picked the right story. The tale of the soldier's abandoned shield starts in Archilochus, before Alcaeus, and Horace had occasion to renew it: *Odes* 2.7. For the burden which a shield was, see Hanson 63–71.

16.

the **Alcmeonids:** for details of this remarkable family see Davies 368ff; Hart 1–16 also discusses them. Their fame starts with Megacles, archon *c*.630, who brought the curse upon them (H. 5.71 and Thuc. 1.126 both omit his name and try to dilute the blame; see also P. *Life of Solon* 12); their great wealth starts with Megacles' son Alcmeon, who got it at Sardis (H. 6.125; the king, however, should be not Croesus but his father Alyattes: Greek stories concerning wealth and Sardis tended to become Croesus stories). But the Alcmeonids' position in Athenian society was not secure, even without the curse: they held no priesthood, which would give prestige and some income, and prove antiquity. Hence their opportunistic marriages and politics, and the importance of Alcmeon's victory at Olympia in 592 (6.125.5), the first in the four-horse chariot race (the prestige event) by an Athenian.

Alcmeon's son Megacles married Agariste, daughter of Cleisthenes tyrant of Sicyon (6.126–30). Their daughter, whose name is not known, is the one used to make alliance with Peisistratus; a son Cleisthenes, archon in 525/4 (see 23/860Cn), set up the Athenian democracy (5.66.2). To get the Peisistratids out they were said to have bribed the oracle at Delphi (5.63.1, but see 23/860Dn); to save their new power in 507 they appealed to Persia (5.73). Whatever happened at Marathon (6.115 and 121), they reaped an unhappy reward: ostracism kept several of them out of the way, which would be an irony if Cleisthenes invented it ([Ar.] *Ath. Pol.* 22.1), and in H.'s own generation, though their wealth and fame persisted (see Aristophanes *Clouds* 46f), they hardly appeared in politics, except for Pericles, an Alcmeonid by his mother (H. 6.131). For an up-to-date discussion with references, see C.W. Fornara and L.J. Samons II, *Athens from Cleisthenes to Pericles*, Berkeley 1991, 3–22.

P.'s spelling of Alcmeonid appears to vary according to whether he is quoting H. (Ἀλκμε-) or writing it for himself (Ἀλκμαι-). See Hansen's *apparatus criticus* 28 and Häsler XI.

he accuses: H. merely narrates. Nor is the story to be doubted: the Alcmeonid opportunism fits.

Peisistratus ... back in power: amongst those who helped were the Thebans (1.161.3), but P. has overlooked that!

C   **the girl said:** oddly, she doesn't. P. has constructed her words himself. Possibly he was still working mostly from memory (see Intro. 19) and assumed that H. used direct speech as he often does. Frost 55 suggests that P.'s familiarity with the story caused the error.

17.

Spartans ... as much as ... Athenians: P. may still have had hopes at this stage of imposing a form of his own on the essay (see Intro. 13 and 14) rather than follow H.'s sequence. In fact he does produce a fair balance: the Spartans are prominent in 21, 23, 25, 26, 29, 31, 32, 41 and 42, the Athenians in 19, 23, 24, 25, 26, 27, 34, 37, 39, 40 and 42; but the balance is owed to H. in the first place, and between them the Spartans and Athenians rather overshadow the Boeotians and Corinthians.

"The sole survivor" ... he says: H. sets up the story with λέγουσι, 'they say'. In context that means 'the Spartans say': de Selincourt's "It is said" obscures the fact that H. uses λέγουσι specifically; if he needs to be vague he uses λέγεται (for what looks like deliberate vagueness see 7.150 and 28/863Cn). After λέγουσι H. uses the infinitive structure for indirect speech, as he often does (see *Lexicon* 206). P.'s word here for 'he says' is φησί, which always takes the infinitive: and that obscures H.'s intent. P. should have said 'H. says that the Spartans say', but that would spoil the attack. P. has also ignored the fact that H. tacks the story on right at the end, weakening its importance just as he does the tales of Eurymachus' execution in 7.233.2 (see 33/867An) and of Adeimantus' cowardice in 8.94 (see 39/870Bn). Were this story to be the evidence that the Spartans lost the battle, as P. says, it would not be worth much, presented as it is; but H. has already declared the Spartans the winners of the second fight (1.82.7), and he adds this tale as a curiosity.

18.

This chapter recalls 13 in its assembly of scattered points, its paraphrase of the Pantaleon story, and the apparent quotation of a brief phrase.

D   **Cyrus ... generosity:** the treatment of Croesus by Cyrus matches the treatment of Astyages (1.130.3). Whether the motive was generosity rather than the need to keep ex-kings under control is another matter. In *Life of Solon* 28 P. accepts Croesus' role as counsellor to Cyrus.

E   **even this ... entirely ungodly:** H. is careful to distinguish the dedications Croesus made from his own resources and those from the estate of Pantaleon's friend. P. implies that they all came from the same source, though there is tacit correction at the end.

one of the nobles: Nicolaus of Damascus, a first century historian, says (*FGrH* 397) that the man's name was Sadyattes: he had offended Croesus by refusing to make him a loan, and Croesus, not then king, vowed that if he came to power he would devote Sadyattes' property to Artemis. That would put it beyond recovery by the man or his family, and even more so if, as H. says, it was split between several gods.

carding-comb: P., paraphrasing, normalises H.'s form of the word.

Deioces ... his justice was a pretence: Lachenaud attributes his reading of the text here to Abresch who cited in support of it P.'s *Life of Publicola* 3.5, but H. himself is P.'s model for ἐπιτίθεσθαι + acc.: see 1.96.2.

"ambition for power": the syntactical quotation noted above helps to fix this as a verbal quotation. H.'s language is strong: 'passion for power' would not be too much. He could have had in mind the lines of Archilochus (25 Bergk) on the power and wealth of Gyges.

19.

F **But enough ... of non-Greeks:** from now on P. confines himself entirely to H.'s Greek stories. Hence nothing more from book 2, little from book 3 (see 21 and 22), and nothing at all from book 4.

most of the other Ionians: they cannot have been very numerous, since H. excludes the twelve principal Ionian communities (1.142.3–4) from them, and several of the twelve were very small: Teos, Myus and Lebedos, for instance (see Emlyn-Jones 13 and 24). By jumping to a passage some 40 lines further on P. has omitted the sentence with which H. balances what he says about the Athenians and the others: "the twelve cities, on the contrary, were proud of it" (the Ionian name).

"ashamed of the name": H.'s view of the Ionians and P.'s perception of it are two different things. P. has lit upon one section of H. on the Ionians, which concerns the remote origins of the central Greek settlements in Asia Minor. He objects first that H. speaks of some Ionians being ashamed of their name; second, that he says some were of mixed stock; third, that the Ephesians and Colophonians are denied some of their Ionianness when H. says that they do not celebrate the Apaturia.

As to the third, H. says the exclusion was due to a murder, which is possible – P. does not rebut it – and could be cause enough if the guilt bore upon the two communities as whole communities in some way. But Ephesus and Colophon seem to have lost some of their Greekness early (Emlyn-Jones 19 and 21/2), and the murder story could be an attempt to explain an existing divergence. In any case, P. entirely misses the amused contempt of H.'s comment (147.1) about purebred Ionians which precedes the remark about Ephesus and Colophon (see 14/856En).

As to the second, H. establishes (146.1) mixed blood for the immigrants even before they emigrated. He himself probably had some non-Greek blood (see 23/860En), which is perhaps what excited his contempt for, and exposure of, the claims being made. The story of the women's oath may also be a construction after the event.

As to the first, H. established no evidence, and he contradicts himself when he has Aristagoras use the blood-tie successfully when seeking Athenian help for the Ionian revolt (5.97.2). P. in objecting might have observed that; he might also have cited the Athenian Thucydides (as he does well in 39/870D) who uses Ionians to include Athenians without demur (see Thuc. 6.57.2 and 9, for instance, despite 4; and especially 3.104.3. The disparaging reference in 6.82.3 is qualified by the context).

We must not ask of P. what he could not give: hence the mention of arguments which were within his grasp. But when he objects to H.'s treatment of the Ionians, he puts his finger on what modern readers of H. have seen as H.'s clearest bias, often repeated (see Hart 89/90 and 181/2). His view emerges as much in his merely factual references as in his obviously contemptuous ones. A good example is noted by Tarn 216 and 224 (where Tarn rejects the story's truth): the exploit of a Samothracian ship at Salamis rescues the Ionians from blame; H. saw no need to observe how unIonian Samothrace was: he lets the irony speak for itself. The most that H. seems to say for the Ionians is that some, Miletus and Chios for instance, were not always as bad as the others (Samos was a special case because of the close knowledge H. gained of it as a young man in exile); on the Aeolian settlements to the north and especially on the Dorian towns to the south H. has so little to say that his view can hardly be established. What he thought of his own Halicarnassus is particularly elusive: he may have recognised that his Artemisia stories were anomalous. His failure to say anything about the Dorians of Asi where it could be said comfortably, after 1.151, is noticeable: in 1.144 he surely says less than he knew.

"Government House": there is similar anachronism in Thucydides (2.15); earliest archaeological evidence for a Prytaneum in Athens is a 'house-like building dating from early in the period of the tyrants' (*c*.550) which 'preceded the Tholos at the southwest corner of the square; like the Tholos it appears to have served the domestic needs of the Councillors'. (*The Athenian Agora, a Guide*[3] 23). Earliest archaeological evidence for Greek settlement at Miletus is of the eleventh century: see V.R. d'A. Desborough, *The Greek Dark Ages*, London 1972, 179/80.

859A **he remarks "they all keep ...":** Rosén 96 judges part of what P. quotes not to be what H. wrote (see Rosén LIII also). If it is not, then the corruption either took place early (see 23/860En) or, as Rosén suggests, is derived from P. The sense of the passage is not affected.

20.

Cyme <...> and the Mytileneans: in H.'s account only the Mytileneans offered Pactyes for a reward; the men of Cyme merely passed him on to them and then took him away to Chios. P.'s text could be emended to make the distinction, but it is more likely that they are lumped together in error. P.'s protest shows how little he appreciated the pressures acting upon the different Greek communities or their tendency to react selfishly.

B **district of Atarneus:** the district is a broad and fertile coastal plain on the mainland east of Mytilene. Its town, which lay close to the coast, had a strong site (Diodorus XIII 65), and is now succeeded by the small Turkish seaside town and port of Dikili. Demaratus, ex-king of Sparta, had his Persian estate in the area.

The natural economic interdependence of the east Aegean islands and the Asiatic mainland, sadly disrupted nowadays, is well shown in the case of Samos by Shipley 31–37: the mainland was vital to the islanders for grain, and the Samians had to fight at times to keep their bit of it. It is less clear how Chios, an Ionian settlement, held on to land so far away in Aeolis; perhaps Lesbos had grain enough of its own and from the north (see J.M. Cook, *The Greeks in Ionia and the East*, London 1962, 27/8) not to want Atarneus for themselves; but hold it the Chians did. 150 years later Xenophon records it (*Hell*. 3.2.11) in the possession of some Chian exiles; the same thing happened from time to time with the Samian peraea. Chios' need to hold Atarneus may be one reason why she continued to build ships as a member of the Delian league rather than contribute money.

Charon of Lampsacus: this is P.'s first citation of alternative evidence by author's name. Charon is one of eight historians, not including H., named by Dionysius of Halicarnassus (*Essay on Thucydides* 5; Dionysius lived in the first century) as having lived before the Peloponnesian war. All but one came from east Greece, as did all four of their younger contemporaries also named by Dionysius. Of all those whom P. cites in evidence, he quotes only Charon, twice, here and in 24. (Ephorus is quoted, but in the preface: 5/855F). Many works are attributed to Charon; he certainly wrote local history and an account of the Persian wars. P.'s quotations of him cannot be checked for accuracy since no text of Charon survives, but their worth to P.'s arguments is nil: if Charon knew what H. reports, then he has simply anticipated P. in excluding details he thought objectionable. The blandness of his version is striking!

an older writer: it is now thought that Charon did not write before the Peloponnesian war (*FGrH* 262 F9 commentary), which could be strictly true of H. as well: his period of composition may have been long and largely oral, and he may not have set pen to paper till as late as 430. See Powell 85/6 and Evans, essay three.

his text reads: twenty-three words of bald prose is a lot to remember accurately by heart; presumably (the superfluous δέ suggests it) P. excerpted Charon as he excerpted H. See Intro. 15 and 20.

21.

C **Samian help against the Messenians:** Sparta's first attempt to get control of her western neighbour belongs to the second half of the eighth century. Forrest 36/7 dates Samos' help to this campaign. A second war was fought two generations later (Tyrtaeus, 5 Bergk). *H & W* think this war the more likely occasion of the help, and Cartledge (1982) points out that help arriving by sea better fits the campaign which completed the conquest: the first campaign probably did not push through to the sea.

mixing bowl: the superb specimen of Laconian craftmanship found at Vix in France in 1953 gives us some idea of what Croesus might have received. See Hooker 90–1 and fig. 21, or R. Joffroy, *Vix et ses trésors*, Paris 1979, 40 and 150 (colour plates and black and white).

corslet ... Amasis: a similar corslet was sent by Amasis to the temple of Athena at Lindos on Rhodes (H. 2.182.1 and 3.47.3). The journey taken by the Spartan bowl from Laconia to Sardis was bound to go at least close to Samos; the considerable finds of Laconian pottery on the island show that the route had been established for a good century already (see Cartledge (1982), and Shipley 51 for references). Between Egypt and Sparta there seems to be less opportunity for Samian intervention; but Amasis was on good terms with Polycrates till shortly before 525 (3.39.2 and 43), and Amasis' carrier may well have aimed for Ionia in the first place. The prevailing current and summer wind (see 5.33.1, and *Mediterranean Pilot* IV 19 and 31) would then assist the voyage onward to the Peloponnese.

hostile to tyrants: one word in the Greek, μισοτύραννος. P. has borrowed it from H., who seems to have coined it specially for the Alcmeonids: see 6.121 and 123, and 27/863A.

What ... corslet ... made them expel: P.'s scorn is nicely focussed, and his preference for the Samian version is sound. Not only do the Spartans seem to have had an obligation to help the Samians displaced by Polycrates' tyranny, but Polycrates was also medizing, as is revealed in the tale of how he tried to send his Samian dissidents to Egypt (3.44). The second reason was well within P.'s grasp.

The tradition that Sparta moved against tyrannies where she could in the two or three generations before Marathon is accepted by Thucydides (1.18.1); the Spartan claim in the Peloponnesian war to be liberators is a renewal of that tradition (1.139.3). P.'s list of these earlier moves, nine in total, is important, since he offers us information not otherwise known. It is correspondingly difficult to handle. H. himself contributes little: he has this tale, whose likely motive he obscures, and the liberation of Athens. Through the mouth of Socles, however (see 23/860F), he attests the Spartan record on tyranny.

H.'s comparative silence is puzzling. Even the ejection of tyranny from Athens is not told to the glory of the Spartans (rather the opposite: they were duped into it, and tried to reverse it; see 5.90); H. tells the story principally because he saw the effect of democracy on the Athenians as a vital element in the Greek victory over Persia: see 5.66 and 7.139. The period of most vigorous Spartan interference coincides more or less with the reign of Cleomenes, whose record seems to have embarrassed the Spartans. Perhaps H.'s inquiries were obstructed. It is worth note that Chilon, ephor in 556, with whom the policy of ousting tyrants is reckoned to begin, is mentioned by H. only twice (1.59 and 7.235), and then on different and comparatively trivial issues.

D Corinth ... Ambracia: the Cypselid tyranny failed in Corinth soon after Periander's death c.585; his nephew Psammetichus inherited but held power for only three years ([Ar.] *Pol.* 1315b). His fall is a generation too soon for Chilon's policy to be at work. If, however, the tale of Chilon's intervention at the conception of Peisistratus is true (H. 1.59), then Chilon became ephor late in life: his office might have been more reward than opportunity. Peisistratus was born c.600 (see J.G.F. Hind, 'The tyrannis and the exiles of Peisistratus' *CQ* 68 (1974) 1–18): that puts Chilon's own birth no later than c.625. He became ephor, then, in his seventies.[2] Perhaps the Corinthians in the 580s had inquired about Spartan help, and so suggested what slowly developed into a policy. But Sparta's position in the Peloponnese was too uncertain for them to apply such a policy until the 550s at the earliest; and the silence of Socles about any Spartan help actually given to Corinth is significant, since it would greatly have assisted his argument to mention it if it had happened. As for Ambracia, Aristotle (*Pol.* 1304a) says it was liberated by a popular uprising against Periander: that means before 585.

Naxos: Lygdamis is described by H. (1.61.4) as an ally of Peisistratus in his third attempt on Athens in 546, but not as tyrant of Naxos then. Probably Peisistratus helped him to power there soon after his own success: he placed his Athenian hostages with him. By 500 Naxos was an oligarchy (5.30), and probably had been since at least 515, for between 515 and 505, according to the list of rulers of the sea preserved in Eusebius (vol I ed. Schoene 225;[3] see 26/862Bn), Naxos was top naval power, in rapid succession to Sparta, which had held the position for two years after the fall of Samos to Persia in 517. We may doubt what role Sparta exercised at sea – for those two years there was probably no dominant power at all – but presumably her power was enough to see that power did not pass to anyone who, like Polycrates earlier, might look to Persia for support. Lygdamis was gone, then, by 515, and might have been ousted ten years earlier, at the time of the Spartan expedition to Samos. D.M. Leahy, 'The Spartan embassy to Lygdamis' *JHS* 77 (1957) 272–5, discusses the timing and the political context; evidently the sons of Peisistratus did not protect their father's helper.

Athens ... Sicyon: the fall of the tyranny at Athens is well recorded (H. 5.62.2–65, Thuc. 6.59.2, and [Ar] *Ath. Pol.* 19). As for Sicyon, we know nothing of Aeschines. A papyrus fragment (*FGrH* 105 1) mentions him: the coherent portion reads Χίλων δὲ ὁ Λάκων ἐφορεύσας καὶ στρατηγήσας ᾿Αναξανδρίδης τε τὰς ἐν τοῖς ῞Ελλησιν τυραννίδας κατέλυσαν ἐν Σικυῶνι μὲν Αἰσχίνην, ῾Ιππίαν δὲ... Πεισιστ ..: 'Chilon the Spartan, who was ephor and army commander, and Anaxandrides put down the tyrannies among the Greeks, in Sicyon Aeschines, Hippias ... the Peisist ... .' Chilon and Anaxandrides could together have put down Aeschines, but not much later than 550 if Chilon was to play any physical part; but Hippias fell in 510, by which time Chilon and Anaxandrides were both dead. The author of the fragment may simply be wrong; at best he is implying a long-lasting policy, but to select two examples of it forty years apart is

2 If Chilon was still alive to have a say in Anaxandridas' second wife (5.39), he might by then be over 80, but at least that would allow the chosen girl to be his great-granddaughter, which seems likely. She was the granddaughter of a certain Demarmenus (5.41.3); a certain Demarmenus named a son Chilon (6.65.2). If the naming was done in usual fashion (see Plato *Laches* 179A, and 27/863An!), after the grandfather, then we have one and the same family. This younger Chilon had a daughter Percalus, who was taken to wife by Demaratus. Thus kings of each royal house, but of different generations, married Chilonian cousins; Chilonian policy, however, did not pass down equally, as the quarrels of Demaratus and Cleomenes show.

3 For convenient text and discussion see J.L. Myres, 'On the list of Thalassocracies in Eusebius' *JHS* 26 (1906) 84–130, with the comments of J.K. Fotheringham and Myres' reply in *JHS* 27, 75–89 and 123–130; also W.G. Forrest, 'Two chronographic notes' *CQ* 63 (1969) 95ff.

odd; perhaps he had other examples but muddled the chronology. Aeschines' fall could be dated down towards that of Hippias in order to bring the two events closer together, but then Chilon and Anaxandrides would be out of it; and the survival of a tyranny in the Peloponnese is unlikely so late. P.'s own list has some degree of chronological order, but Hippias precedes Aeschines in it. Our ignorance about some of its other names makes a chronological argument impossible to press.

Thasos ... Phocis ... Miletus: we know nothing of the tyrannies here. All are further afield, and two are overseas, where the Spartans were reluctant to venture. Miletus had been in treaty with the Lydians since before Croesus (H. 1.22.4), and after his fall the town promptly came to terms with his successor Cyrus (141.4). Spartan intervention there would have been as foolhardy as they thought Athenian intervention was in 498 (8.142.2), when Aristagoras stood down from his tyranny. **Thessaly:** king Leotychides' expedition (6.72) took place after the Persian wars, c.478, and was made in accordance with the allies' oath (7.132) to tithe the medizers. It should not be in this list.

In sum P. mentions nine ejections. The first two are doubtful; the third is acceptable, the fourth is sure, and the fifth is acceptable; the sixth and seventh are wholly obscure; the eighth is very unlikely; and the ninth does not belong in the same category.

other writers: P. leaves us guessing who they were, but their existence is not to be doubted.

E **petty vindictiveness:** P.'s best material for arguing against H.'s reason for the Spartan expedition is deployed at the end of the next chapter, which mostly deals with the participation of Corinth. It would fit better here instead of the abuse. H.'s account of the affair of 525 may have been influenced by the affair of 440–39, when the Peloponnesian league considered going to the help of Samos and Corinth argued against (Thuc. 1.40.5 and *HCT* I 349).

22.

For an analysis of P.'s composition in this chapter, see Intro. 37.

Periander ... Alyattes: Periander died c.585 after more than forty years of power; Alyattes ruled Lydia for 57 years (H. 1.25.1), dying c.560. So great an overlap prevents a precise date for the incident, but trouble between Periander and the Corcyreans is more likely to belong to his later years, which is where it needs to be to fit with the measure of time noted below (860A) between his action and the Corinthian reaction of 525.

F **temple of Artemis:** its site is near the ancient town, whose successor is now called Pythagorio. See Shipley 78n. This temple is earlier than the most famous one on Samos, the temple of Hera at the sanctuary seven miles west of Pythagorio.

sesame seed and honey: halva.

860A **two generations later:** literally, 'after three generations'. P. is counting inclusively of both ends.

H.'s MSS at this point say γενεῇ, 'a generation' (3.48.1). In the early nineteenth century it was suggested that τρίτῃ, 'third', in the form of γ', meaning 3, should be added before γενεῇ, to correct H.'s chronology: from 585 at the latest to 525 is two generations on any reckoning. This suggestion is adopted by the Budé editor, but not by Hude or Rosén. H. may simply have got the chronology wrong. There is no papyrus evidence to point either way (see Intro. 24). P. probably worked it out for himself and corrected H. silently; but it is just possible that he had a text with the 'missing' γ'.

abolish every memory: Socles' speech in 5.92 shows that if they tried they failed; moreover, there the memory is made to serve a useful purpose. The Athenians did not forget the Peisistratids.

spurred on the ... expedition: P.'s objection is not to revenge itself as a motive but to the particular cause of revenge which H. proposes. The objection is justified, but P. ignores what H. offers to explain the Corinthian motive (the strained relations between Corinth and Corcyra), argues only from probability, and has no better cause to propose himself. One may be found, however, in the interrelationship of Sparta, Corinth and Samos. One of the stabler features of Greek politics in the sixth and fifth centuries is the basic accord between Sparta and Corinth; it survived some sharp disagreements and a goodwill towards Athens on the part of Corinth which persisted until 460 (see 23/860Fn). The joint expedition against Polycrates, which presumes the accord, is also the first historical evidence for it: see Salmon 240–51. We cannot tell how long they had been on terms already; P. in *Life of Lysander* 1 records that the Corinthian nobles displaced by Cypselus' seizure of power *c.*657 found refuge in Sparta. The relationship between Sparta and Samos has been noted above (21/859Cnn). As for Samos and Corinth, they seem to have worked in common in the late eighth century, backing Chalcis against Eretria in the so-called Lelantine war. Corinthian pottery was being imported into Samos in some quantity by then (see Shipley 55 with references). The estrangement between them was probably caused by the activities of Polycrates: his piracy and his medism were good reasons for both Sparta and Corinth to take action, to restore the status quo. See Cartledge (1982).

B   **the Cnidians:** the evidence P. reports is unique to him and cannot be proved or disproved. Texts of Antenor and Dionysius have not survived, nor have any relevant inscriptions been discovered in Corcyra; P. might possibly have seen some for himself, on a journey to Rome, for instance. P.'s account and H.'s account are simply at odds. At the end of 23 P. himself seems to forget the Cnidian contribution. Perhaps the Samians commissioned some available Cnidian boats. See Salmon 225n.

Antenor ... Dionysius: P. cites these two writers only here. Antenor's date is not clear; he was probably a late or very late Hellenistic writer, and may have overlapped P. himself. Dionysius wrote five books on foundations of cities; he belongs to the middle of the fourth century.

C   **Archias ... a tomb ... its honours:** by delaying the evidence of H. to the end of the paragraph P. makes it seem as if he has a different primary source for the Archias story, and H. is mentioned merely in confirmation of it (see 35/868F for the same sort of delaying tactics). But the details are just as H. gives them, though H. refers them to his own conversation with Archias' grandson, whereas P.'s 'they say' refers to the Samians. P.'s Greek does not make it clear whether the tomb and its honours and the relationship, as well as the story, had survived to his own day. Nevertheless the point made is a good one, and clinches what was said in 21.

23.

he says that Cleisthenes ... "bribed the priestess": H. does not mention Cleisthenes till 5.66.1; in 62, where the story begins, the Alcmeonids (see 16/858Bn) are treated as a group. The story is told in direct speech, but just before the bribery episode (63.1), H. says "As the Athenians say" and when Cleisthenes is named, in 66.1, there is a similar qualification, adequately represented by de Selincourt's "the story goes." When the story is mentioned later, in 6.123.2, H.'s language again calls its veracity into doubt. P. has overlooked H.'s reservations.

From a fragment of the official archon list inscribed *c*.425 (*M–L* 6) we learn that a Cleisthenes, undoubtedly this one, was archon in 525/4, shortly after Hippias inherited power. H.'s picture of a family determinedly in exile throughout the tyranny (5.62.2 and 6.123.1) cannot be right. Cleisthenes was presumably head of the family when he was archon but his leadership is not clearly recorded till after the expulsion of Hippias, in the period of rivalry with Isagoras. In [Ar] *Ath. Pol.* also, he is not mentioned till after the tyranny is over (21.1).

D   **a false response:** it is not called false by H., who approved of the liberation of Athens as P. does. Alcmeonid money (their significant expenditure at Delphi was on the new temple of Apollo) had some impact, but Delphi already took a dim view of the Peisistratid tyranny (see Parke (1956) I 144/5), and the Spartans were ready to act against it (see 21/859Cn); the Athenian exiles were pushing at a half-open door, and nothing improper needed to be done. H.'s reservations, noted above, may reflect Alcmeonid dislike of a rumour against them which persisted in the fifth century; more notably, for this affair H. has no names of guilty Delphians, whereas he does for the considerable scandal of Cleomenes' dethrone-ment of Demaratus (H. 6.66). P. makes no protest at H.'s mention of that affair: the fate of Cleomenes was presumably seen as confirmation of the outrage (see Pausanias 3.4.5/6, for instance), and P. could hardly have required H. to omit the story (see 3 and 5 for categories of omission). Here P.'s real protest is on behalf of the Alcmeonids and the Spartans; benefit to Apollo is incidental. See Intro. 9, and for a similar protest 40/871D.

The absoluteness of the oracle tends to be overrated by those who have the famous tales of Oedipus and Orestes in mind. Oracles gave advice and opinion rather than commands, and could be challenged, as Delphi was by the Athenians, successfully, before Salamis (7.141), and as Didyma was by Aristodicus, unsuccessfully, after the fall of Croesus (1.159).

Themis: the personification, and deification, of an abstract fem. noun meaning 'established custom', 'sanctioned practice'. Themis has divine status in Homer (*Iliad* xv 87ff, for instance); for her place at Delphi see Aeschylus *Eumenides* 2.

praise with ... disapproval: see 9.

Isagoras son of Tisander: Tisander was not a common name in Athens (see Davies *s.v.*). Hippocleides who danced away his marriage (6.127.4) had a father called Tisander; they were Philaids, of the clan to which Miltiades belonged, ri-vals of the Alcmeonids. It is tempting to put Isagoras with them, but if the evi-dence had existed, H. would surely have done it himself instead of refrain rather obviously. See D.M. Lewis, 'Cleisthenes and Attica' *Historia* 12 (1963) 22–40.

E   **Carian Zeus:** P. clearly thinks that the Carians of south-west Asia Minor are meant, allies of the Ionians in the rebellion of 499–4; they were not Greeks but were considerably hellenized. H. himself presumably had some Carian ancestors: his father Lyxes and his uncle the epic poet Panyassis bear Carian names. But inscriptional evidence from the Attic deme called Icarion suggests that we are dealing with a local cult: see D.M. Lewis as cited above, and *IG* 1³ 253/4 for his more detailed note on the text of the inscription. H.'s text has the phrase "Carian Zeus" in the dative: ΔIIKAPIOI. It is easy to see that as a miscopying of ΔIIIKAPIOI: Icarian Zeus. P. then becomes the victim of a misreading of his own, or of a corrupted text, and his protest is null.

carrion of Caria: not a great pun, but it matches P.'s. 'Carrion' represents P.'s κόρακας, 'crows'. 'Go to the crows' (a phrase familiar to readers of Aristophanes) meant 'Go to hell'.

The Gephyreans: what H.'s investigations were, and why he came to a different conclusion from that of the family about their origins, we cannot tell. *H & W* have a variety of suggestions; they come down anyway in favour of the family's view. P.'s objection has nothing to do with the soundness or unsoundness of H.'s view: it is the familiar complaint that things Greek are having their Greekness diluted. See 13, 14 and 15 on the gods and Perseus and Thales.

He may not be able to deny: nor does he try! But P.'s implication that H. would like to is a momentarily effective piece of rhetoric.

F **they had "made a mistake":** the Spartans had expected oligarchy to replace tyranny, as happened elsewhere. Cleisthenes' initiative took them by surprise; hence their attempt to sustain Isagoras as archon in 508/7, and when that failed, the attempt to take a Peloponnesian force into Attica, probably the next year. The passage which P. quotes belongs to a further attempt on Attica, when the Spartans proposed to restore the original tyranny. The Athenians themselves had resisted the first attempt successfully (5.72.2); the second attempt was collapsed by the Corinthians and Demaratus (75.1); Socles' speech at Sparta undid the third before it got under way (93.2). P. has telescoped events. If the Spartans had learnt of the Alcmeonid mission to Sardis (73), they had good cause for their worry.

"oracles ... a swindle": even though the episode was perhaps ten years old and the degree of corruption slight (see 22/860Dn), the claim of corruption made an adequate pretext for interference.

the Corinthians: Corinthian goodwill towards Athens during the time-span of H.'s history is in sharp contrast with the relationship H. knew in his own lifetime (see de Ste. Croix 211/2). The change came when the Megarians sought Athenian help c.460 (Thuc. 1.103.4). In addition to the two interventions noted above, H. reports Periander's arbitration over Sigeum (5.95; see 15/858An), the attempted protection of Plataea as an ally of Athens (6.108.5), and the cheap sale of ships for Athens' war with Aegina (6.89). H. chooses the last of these to make explicit comment on the Corinthian friendliness towards Athens.

Socles: so he is spelt in P.'s MSS. H.'s MSS are divided between Socles and Sosicles.

861A **the despatch of those three hundred:** P.'s return to this topic is abrupt and somewhat confusing. His reasoning appears to be that the pot is calling the kettle black, as follows: Sparta, despite her record on tyrants hitherto, is behaving wrongly in trying to re-impose tyranny in Athens, but the Corinthians are in no position to protest when they, in alleged pursuit of a quarrel of their own tyrant Periander, try to impose their will on Samos. A. Ferrill, 'Herodotus on tyranny' *Historia* 27 (1978) 385–98, suggests that Socles meant the Spartans to see their own Cleomenes as a Periander.

"bore the Samians a grudge": P. uses the verb μνησικακεῖν, a word first recorded in H. In 3.49.2 H. prefixes it, uniquely, with ἀπο-, which P. omits here, but he is surely quoting. See Intro. 19.

24.

"the beginning of evil": P., literary man, quotes Homer (*Iliad* v 63). H. himself undid Homer's compound adjective ἀρχέκακος into ἀρχὴ κακῶν and avoided the direct quotation; so did Thucydides later (2.12.3). P.'s complaint here is that H. should at least have praised Athenian boldness (not that it lasted long: see 5.103.1); but H. has in mind the ultimate failure of the Ionian rebellion and the consequent threat to Athens and to Greece: a realistic viewpoint.

B **Since Ionia ... Pamphylian waters:** Hansen obelizes the whole sentence. Though its sense is mostly clear, it is defective in syntax and inadequate in expression of the apparent sense. First problem is ὡς: Hansen thinks it was intended as a conjunction, and that its finite verb has got lost; but it could be giving causal sense to the two participles συγκεχυμένων and προσπλέοντος (Goodwin 864: Goodwin's examples are confined to fifth and fourth century authors, but they were P.'s models), except that it is questionable whether causal force is appropriate: temporal force for both seems better ('since' offered in translation is conveniently ambiguous). Second, ἀπαντήσαντες, 'encountered', needs something to complete its sense. Third, ἔξω, 'outside', lacks definition. Fourth, Κυπρίους, 'some Cypriots', if it refers, as is probable, to the Cypriote division of the Persian navy, is very brief; if to anything else, too brief. Hansen thinks ἔξω Κυπρίους can stand, and he proposes one lacuna after προσπλέοντος for the missing clause verb and another after κατεναυμάχησαν for words to prevent the Eretrians remaining sole subjects of what follows. Certainly, other Greeks took part in the attack on Sardis, but it is possible P. took that as read.

For want of other information about the Eretrian exploit, no reconstruction of the text can be sure. But the Byzantine humanist George Gemistus Pletho, who died at Mistra aged nearly 100 two years before the fall of Constantinople, made about 100 excerpts from this essay of P., paraphrasing mildly. One of them is an excerpt of this passage. Pletho writes στόλῳ βασιλικῷ ἐκ Κύπρου τῇ 'Ιωνίᾳ προσπλέοντι ἔξω ἐν τῷ Παμφυλίῳ πελάγει ἀπαντήσαντες κατεναυμάχησαν, 'the royal fleet was sailing from Cyprus to Ionia; they met it outside in the Pamphylian sea and beat it in a sea-fight'. Whatever the relationship may be of Pletho's paraphrase to his text of P., in itself it makes good sense. Cypriote ships were part of the Persian navy; failing the Ionian ships, these were nearest to the troublespot. Artaphernes perhaps had power as satrap on the spot to summon them without first seeking the authority of the king at Susa. The rebels anticipated them, and the Eretrians, probably with others, met them and disposed of them before they could get to Ionia. The victory would explain how next year the Ionians landed in Cyprus without opposition (H. 5.109.2: no Cypriote ships) and with some welcome.

The manoeuvre is strategically likely (see *PG* 199/200). As for Eretrian leadership of the manoeuvre, the list of rulers of the sea (see 21/859Dn) has Eretria as chief naval power from 505 to 490, in succession to Naxos; but H. reports (5.99) only five ships joining the twenty of Athens to help the Ionians in 498: if the bulk of her fleet was deployed further east and a token few went to Coressus, everything fits. The difficulties of P.'s text do not obscure the probable important addition to our information about the Ionian revolt.

left their ships at Ephesus: at this date the city of Ephesus had a site provided by Croesus (Strabo 640), under the hill now called Ayasuluk by modern Selçuk. There the famous temple of Artemis was built. The harbour of Ephesus was under the hill called Coressus (H. 5.100), half an hour's walk away west-south-west. There the town was re-sited *c*.300; that was the town of P.'s day. The site is now three miles inland, but reedbeds mark the old harbour and its channel.

C **swamped by superior numbers:** H. speaks only of large numbers gathering against them (101.3). P. probably felt that a clearer reason was needed for the Greek retreat from Sardis.

Lysanias of Mallos: this is the only record of him. No date can be set for him. Mallos was near Tarsus in Cilicia, north of Cyprus.

defeated ... and ... pursued: P. has adjusted H.'s account to suit himself. H. says 'followed', not 'pursued', and he puts the defeat at Ephesus, not Coressus.

Charon of Lampsacus: see 20/859B. In the quotation here there is the same bland simplification as before.

(I quote): P. uses the phrase κατὰ λέξιν, 'I quote' four times, twice for his quotations of Charon and twice in quoting H. (31/865E and 37/869D). We cannot check how accurately Charon is quoted, but P.'s use here of the Ionic form for 'royal', βασιλη[ου, is to be noted. Two very similar phrases introducing quotations from H. occur elsewhere, apparently for emphasis: in 35/868B αὐτοῖς ὀνόμασι and in 37/869E αὐταῖς λέξεσι. See Intro. 21 and 23 for P.'s accuracy in the Herodotean passages.

25.

D   **In the sixth book:** in H. the story of Plataea's link with Athens is a digression within the Marathon narrative. P. shows good sense in detaching it for comment here; likewise with the Ameinocles story in 30. To put the Argos chapter (28) where it is has less obvious justification; at the end of 27 P. has a good cue to go on with Athens, and his comments on Argos could easily come after 29 and keep H.'s sequence. See Intro. 14.

the Plataeans' offer of themselves to the Spartiates: P.'s use of the word 'Spartiate', Σπαρτιάτης, is odd. H. says (6.108.2) that they offered themselves to Cleomenes and the Spartans, Λακεδαιμονίοισι. P. reverts to 'Spartans' in five lines' time. See 31/864Fn. I have translated Σπαρτιάτης as 'Spartiate' wherever P. uses it, adjusting de Selincourt as necessary (see 31/865E = H. 7.220.4); Λακεδαιμόνιος I have mostly translated as 'Spartan', as is usual in English.

not as a suspicion ... but as if ... for sure: H.'s narrative is in direct speech; P. makes the most of its directness!

"advice ... not ... from goodwill": P. objects to the cynicism which H.'s analysis attributes to the Spartans. We are not well enough informed about relations between Thebes and Athens before this event to know whether the Spartans could have reasoned as H. says they do: but see 31/864En. The date of the episode is probably 519: the Athenian who accepted the alliance is then Hippias. He may have thought it better policy not to disappoint the Spartans than to upset the Thebans, despite their generous support of his father thirty years earlier (1.61.3). In the event, the Plataeans justified the alliance by joining the Athenians at Marathon.

26.

E   **in the first half of the month:** any Spartan ban on military action in the first half of a month (6.106.3) seems to be confined to the month called Carneius (7.206.1 and Thuc. 5.54), which corresponded roughly to the Athenian month called Metageitnion, second month in the calendar. The year began at midsummer as nearly as the state of the moon allowed. The Spartan feast Carneia in honour of Apollo was celebrated in the week leading up to the full moon: full moon fell in the middle of the month. Military inaction was prolonged by the Gymnopaediae (Thuc. 5.82.2/3), which preceded the Carneia. In H. 7.206 we see the additional impact of the Olympic festival in the year of Thermopylae. The Hyacinthia, which partly delayed action in 479, fell earlier in the year (H. 9.7.1 and 11.1). But if the need was pressing enough, the Spartans could respond: they did send men to Thermopylae, and the battle of Leuctra in 371 clearly fell during the Gymnopaediae (Xen. Hell. 6.4.16). Marathon may have been the first occasion on which the Spartan army was needed away from home at a time not of their own choosing (the exiled Demaratus may have offered advice!); the Spartans may have felt that if the Athenians could hold the position for a week (no doubt Philippides confirmed the strategy), they could do it for two or three days more. In 480 the need was much more pressing.[4]

the sixth day: on 6th Boedromion (the Athenian month next after Metageitnion) there was a festival of Artemis, and it was used by the Athenians to commemorate Marathon. P. has concluded that the day of commemoration was the day of the

---

[4] Plato, Laws 698E, says that the Spartans were distracted in 490 by war in Messenia. P. knew Laws well, but, as L. Pearson observes ('The pseudo-History of Messenia and its authors' Historia 11 (1962) 397–426), presumably he discounted the testimony. Plato is not reliable as a historian. See below 862Bn!

fight. It may have been a common opinion in his day. The error makes nonsense of most of the rest of the chapter. The probable day of the battle is the morning after the Carneian full moon or the morning after that: 12th or 13th August in our calendar. Burn *PG* 240/1n and 257 gives a clear discussion of the difficulties and possibilities.

F   **"the ninth day":** of the Spartan month. See below.

862A   **Agrae:** it was close outside the walls of Athens to the south-east, just beyond the site of the great temple of Zeus begun by Peisistratus and completed by Hadrian, on the left bank of the Ilissus.

Philippides: this, not the better known Phidippides, is probably the right form of the runner's name. See *H & W* on 6.105.1, and K.J. Dover, Aristophanes *Clouds*, Oxford 1968, xxv.

summoning ... on the ninth: P. has combined H.'s Spartan date with 6th Boedromion, and argues as if Philippides set off on the eighth day of both months.

B   **Diyllus ... Anytus ... ten talents:** Diyllus lived from 357 to 297 and wrote 26 books of history which followed on from Ephorus (see 5/858En). Ten talents would be a considerable sum: 60,000 drachmae, when a generation later a stone-mason working on the Acropolis was earning 1 drachma a day (*IG* 1³ 475)⁵. Pindar the poet is said to have received a present from the Athenians of 10,000 drachmae (Isocrates *Antidosis* 166); the same sum was charged by H.'s contemporaries the sophists Protagoras (Diogenes Laertius 9.52) and Zeno (Plato *Alcibiades* 119A).

The sum is possible; the circumstances are problematic. The award would be related to public recitals. H. was probably in Athens in the 440s and in 430. Eusebius, a bishop of the fourth century A.D., says H. was officially honoured in 445/4, but the Histories were certainly not in their present form so early: see 33/867An and 39/870Bn. H. could have been trying out an early version. The Anytus best known to us is the man who took part in the prosecution of Socrates in 399; if the award happened as early as Eusebius says, then some other Anytus is likely: the name is not uncommon.

as most people say: the phrase suggests a large critical literature on H. (see 27/862Dn). But the text is doubtful.

numbers of the dead: H. gives no figures for the size of Datis' original force. Later writers were less scrupulous. Nepos the Roman, who lived from *c*.99 to 24, says 10,000 cavalry and 100,000 infantry, and that, as Burn (*PG* 244n) says, is the most modest estimate. Plato *Menexenus* 240A says 500,000! A toll of 6,400 dead (H.6.117.1) from that would not be much. But if Datis' numbers were about 20,000, as is commonly accepted, and if about half of them were on their way by sea to Athens when the battle took place, then 6,400 is over 50%.

Artemis Agrotera: Artemis of the Wilds. See *Iliad* xxi 471. The title is often interpreted to mean 'huntress': see *LSJ* ἀγρότερος. The compromise sacrifice is mentioned by Xenophon, *Anab.* 3.12.2.

27.

C   **Eretrians ... proud ... determination:** P. ignores H.'s evidence of a people divided and a town betrayed from inside (6.100 and 101). The word translated 'slave' which P. objects to, ἀνδράποδον, is first recorded in H. and means 'prisoner of war fit for use'.

D   **his slander of the Alcmeonids:** see 16. H. says plenty that is ambiguous about the family. The famous passage referred to here (6.121.4), ostensibly a refutation of the charge that they communicated with the Persians, can even be read as the

---

⁵ See M.M. Markle, 'Jury Pay & Assembly Pay at Athens' (Appendix), in *Crux* edd. P.A. Cartledge and F.D. Harvey (London 1985) 293.

opposite: see Hart 12. The slander as P. sees it is for H. to have mentioned them at all in the context; to defend them, or to seem to do so, after attacking them is worse: H. is guilty of the offence mentioned in 8. See Evans 93/4.

just a brief clash: H. says (6.113) that the fighting took a long time. Burn *PG* 251 observes 'the time of a hand-to-hand mêlée must be counted in minutes rather than hours'; see also Hanson chs 13 and 15. H.'s "long time" starts with the impact of the charge on the Persians and continues to the fighting by the ships; the encounter had several stages. But P. does not mean to discount all that; his objection is rather that H. (who plainly was short of hard facts about the whole affair: hence to some extent the elaborate digressions in the Marathon narrative) did not produce a story to match the achievement; if he had, the 'jealous and disparaging critics' (we should like to know more about them: was Theopompus one? See 1/855An) would have had no chance to disparage. But they probably wrote in reaction to later exaggeration. The consequences of Marathon were greater than the event itself.

after their landing: P. in his excitement gives the impression that the Athenians and Plataeans hit the Persians almost as they disembarked. H. (110) indicates that several days separated the landing from the fight; the despatch of Philippides would make no sense if not. P. accepts this in *Life of Aristeides* 5.

the wind that would take them furthest from Attica: in *Life of Aristeides* 5 P. says that the wind and current carried them 'inwards, towards Attica'. This is likely: the prevailing wind should have helped during the daytime, at least as far as Sunium; see *Mediterranean Pilot* IV 31 and 339, and *GH* I 84 and 88. Either way, P. fails to account for the Athenians' hasty return to Athens. His picture here of a panic-stricken Persian flight accords rather with what H. says of Xerxes' return after Salamis (8.115) and with what Aeschylus says (*Persians* 480–512). Aeschylus was writing in 472, only eight years after the event, which shows how soon distortion could develop: H.'s statement that Xerxes took 45 days to reach the Hellespont reveals that there was no great haste.

E   **He ... lays the charge against others:** P. makes a good point, provided we accept that a shield was shown deliberately . The practical difficulties are well explored in articles by P.K.B. Reynolds, 'The shield signal at the battle of Marathon' *JHS* 49 (1929) 100–05, and by A.T. Hodge and L.A. Losada, 'The time of the shield signal at Marathon' *AJA* 74 (1970) 31–36. It may be that the whole tale is derived from an accident, but the story would not have taken hold unless it were plausible: Athenians then and later thought it likely that there were medizers. That thought is what P. objects to: but he tells a similar tale himself of an incident at Plataea in *Life of Aristeides* 13 (see 42/872Bn).

a decisive victory: P. deludes himself. If the victory was decisive, there was no need to rush back to Athens, and the Spartans' inspection of the Persian dead becomes mere curiosity instead of sensible preparation against a further invasion (see *PG* 253), which Darius ordered as soon as Datis had reported the fate of the first (H. 7.1). The Greeks were lucky it was so long delayed.

it could not have been seen by the foe: it could, but it came too late. Datis had committed himself.

F   **'Wait, little crab ... let you go!':** for 'piece of verse' P. says 'paroemiac': the word means proverbial, but is also the proper term for the metrical unit of the quotation, which is an anapaestic dimeter catalectic.

863A   **"tyrant-haters":** see 21/859Cn and 16/858Bn.

B   **Callias son of Phaenippus, not omitting his son Hipponicus:** P. is muddled; see Davies 254ff. Of Phaenippus nothing is known; his son Callias was a contemporary of Peisistratus, but though the family was noble and very rich, it identified with the democracy at all stages. Callias had a son Hipponicus; Hipponicus had a son Callias, born c.520, who late in his life helped to negotiate both the terms with Persia which are usually called the peace of Callias and the 30 years' peace with Sparta three years later in 446/5. This Callias, the peace-maker, had a son Hipponicus in the fifth generation from Phaenippus, and he is H.'s contemporary. When H. was first in Athens, Callias the peace-maker was probably still alive; by 430 (see 26/862Bn) Hipponicus was head of the family. He died c.422, having been secretary to the Council in 444/3 and a general in 426/5. He campaigned successfully in Boeotia (Thuc. 3.91.4–5), a fact which could have nettled P., but the Hipponicus whom H. mentions in the passage P. quotes is the grandfather of H.'s contemporary. Hipponicus the grandson may well have played host to H. in Athens, but H. mentions very few people or events of the years after 479 (the most thorough note is in Macan, I li–lii); his mention of Callias the peace-maker is remarkably coy (see 28/863Cn), and that is Callias son of Hipponicus, not son of Phaenippus.

28.

Everybody knows: P. uses a rhetorical ploy; its intent is that those who know differently won't dare say so, or they will be shouted down if they try by those who share the speaker's view.

their bitterest enemies: hostility between Argos and Sparta goes back before 700. King Nicander of Sparta ravaged the Argolid c.720, but the Argives destroyed Asine in revenge, and under their king Pheidon reached their greatest power in the Peloponnese, defeating the Spartans heavily at the battle of Hysiae c.669. Pheidon died c.655, and Argos declined, but for a century Sparta struggled, until she gained Orestes' bones (H. 1.67/8) and c.546 defeated Argos in the battle of the Champions (1.82 and see 18). Cleomenes' victory at Sepeia c.494 (6.76–80) reduced Argos to virtual impotence. Sparta's response to the Persian threat was impeded by Argive medism but not obstructed (see 863Fn).

P. accepts the relationship between the two states, and later in this chapter (E) admits that the Argive behaviour was disgraceful. His protest at H.'s interpretation is weak anyway because he cannot produce a more convincing one of his own; but he conducts his thin case with some skill. The reference to the Ethiopians is irrelevant but diverting, and the rhetorical questions at the end, though answerable, are focussed on relevant issues.

C   he **"cannot guarantee the story":** P. has put his finger on an important spot. H.'s narrative starts at 7.148 on a course which leads him, rather incidentally and rather late in the day, to his most significant methodological statement as a historian, the declaration in 152.3 which P. quotes next. H. in the course of his inquiries came to a sophisticated understanding of the fluidity of the record, and in preserving the record he decided to preserve also some of its fluidity. Hence the various and even contradictory versions of some events. P., taking a more Thucydidean line, and working to moral criteria, looks for a single canonical version (see Intro. 11). But in this instance P.'s preoccupation with the general issue of Argos has blinded him to a particular weakness in H.'s account: the "story" that H. "cannot guarantee" is a combination of two stories, one of which belonged to H.'s own day: H. should have been able to speak of that without uncertainty.

In 7.148.2 H. starts to recount the Argive version of affairs: Ἀργεῖοι λέγουσι, "the Argives say". He maintains indirect speech for over a page, renewing it at 149.1 (ταῦτα λέγουσι, "this is what they say") and at 149.3 (οὕτω δὴ οἱ Ἀργεῖοί φασι, "that is how the Argives put it"), and closing it at the end of 149.3: αὐτοὶ μὲν Ἀργεῖοι τοσαῦτα τούτων πέρι λέγουσι, "so much for what the Argives themselves say about the incident." At 150 he starts an alternative version (ἔστι δὲ ἄλλος λόγος, "there is however another story"), renewed twice by λέγεται, "the story goes". 151 starts συμπεσεῖν δὲ τούτοισι καὶ τόνδε τὸν λόγον λέγουσί τινες 'Ελλήνων, "Coinciding with this there is also the following story told by certain Greeks." This is a third story. The first two stories, the Argive version and the generally accepted version, are of an incident which happened when H. was a small child in another place; he has made his inquiries, found two conflicting versions, and reports both, in customary fashion. The third story, however, belongs to his own times and concerns a man he very probably knew, the negotiator of treaties Callias (see 27/863An). "Certain Greeks" can hardly be other than Callias and his fellow Athenians who went to Susa.

When in 152.1 H. says that he "cannot guarantee the story", he is speaking of the first and third stories together. De Selincourt undoes H.'s single sentence into two: the combined sentence says "Whether Xerxes sent a herald with that message to Argos and whether Argive messengers went to Susa and asked Artaxerxes about friendship I cannot say for sure". An incident of 481 is thus put together with an incident of 449/8, and H., who admits the difference in time (151), confuses the issue further when he adds "I express no opinion on this matter other than that of the Argives themselves". The first story is the Argive "opinion"; the third story is, as H. puts it, strictly anonymous ("people in Greece", says de Selincourt), but is surely owed to the Athenians who went to Susa. H.'s coyness about them is curious; at least it fits with the apparent contemporary lack of acknowledgement of the mission.

D   **"their war with Sparta was going badly"**: since Cleomenes had killed virtually all the fighting men of Argos in the Sepeia campaign (6.78–80, 83), there could be no continuing war.
    what Herodotus himself says: see 33/867B for a neat quotation of H. against himself.

E   **'all twisted ... back to front'**: from Euripides, *Andromache* 448. The fact that P. quotes it without attribution suggests that it had become a commonplace.
    like painters using shadow: the comparison of writing with painting goes back into the Greek language itself; the root γραφ- (graph-) serves for both, meaning basically 'make a mark'. Lachenaud 116 notes the use P. makes of the idea in other places and points back to a Platonic example (*Politicus* 277C); Russell 71/2 in quoting from P.'s 'The Face in the Moon' (934D–935A) notes P.'s care for colour.
    descent from Heracles: see 14/857Fn.
    Siphnos and Cythnos: on the Serpent Column dedicated at Delphi but now, in a reduced condition, in the hippodrome in Istanbul are the names of the thirty-one communities who (give and take a few: see *PG* 543/4) fought on the Greek side at Salamis and Plataea. Cythnos and Siphnos are twenty-eighth and twenty-ninth respectively. Cythnos provided one trireme and one penteconter to the fleet (8.46.4) and Siphnos one penteconter (8.48).

F   **why did they not medize openly**: P.'s question is intended to throw doubt on H.'s statement that Argos medized at all. If they medized, what did they do for Persia? Answer, nothing. Therefore they did not medize. But they did nothing because they could do no more (9.12.2); they had not recovered from Sepeia. Even so, uncertainty about Argive will and capacity to act helps explain both why the Spartans were so long and secretive in mounting the campaign of 479 (other parts of the Peloponnese were also unreliable: see 42/872Fn) and why the Spartiate hoplites who went were only 5,000 in number. It is usually reckoned that the total then available was greater: see 41/871En.
    why ... not ravage Laconia: P. has forgotten the Spartiates who did not go but stayed as a garrison force.

or seize Thyrea again: Thyrea was a bone of contention till the battle of the Champions (1.82). It is difficult of access by sea and more difficult by land. The area is distinguished nowadays by having a dialect of Greek not descended from the Koine (which was established in the fourth century as the standard form of Greek and was based on the Athenian dialect, Attic): Tsaconian, as it is called, is uniquely descended from ancient Spartan.

864A **interfered with the Spartans' march:** H. mentions the possibility in 9.12. P. seems to be suggesting guerrilla action, to which Greek terrain is well suited, but hoplite warfare is not, and in the classical period there is very little guerrilla action. Thucydides (3.94–113) shows the Athenian general Demosthenes coming to terms with it.

29.

all the defamation amid the praise: the defamation is that the Athenians were among those who would have abandoned the struggle against Persia. Themistocles made a powerful threat to do so before Salamis (H. 8.62), and the topic is renewed in 8.141, 9.6 and 7, and 9.11.1/2.

B **he praises Athens:** H.'s praise of Athens has two components. There is the praise itself, in 7.139.5, and the apologetic context in which it is set (139.1). P. has probably misunderstood the second component, which is not part of the events of 480 and 479 but arises from the conditions of H.'s own lifetime. The importance of the Athenian contribution in 480 and 479 is beyond dispute, but in the years afterwards, as Athenian power and Athenian pretensions grew, other Greeks, feeling oppressed, may at least have wished to dispute it, and may have regretted its consequences.

Thebes and Phocis: for P.'s defence of the Phocians see 35. His own home town Chaeronea lay very close to Phocian territory: perhaps Phocis is benefiting from a surge of P.'s Boeotian sympathies.

attacked for a treachery which never happened: H. knew better than P. the fragility of the Greek alliance. The speculation of 7.139 is something rare in H.'s *Histories*, and P. misinterprets it to suit his argument.

indications ... at Thermopylae: the bravery of those who stayed behind is incontestable, but whether the event had to be what it was is another question. For whatever cause, and lack of troops may be a proper answer, Leonidas failed to see the back door securely shut, and his sacrifice was forced. P. is well content with the ruthless courage of it.

30.

C **Herodotus raised the topic:** the story of Ameinocles is a good example of how H. saw fortune operating; see Immerwahr 76n. H.'s Greek leaves it obscure how Ameinocles' son died: literally, "grieving him there was a son-killing misfortune of no joy". 'Son-killing', παιδοφόνος, is last word of H.'s sentence, usually in Greek a position of little prominence (though Dover observes, 67/8, 'We have the impression that from a stylistic rather than a linguistic point of view one of the most powerful determinants of order in Herodotus is the desire to achieve variety so far as this is consistent with the principles shared by him with other Greek writers and the stock of models available to him.'). The word itself is very rare: it has the authority of Homer, who uses it once, in *Iliad* xxiv 506, the last line of Priam's appeal to Achilles: 'I put my lips to the hand of the man who has killed my sons.' The context is highly charged; so is the use of the word, since compound adjectives like παιδοφόνος are usually reflexive: it should describe people who kill their own children. So Jason uses it of Medea (Euripides *Medea* 1407) in a final outraged protest; the play, produced in 431, is closely contemporary with H.'s own probable time of writing (see 20/859Bn). P. has brushed aside H.'s tact.

"washed ashore": P. uses H.'s word, ἐκβρασσόμενον. H. uses it only in 7.188 and 190; it occurs nowhere else in classical Greek except in the Hippocratic corpus.

31.

Here P. reaches the Thebans. His defence of them is long and vigorous, and is renewed in 33. 31 is second in length only to 42.

Aristophanes the Boeotian: he wrote annals, probably in the early fourth century. Only fragments survive. Though P. cites him with confidence both here and in 33/867A, we have no measure of the man's worth; Hignett (22/3) regards him as positively hostile to H., apparently on internal evidence. H. certainly had contact with Boeotians (9.16.1), but Aristophanes' story could be a product of the sort of malice which P. complains of in H.

asked for money ... tried to talk ... share their studies: the words describe the practice of a sophist, in the fifth century sense of the word: see 15/857Fn. Perhaps H. was making some of his inquiries.

D   **their crude and anti-intellectual nature:** a Boeotian's comment on Boeotians, quoted without comment by another Boeotian!

"the Thessalians ... under compulsion": I have adjusted de Selincourt's translation to get the point of H.'s "at first". The compulsion came from their own leading clan the Aleuads.

E   **The Thebans don't get the same understanding:** the objection is just, up to a point. What H. has to say of the Thebans often seems to carry Athenian colouring. Athens had been at odds with her northern neighbour since the sixth century, when first Eleutherae obtained Athenian protection and then Plataea and Hysiae did (H. 6.108.1 and 6). Oropus soon followed. The Thebans reacted to Plataea's detachment with military force (108.4), and later helped Cleomenes when he tried to impose oligarchy on Athens (5.74.2), with disastrous results for themselves, which H. tells us in some detail. In the same connexion they sought the help of Aegina against Athens (79–81 and 89.1). When Datis came they sat by, and their medism was active in Xerxes' war: at the battle of Plataea the Boeotian contingent was lined up opposite the Athenians (9.31.5) and they took care to maintain the arrangement (47); according to H. it was a Theban who recommended the attack on the allied supply lines (38.2) and Thebans who kept up the Persian cavalry attacks (40). In the battle itself the fighting between the Athenians and the Boeotians was particularly bitter (67), and the Boeotian cavalry continued to help the Persians even when their cause was lost (68). The allied attempt to take immediate revenge on Thebes was frustrated (86–88), but the Athenians got theirs in the end at the battle of Oenophyta in 457, after the bitter battle of Tanagra (Thuc. 1.108.2/3). That victory was undone a decade later at Coronea (Thuc. 1.113); H. may well have been in Athens at the time. Things virtually came full circle in 431 when the Thebans seized Plataea, an event referred to by H. in 7.233 (see 33/867An). For a Theban interpretation of their recent history, see Thuc. 3.62, on which Gomme however comments (*HCT* II 348) 'this simple picture of Thebes governed autocratically by a small group of medizing politicians must be far from the truth'.

Other mainland states medized. The case for Athenian colouring in H.'s account of the Thebans is supported by the comparative lack of disapproval in what he says of Argos and Thessaly. They were not neighbours of Athens, and her later relationship with them took a different course. In 461 all three made alliances with each other (Thuc. 1.102.4), and even though the Thessalians soon changed sides, at Tanagra, and the Argives made their own peace with Sparta in 451, (Thuc. 5.28.2), Athens in reckoning her potential friends and enemies continued to see them as friends.

five hundred hoplites to Tempe under Mnamias: H. (7.173.2) gives only the total size of the joint force, ten thousand; apart from the Spartan commander-in-chief he names only Themistocles. Among the allies a Theban presence at that stage is likely, and though P. gives no authority for his assertion (was it Aristophanes?) there is no reason to doubt it.

as many ... as Leonidas asked for: this is disingenuously put. H. simply says four hundred (7.202) – one hundred fewer than P. says went to Tempe; but with them were seven hundred Thespians, all the Opuntian Locrians (who also sent seven penteconters to Artemisium; see 8.1.2), and one thousand Phocians. The Peloponnesians had their reasons for sending only a few in the first instance; not so the locals, and Theban reluctance to be committed is exposed more surely by the proportionately large contribution of her neighbours than by H.'s patently biased comment in 7.205.3.

when the rest deserted: P.'s choice of word (surprisingly unpatriotic!) conceals H.'s conclusion (220/1) that they went on Leonidas' orders. Later in the chapter P. uses H.'s view four times: 865A, B, D and E.

control of their passes: from the Spercheius valley two routes lead towards Boeotia, the coastal route due east via Opuntian Locris, controlled most easily at Thermopylae (this is the route now taken by the motorway), and the route south up the Asopus valley and over the pass into Phocis and the upper Cephisus valley (this is the route taken by the old main road and by the railway, with spectacular difficulty). It is not obvious from most maps that a control of both routes could be maintained from Thermopylae. Even a detailed map like that in *PG* 408 needs the support of the text: a force defending the southern route need not be visible from the Spercheius plain and could be only a few hours from Thermopylae. Leonidas' Phocian troops were in the right place.

But P. is being disingenuous again. He implies that the Thebans had no other passes and that these were theirs anyway. Though the Locrians, who had given earth and water earlier (7.132.2), now joined Xerxes (8.66.2 and 9.31.5), some Phocians took to the hills (8.32.1 and 9.31.5) and most withdrew to Amphissa (8.32.2); the Athenians were ready to evacuate Attica. The Thebans had various examples before them, and there were roads south.

guest-friendship with Attaginus: these personal cross-border relationships were well established among top families in Greece; they could be used for inter-state business. They were sustained by contact at the Greek festivals, and were occasionally boosted by marriages like that of Megacles and Agariste (6.125–30). P. does not give his authority for linking Demaratus and Attaginus; it is not H., which is a little surprising, since H. is well informed on Demaratus. Attaginus at least gave a banquet for Mardonius (9.15.4). For his later fortunes see 9.88.

on similar terms with the king: medizers of high status could do well. Witness the fortunes of Demaratus himself (6.70.2), of Themistocles (Thuc. 1.138), of Miltiades' son Metiochus (H. 6.41), and even of Histiaeus of Miletus (5.11 and 6.30).

the Greeks were in their ships: which Greeks, and where? It is not clear whether P. has the Athenians in mind evacuating Attica or the allied fleet at Artemisium or the preparations for a stand at Salamis.

not till then did they submit: P.'s accumulation of conditions is impressive as a list but they do not add up to much in fact.

F **accept the king's terms:** P. fails to take account of H.'s statement (7.132) that the Thebans and the other Boeotians, Thespians and Plataeans excepted, had given earth and water much earlier, perhaps while Xerxes was still at Sardis (see N.G.L. Hammond, 'The narrative of Herodotus vii and the decree of Themistocles at Troezen' *JHS* 102 (1982) 75–93).

with only the Spartiates and the Thespians: P. is thinking of the third day's fighting only. In saying Spartiates rather than Spartans he shows himself a victim of Spartiate propaganda about Thermopylae. So to some extent was H.: his battle narrative from 7.208 to 211 mentions only Spartans (not even Thespians), and amongst the dead only Spartiates; he also reports Leonidas' view that the duty (220.1) and the glory (220.4) of the final stand belonged peculiarly to the Spartiates. But Dascalakis argues (25–8) that H. did distinguish between Spartans and Spartiates; at Plataea H. notes the three constituent groups of the force which came from Sparta, 5,000 Spartiate hoplites, 5,000 non-Spartiate (Spartan) hoplites, and 35,000 light-armed helots (9.28.2). At Thermopylae the only corresponding figure we get is that of 300 Spartiate hoplites; but for a helot presence there, see 8.25.1[6] and 7.229.1, and for Spartans as opposed to Spartiates, see 211.3, 225.1 against 224.1, and 227 against 226. H. thus reveals the presence of the expected others from Lacedaemon most delicately, without upsetting the focus on the three hundred. Hexameter verse cannot accommodate the word Spartiate; otherwise the oracle quoted in 220.4 and the epitaphs in 228.1 and 2 might have bent the record further. In quoting the famous epitaph in 228.2 H. shows he knew what was meant; the message of the passer-by is indeed for the Spartans, but the epitaph was for the Spartiates.

865A   their great and glorious deed: P.'s attempt to rehabilitate the Thebans fails above all because he does not allow for division within their state (see 27/862Cn for the same failure with Eretria). He overlooks arguments available from Thucydides (3.62, cited above, 864En), which is strange, for he knew his Thucydides well. He might make a case for the four hundred who fought at Thermopylae, as Diodorus[7] briefly does (XI 4.7), but hardly for the rest. The reaction of the allies after Plataea argues against that, and H. makes it plain in 7.202.2/3 that Leonidas in asking for Theban troops was trying to call Theban bluff. The four hundred were a just adequate response. They may have been Greek loyalists; they may have been sent as Polycrates sent his Samian enemies to Cambyses (3.44.2), a possibility which P. considers below in 865D/E but dismisses.

"detained ... as hostages": P. rightly sees that this is a nonsense, and he unpicks it thoroughly in what follows.

E   "I quote": in fact P. makes two small deviations from H.'s text (three if we read not Λεωνίδην, an editor's approximation of P.'s text to H.'s, but Λεωνίδεα, as in both P.'s MSS); more important, he misses H.'s irony: H.'s sentence reporting this story is cast in indirect speech (see Intro. 22), uniquely in its context.

"fame in which no other city should share": Leonidas has had his wish; few remember the Thespians and the other Spartans.

he considered them sound friends: P. blithely ignores H. 7.205.2/3.

to sleep in the temple of Heracles: H. was interested in dreams. If this story had been known in his day, it is hard to think he would not have heard it, and hard to think he would not have used it. It appears to foretell Alexander's destruction of Thebes in 335. Its source is unknown. Two more unattributed stories follow. All are indications of the growth of the Thermopylae legend.

---

[6] In de Selincourt's translation, the last sentence of 8.25 containing the figures for the dead is unfortunately omitted.

[7] For Diodorus see 32/866An. Diodorus' case for the four hundred is well expressed by Dascalakis, 61/2.

32.

866A **The truth is different:** P.'s confidence in his version is a good sign of the power which such heroical nonsense had. He makes no attempt to account for H.'s version till the end of the chapter.

in the night: The Persians under Hydarnes did not reach the Phocian position till dawn was breaking (7.217.1). H. gives the timing of events with care. The first alarm at Thermopylae came from Megistias' sacrifice, which warned of death in the dawn: clearly the sacrifice took place before dawn. The second alarm was the report by deserters that a march round behind was being made; H. says that this news came in the night, which confirms the timing of the sacrifice. Third came the scouts from the hills "just as day was breaking" (219.1). Only then was the failure of the Phocians clear; only then could the escape plan be started. The fighting began later (223.1), at 'agora-full' time.

they ... set out for the Persian camp: this version of the final fight was probably first put on paper by Ephorus (see 5/858En). It survives to us in Diodorus Siculus XI 9.4–10.4, who used Ephorus extensively. Diodorus wrote in the first century, and compiled a history of the world down to 60, the year of the first 'triumvirate' in Rome.

B **my life of Leonidas:** it has not survived, and there are doubts it was ever written. Some of the material that might have been used may be conveniently found in Talbert. The remark is evidence that the project of the Lives was at least already in P.'s mind; he seems to have begun them c.96 A.D. (see Jones (1966)).

Before marching out ... funeral games: this would be impossibly ill-omened; since they expected reinforcement (7.206.1), it is also ridiculous.

'Plenty enough to die': such heroics do not change: see Shakespeare, Henry V 4.3.20f. This and the following sayings are in P.'s 'Sayings of Spartans' and 'Sayings of Spartan women', both in Talbert. See his introduction 106–8 for the probable origins of the collections, which were made well before P.

his wife ... 'Marry heroes and bear them': Gorgo, Leonidas' wife, was the only child of his half-brother Cleomenes (5.48). She clearly had some reputation: H. reports two good tales of her himself (5.51 and 7.239).

C **two men of good family:** since Leonidas took with him men who already had sons (205.2), the missions proposed for these two lack some of the justification which P. claims.

'I came ... errand-boy': P. quotes it in Spartan dialect.

<'I'm better ..> things': most of the sentence is missing in the MSS but with indication of a gap. The supplement printed was constructed *exempli gratia* by Pearson from 'Sayings of Spartans' 225E.

these omissions ... carelessness and oversight: in quoting for contrast two tales which come in book two P. fails to notice how much H.'s stories change as he comes to times more near his own. He also fails to allow for what H. neatly and adequately does say, in 7.208 (when the Spartans are watched combing their hair), in 221 (when Megistias refuses to leave), and in 226.2 (Dieneces' reply). H. heard plenty of memorable things about Thermopylae; he tells some further stories in 229–232. He also exercised some judgement on how much to say.

33.

In returning to the topic of the Thebans, P. has some further points to make, but mostly he elaborates his indignation.

D **men with whips ... piece of slander:** men with whips at Leonidas' disposal is a splendidly sarcastic inference on P.'s part! For the Greeks of H.'s day the whip marked the relationship of master and slave: see 4.3–4. H. reports Persian use of whips not only here (7.223.3) but also in situations without the same pressure, the crossing of the Hellespont bridges (56.1) and the Athos canal-digging (22.1).

Xenophon attests the practice too (*Anab.* 3.4.25). P. quotes his own great-grandfather for a Roman use of whips in *Life of Antony* 68.7/8.

"the Thebans detached themselves": H.'s reason for the presence of the four hundred at the final fight will not do. But what he describes is nevertheless possible. If it happened, it marks sheer panic at imminent death, the sort of panic which might be individual in origin but which is infectious. It would not be an edifying moment, which is part of P.'s objection, but such things do occur in battle. That said, the story looks much more like a later attempt to tar all Thebans with the same brush, even these possible loyalists.

"approached ... with outstretched hands ... against their will": in the translation I have quoted de Selincourt; but precise representation of H.'s verbs is scarcely possible in English, and in any case P. has failed to copy H. in three of them, two of which matter for his understanding of H. First: for H.'s imperfect προέτεινον (they were stretching forth) he writes the aorist προέτειναν (they stretched forth). This upsets H.'s trio of imperfects, προέτεινον, ἦσαν and λέγοντες (the participial form of ἔλεγον), in which the emphasis is on what the Thebans were trying to do without necessarily succeeding in it. H. presents the scene as a moving picture: 'there they were, stretching out their hands and trying to get closer to the Persians, saying...' Second, when he reports what the Thebans tried to say, he uses an idiom of semi-indirect speech. He might have quoted them, writing 'We are medizing' (μηδίζομεν; pres. indic. 1st. pers. plur.); he might have adapted their words fully to his historic context, writing 'that they were medizing' (μηδίζοιεν: pres. opt. 3rd. pers. plur.). In fact he writes 'they are medizing' (μηδίζουσι: pres. indic. 3rd. pers. plur.). But P. writes μηδίσειαν: aor. opt. 3rd. pers. plur., 'that they had medized'.

P. may have understood μηδίζουσι to mean 'they are medizers' (see Goodwin §20); he may have unconsciously thought that better expressed by an aorist. But if so, it is inconsistent of him to quote H.'s ἔδοσαν, 'they have given', aor. indic., without converting it too to its optative. It is uncommon to revert to the indicative after once going into the optative of indirect speech (Goodwin §690). Perhaps after writing μηδίσειαν he simply glanced back at his excerpt to refresh his memory of it.

Third: for 'they had come' P.'s MSS show ἀπικέατο (ἀπικοίατο in Lachenaud's text is an editorial approximation to H.'s text). ἀπικέατο is a form without warrant (see Legrand (1932) Vol. I 216/7), probably to be reckoned a hyper-ionicism.

E   **that plea being heard:** P.'s objection, that conditions prevented the plea being heard, does not deal with the question whether it was made; but he elaborates his objection well.

F   **'recently in our power ... Lattamyas':** the battle which lost the Thessalians their power in central Greece is mentioned by P. in *Life of Camillus* 19. He dates it more than 200 years before Leuctra, which was fought in 371. His Thessalians are referring to an event a good hundred years old by the time of Thermopylae. There is no other information about the battle or about Lattamyas.

"branded ... with the royal mark": branding was common practice, in Greece as in Persia, for runaway slaves. Those who gave earth and water to the king became his slaves. See 7.132 for the Thebans, and 31/864Fn. These men by fighting against him (they could have deserted Leonidas on day one) had broken their contract with defiance. How many of the four hundred remained alive to be branded we cannot tell (see 42/872Dn).

867A   **Leontiades was not in command ... Aristophanes ... Nicander:** for Aristophanes the Boeotian see 31/864Cn. Nicander of Colophon was a poet, and priest of Apollo at Claros, which is nine miles south of Colophon near the coast;

he lived in the latter days of the kingdom of Pergamum, before it passed to the Romans in 133. He wrote a great deal, principally (in the surviving works) on medical topics, through which P. may first have come across him. See A.S.F. Gow and A.F. Scholfield, *Nicander*, Cambridge 1953. He also wrote on historical matters concerning the areas of Thebes, Aetolia and Oeta, which are all in central Greece. What P. cites him for here has not survived.

Leontiades had a son Eurymachus who in 431 played an important part in the Theban seizure of Plataea (H. 7.233.2 and more accurately Thuc. 2.2.3). It appears that Athenian anger against Eurymachus may have helped the allegation that his father was a medizer at Thermopylae. See H. 8.94.4 and 39/870Bn for the similar case of Adeimantus the Corinthian. H. vindicates Adeimantus; Leontiades he leaves to his scar, and to a context of medism repeated: 7.205 and 233.

before Herodotus ... no knowledge: the argument from silence. But before Herodotus there is little historical record of anything!

B   **having been branded ... still medizing ... at Plataea:** the Thebans branded after Thermopylae were the survivors of the four hundred, not the rest of the population, who no doubt made their explanations to Xerxes. Again P. fails to distinguish. It is possible that survivors of the four hundred fought at Plataea, but see 42/872Dn.

Hippocleides: P. makes a neat ending, quoting the scripture to his own purpose. See 28/863D.

34.

"turned coward": P.'s word is not H.'s word. H. uses one of his favourites, καταρρωδεῖν, 'to dread'; P. uses καταδειλιᾶν; but cowardice is not the same as the dread which men may well feel before battle and yet fight bravely. *LSJ* quote P.'s word only twice, in fourth century prose, but P. himself uses it three times. The variation from what H. writes is particularly odd in that the word is head word of the phrase.

the Euboeans ... paid money: to the several reasons which *H & W* give for disbelieving this story, add the difficulty of the different communities on Euboea (the island is 100 miles long) getting together and agreeing the money in the time. Carystus may have been ready to accept the Persians anyway: see H. 6.99, and 8.66 and 121. P.'s objection (he tells the story slightly differently in *Life of Themistocles* 7) is made partly on patriotic grounds, in that it demeans those concerned, and partly because H. offers no other reason for the allied fleet remaining on station at Artemisium. That is a good ground of objection.

Adeimantus the Corinthian commander: P. comes to his rescue in 39.

C   **Pindar, from a city ... accused of medism:** Pindar was a Theban, and a contemporary of the wars; his first ode, the tenth Pythian, was written in 498, and his last datable ode, the eighth Pythian, belongs to 446. Where he was when the Persians came we do not know; he praised the victory of Salamis in his fifth Isthmian ode, written soon after the war, and his praise of Athens is said to have provoked the Thebans to fine him: the Athenians paid. The phrase quoted here is a favourite with P., who quotes it on three other occasions; it is not from a surviving whole poem.

Almost everyone agrees: it is not clear whether P. is referring to alternative sources or just to readers of H. like himself.

D   **at Artemisium the Greeks won:** H.'s narrative indicates two small wins (8.9.2 and 14.2) and a Pyrrhic draw, after which their position was untenable: in sum, they lost. P.'s determination to have the Greeks victorious has made him impatient of H.'s more careful account; so too at Marathon (27/862En).

"they determined to quit": "they began to consider quitting" would be a better translation. The military operation at Thermopylae and Artemisium was a joint operation: if one fell, both fell. P. recognizes the point clearly in his previous sentence. H. for convenience divides his narrative of the events in detail so as to produce a Thermopylae story and an Artemisium story, but he understood the joint strategy (7.175.2, and 8.15.2 and 21), despite the comment of J.B. Bury, 'The campaign of Artemisium and Thermopylae' *ABSA* 2 (1895/6) 83–104. If the ships were not up to another immediate fight, then they had to withdraw.

E   **quitting**: P. makes some play with the word (δρασμός; δρησμός in H.'s Ionic Greek). It is not common in prose, except in H.; the tragedians also use it. Notably, Aeschylus uses it twice in *Persians* (360 and 370) when reporting Themistocles' false message to Xerxes of what the Greeks at Salamis were planning to do. H. may have followed that lead. He uses it eight times, six times with the verb βουλεύειν, 'to plan': once of Aristagoras quitting the Ionian revolt (5.124), once of Demaratus quitting Sparta (6.70), and six times in book eight: 4.1, 18 and 23.1 of Artemisium; 75.2 as in Aeschylus; 97.1 and 100.1 of Xerxes quitting Greece after Salamis. The verb of the same root in standard use is ἀποδιδράσκειν; it carries the connotation of running away by stealth, and is quite common in H. P.'s objection is patriotically inspired; but H.'s narrative of Artemisium has several odd features anyway, in particular reports of panic in 183.1 followed by a puzzling withdrawal to Chalcis (see *PG* 387 and Hignett 166), and panic again in 8.4.1. Either there was some discreditable irresolution on the Greek side, and H. picked it up, or perhaps the story suffered from the glorification of Thermopylae, and of Salamis, by deliberate contrast.

    Hestiaea: H.'s form of the word is Histiaea. P. uses the standard spelling.

F   **Artemis Proseoa**: the temple (for traces see Podlecki 176) gave its name to the anchorage, which is further west (7.176.1). The title Proseoa, which means 'looking dawnwards', is confirmed by an inscription found on the site (*IG* xii(9) 1189.5). The site itself looks more north than east, to Skiathos and Magnesia. See Frost 109–11.

    The inscription which P. quotes (he had seen it himself *in situ*, as *Life of Themistocles* 8 shows) is like Pausanias' inscription at Delphi in giving all the glory to the inscribers. Perhaps it was not set up till some years later, when Euboea was an established member of the Delian league and no one could make much protest, or not until 445, when Athens had put down a revolt in Euboea which was particularly strong in the north of the island. For its authorship see 36/869Cn. There is a useful discussion of Athenian commemoration of their dead by F. Jacoby: 'Some Athenian epigrams from the Persian Wars' *Hesperia* 14 (1945) 157–211.

868A   **he failed to give the Greek dispositions**: this is the objection of a serious historian, but it has no obvious place in the argument P. is conducting about bias. H. gives detailed dispositions for Salamis, Plataea and Mycale, and for Lade in 494 (6.8). Perhaps the details of Artemisium had faded from memory by the time H. was inquiring: a pity, given the fact that unlike Salamis it was a fight in fairly open waters, and, as Hignett says (189), the most serious for its size to date.

    "the Corinthians led": P. quotes this without comment. He deals with the slur on Corinthian courage in 39. In *Life of Themistocles* 9 he uses this incident to point up Athenian courage.

35.

    only a Thurian: in 510 the rich town of Sybaris in south Italy was overthrown by its neighbour Croton (H. 5.44 and 6.21). In 452 efforts were made to refound it which failed (Diodorus XI 90.3–4). In 443 Athens made a new effort (Diodorus XII 10/11); the settlement was named Thurii. H., presumably seeing his exclusion from Halicarnassus as permanent, and needing a citizenship, joined it (but perhaps not at once). P. comments on the question whether H. is rightly called a

Halicarnassian or a Thurian in his work *On Exile* (604F); Thurian was the common label. P. uses Thurian in order to sneer at H.: the Greeks of the west made almost no contribution to the campaign against Xerxes. Croton sent one trireme (8.47).

his own attachment: P.'s word for attachment is strong: περιέχεσθαι means 'to cling to'. H. in fact is remarkably free of particular attachment: hence P.'s complaint that he was not attached enough to the Greek cause. H. does, however, show some partiality towards Artemisia (see 38/869Fn).

Dorians: according to H. (7.99.3) they were Dorians from Troezen in the northeast Peloponnese. In discussing the early migrations across the Aegean (1.142–151) H. observes that the so-called Ionians were a mixed lot by origin: Dorians from Epidaurus were among them. Whatever the exact origins of the settlement at Halicarnassus, by H.'s day they used Ionic Greek in their public inscriptions, as H. does in his *Histories*. P.'s sneer this time is that H. really belonged to the other side; if he was born c.485, which is likely, then he began life under the Persian empire.

harem in tow: Artemisia led her contingent.

B **for fifty talents:** Phocis is not a rich area. Miltiades the Athenian was fined the same sum in 489 (H. 6.136.3).

and I quote: see 24/861Cn.

"in my considered opinion": I have added 'considered' to de Selincourt's translation for the sake of the weight which P. attaches to the phrase when he quotes it in E below.

thirteen Phocian towns: H. names only twelve, including Abae; except for Abae he has them in order as the Persians would have reached them. At Abae at least some statues survived for H. to record (8.27.5); destruction was not total.

C **to excuse Thessalian medism:** P. nicely stands the argument on its head. There is a good discussion by H.D. Westlake: 'The Medism of Thessaly' *JHS* 56 (1936) 12–24.

D **good reasons for bad deeds:** P.'s argument is only justified if it is right for neighbours to react to neighbours with contrary action, and that is what P. is complaining about in the first place!

E **He should have declared ... cowards:** P. constructed his *Lives* in accordance with a basic theory that individuals behave consistently. The extension of that to behaviour of communities is less satisfactory, but widely accepted (see the speech of the Corinthians comparing Spartan and Athenian characteristics in Thuc. 1.68–71, for instance); it lies behind P.'s protest here.

mutual enmity: neither P.'s experience nor his ideals could make much sense of the quarrelsomeness of classical Greece. In the case of Aegina and Athens he underrates the danger which Aeginetan medism posed (H. 7.145.1); an island base in the Saronic gulf would have made a Persian conquest of Greece comparatively easy. P. ignores the difference between the 490s, when Cleomenes had to go in (6.49–51), and 480, when Athens' huge new fleet probably had some coercive effect on Aegina (7.144). As for Chalcis, she had been defeated and weakened for ever by Athens in 506 (5.77.2), and Eretria was wrecked by the Persians in 490 (6.101.3): neither could offer much to the alliance (8.2). The Chalcidians who manned the twenty Athenian triremes in 480 were presumably Athenian cleruchs in large part: see 6.100.1. The quarrel between the two communities had erupted in the late eighth or the early seventh century. Corinth's differences with Megara mostly concerned the Perachora and their frontier, and had been settled in Corinth's favour by the early sixth century. Burn observes shrewdly that both at Salamis (*PG* 459) and at Plataea (*ibid.* 524) some allowance for local antipathies may be seen in the battle arrays.

the Macedonians: they had medized earlier, when Darius established a Persian base at Doriscus in Thrace c.514. H.'s story in 5.17–21 is best seen as a later Macedonian attempt to prove the Greek loyalties of Alexander despite his father's medism; the marriage of his sister Gygaea exposes it.

F   Lacrates the Spartiate: nothing else is known of him, which is a pity; a Spartiate historian would be a notable figure. But P.'s aorist 'bore witness' together with the word 'direct' make it likely that Lacrates was a soldier whose words on the spot were recorded by someone else. No sayings of a Lacrates are recorded in 'Spartan sayings' (see 32/866B).

Phocians on the Greek side: H. (9.31.5) does not put Phocians in the Greek battle array, but he says that some raided the Persian position from their base on Parnassus. On the other hand, 1,000 Phocians fought on the Persian side (9.17–18). The community like many another was divided. Their name is not among those on the Serpent Column.

36.

869A   Naxos sent ... with the Greeks: P. paraphrases H.

three triremes: H. says four. Either P. was working from memory, as the use of paraphrase suggests, or he had made a faulty note; or he was distracted by the alternative figures of Hellanicus and Ephorus.

a whole city ... a bad name: P. implies that all Naxians except Democritus remained in favour of Persia; but at least a fair majority of his own fellow sailors must have agreed with him. (What happened to the Persian marines which H. says (7.184.2) every trireme carried? Tarn 216 notes the effect they would have on would-be medizers.)

Hellanicus: he is one of the four historians said by Dionysius of Halicarnassus (see 20/859Bn) to have lived a little before the Peloponnesian war, overlapping the time of Thucydides. Though Hellanicus was interested in chronology, he was attacked by Thucydides for lack of it, and for brevity, in his account of the period from 479 to 431 (Thuc. 1.97.2). P. does not cite him much, and not at all in *Life of Pericles*, where some use of him might be expected. See Stadter (1989) lxxvii.

Ephorus: see 5/855En.

six ... five: H & W have an ingenious suggestion for the cause of the muddle; but the reasons for it could be as simple as those suggested above for P. himself.

B   the Naxian chroniclers: this citation gives us a glimpse of how widely P. read. He cites them also in *Life of Themistocles* 20.8. The name of one of them is known: Andriscus. For the breadth and thoroughness of P.'s reading see Stadter (1965) 128–40. Stadter uses P.'s essay *Courageous Women* as his base.

after burning ... to do harm: some text has been lost after the word 'burning', though no gap is indicated in the MSS. What Datis did is in H. 6.96. If the chroniclers merely repeated H., P. would not cite them. When they say Datis was repulsed, we get a clue. Datis was not repulsed: he moved on, after adequate success, to other tasks. But the fact that he left Naxos without causing total destruction of the island could be interpreted as failure, in line with Megabates' obvious failure: if Datis burnt the shrines and the town, then there were acres elsewhere he did not burn: if he enslaved some, then there were some he did not. Such may have been the patriotic argument, but no reconstruction of the text can sensibly be attempted.

as H. has said elsewhere: P. combines H.'s mentions of Naxos well.

what a fine cause: the irony is heavy, a mark of P.'s confidence in his argument...

their destroyers: ... but hardly, if Naxos could still produce triremes!

not to praise ... to disgrace Naxos: see 29/864B, and 9.

omission and suppression: since H. knew his Simonides (see 7.228.3, and the next note), it is reasonable to think that he chose to omit these verses. Faced, it seems, with a multitude of anecdotes (see 32/866Cn), he reports the disagreement between the Athenians and the Aeginetans about who was first into the fighting at Salamis (8.84); Democritus, 'third man in', just failed to make it into H.

C **Simonides:** he lived from 556 to 468, and was the first poet notorious for making a living from his work (see P. 786B). He had made his name long before the Persian wars, in Ionia and when he was taken up in Athens by Peisistratus, but the Persian wars brought commissions for praise and commemoration which he was peculiarly able to fulfil. The wars brought many commissions; how many Simonides wrote of all the verses eventually attributed to him is impossible to tell: see Campbell 519/20 and A.S.F. Gow and D.L. Page, *Hellenistic Epigrams*, Cambridge 1965 II 516. War epigrams of the period, unless they were firmly attached to some other poet, gravitated towards Simonides. A.J. Podlecki, 'Simonides: 480' *Historia* 17 (1968) 262–74, is even able to cast doubt on the ascription of the war's most famous couplet of all, quoted by H. in 7.228.2 second of three commemorating Thermopylae: H. attributes only the third of the three to Simonides. Burn, *PG* 422, agrees in scepticism.

P. ascribes to Simonides three of the ten sets of verses that he quotes in this work: the three are (in his order) the second, here, the seventh (39/871B), and the eighth (42/872D). The seventh is attested elsewhere as Simonidean, (see *ad loc.*) but for the other two we have only P.'s authority. It seems likely that when P. names Simonides as author he does so simply for emphasis in the context, and with no implication that Simonides was not the author of the other seven.

Mary Renault's historical novel *The Praise Singer* is an attractive and well considered re-creation of the life and times of Simonides.

37.

Themistocles' battle plan: P. accepts the general view, that at Salamis Themistocles did the important strategic thinking. The tradition is first recorded in Aeschylus *Persians* 362. In this chapter P. starts by protesting against the idea that anybody else had a part in it; by the end the protest has changed: if Themistocles was to any extent prompted by another, he should not have taken all the glory to himself.

D **Melite:** it was an area of Athens west of the agora, just beyond the temple of Hephaestus and within the city walls, a deme of the tribe Cecropis (see D. Whitehead, *The Demes of Attica*, Princeton 1986, xxiii). Themistocles had his house there (P. *Life of Themistocles* 22).

temple of Artemis: P.'s comment about Themistocles' temple-building reveals his appreciation of this sort of evidence; he remarks upon seeing a small portrait statue of Themistocles in the temple in the passage noted above, and gives other details. See 7/856Bn. One side of a shrine almost certainly to be identified as this temple was discovered in 1958; see J. Travlos, *A pictorial dictionary of Ancient Athens*, New York 1971, 121 and Podlecki 174–6.

Mnesiphilus: he was prominent enough in Athenian life to be a candidate for ostracism (D.M. Lewis *ap. PG* 603–6); the ostraca confirm P.'s statement that he was a member of the same deme as Themistocles, Phrearrhii (*Life of Themistocles* 2). P. says he was an intelligent man who had applied his intelligence to politics: an early sophist. H.'s story of Mnesiphilus' contribution to the plan of Salamis is surprising, but then, his whole treatment of Themistocles, from its late start in 7.143 to its early finish in 8.125, is puzzling. Mnesiphilus' role is comparable with that of Cheileos of Tegea before Plataea: see 41/871Fn. In *Life of Themistocles* P. suppresses Mnesiphilus altogether in his Herodotean role. See

F.J. Frost 'Themistocles and Mnesiphilus' *Historia* 20 (1971) 20–25 for a full discussion of the man.

E **"with many new ones added":** this is H.'s text; the effect is to reduce the apparent importance of Mnesiphilus' contribution. P.'s MSS omit 'many'.

38.

F **nicknamed Odysseus:** there is no other evidence for this; P. did not use it in *Life of Themistocles*.

Artemisia ... compatriot: the pride of kinship that led P. to defend the Thebans is made a reproach to H. Monarchical rule in Halicarnassus survived the Ionian revolt and Xerxes' war; Artemisia had taken over when her husband Mausolus died, because their son Pisindelis was too young (H. 7.99.1). Pisindelis' son Lygdamis is said in the *Suda* (see 43/873En) to have been responsible for H.'s exile. H., child himself of an important family, would perhaps remember Artemisia's return from war, and the stories that spread of her contributions both in council and in battle. Despite his own exile he has preserved his admiration for her. For her thematic importance in the *Histories*, see R.V. Munson, 'Artemisia in Herodotus' *CA* 7 (1988) 91–106.

870A **Herodotus should have used verse:** what H. says is remarkably similar to what Aeschylus says (*Persians* 728), as Tarn observes, 222n80.

as a Sibyl predicting: the Sibyl was located at Erythrae or Cyme; she was a familiar figure (see Aristophanes *Knights* 61 and *Peace* 1096). Later she was multiplied, but P. refers to her in the singular, without location, as elsewhere in his works.

Xerxes gave her his children: P. has telescoped events. Xerxes gave her his children (his bastards, in fact: 8.103) after Artemisia had commented on Mardonius' plan to continue the campaign in Greece after Salamis (101), not after her comments before Salamis (68), which P. quotes here. What the children needed was reliable escort to a safe port; Artemisia's sex was a secondary recommendation. Xerxes was presumably doing her an honour.

39.

B **malicious falsehoods ... Adeimantus:** in this chapter P. best justifies his attack on H. H.'s record on Adeimantus is shabby. He mentions him five times, on four occasions, and all are to the Corinthian's discredit.

First (7.137) he mentions, without explanation, the fate of Adeimantus' son Aristeas (P., like Thucydides, calls him Aristeus), who was put to death by the Athenians in 430 together with three Spartans, a Tegean and an Argive. Thucydides (2.67) has the story in detail; he also has the fact (1.60) that Aristeas had commanded the Corinthian forces which went to the aid of Poteidaea in 432; hence, no doubt, special Athenian pleasure at his capture. H. is more interested in the fate of two of the Spartans: they illustrate divine requital, *tisis* (see Immerwahr 324), more precisely than Aristeas, whom he could comfortably have omitted from his text. See 33/867An for the similar treatment of Eurymachus the Theban in H. 7.233.2.

Adeimantus' second appearance, and first in his own right, is at Artemisium (8.5) as recipient of a small part of the Euboeans' bribe to Themistocles. The third occasion is the reconvened council of commanders at Salamis (8.56ff): first (59) Adeimantus rebukes Themistocles for speaking out of turn, and then (61) tells him to shut up because he has no city. Finally (8.94) comes the tale of attempted desertion at the battle itself. H. introduces it as an Athenian story; only at the end does he say it is a purely Athenian story, and disputed. Moreover he tells the story outside the battle narrative proper, and he follows λέγουσι, 'they say', with infinitives (see Intro. 22). P. uses indicatives, normalising the structure but obscuring what H. keeps plain, that the story is only as sound as the source.

P. has selected the stories in 8.5 and 8.94 for counter-attack, and he attacks thoroughly. Since he acknowledges that H. himself undoes the story of desertion, his attack on it is mostly designed to expose in H. the sort of malice classified in 8. Adeimantus does not need the rescue P. offers, but P. has asked himself, after a fashion, why H. first tells the story and then undoes it, and the question remains. As P. proceeds in this chapter, he mostly argues well; only the last argument of all is of uncertain worth.

In *Life of Themistocles*, where his focus is different, P. reacts differently: he omits Adeimantus from the Euboean bribery story, he gives to Eurybiades the protest about speaking too soon, he makes the other protest anonymous, and he makes no mention of the Corinthians in the battle of Salamis at all.

The name Adeimantus means dauntless, unafraid. When H. starts his last Adeimantus story, he uses two participles to describe Adeimantus' reactions, ἐκπλαγέντα, 'shocked out of his wits', and ὑπερδείσαντα, 'hyperpanicky'. P., paraphrasing, nearly quotes them. The second, unique in classical prose, contains the same root as the man's name. Perhaps H. is mocking the story from the start.

brazenly raised his sails: this, what Burn (*PG* 458) calls a public fact, shows that the move was part of the battle plan. Triremes did not go into battle with their sails on board: see J.S. Morrison and J.F. Coates, *The Athenian trireme*, Cambridge 1986, 85, 97 and 177n.

C **heaven-sent:** P.'s word οὐρανοπετής is unique to him, and ironical in context.
deus ex machina: see *Life of Themistocles* 10.1 for another disparaging reference to the device.

D **Herodotus perjuring himself:** if P. had pondered further why H. tells a story only to deny it, he might have concluded that H. does it in order to expose the bias in his informants, but P.'s object of attack is H., and so he concludes that H. has concocted the Adeimantus story himself in order to pass it off on the Athenians, blackening both them and the Corinthians with the one fiction.
At least Thucydides ... battle of Salamis: see Thuc. 1.73–78, especially 73.2–74.4. This is a good piece of evidence: the demolition of the Adeimantus story now starts to go well.
engraved on the war memorial: so it was at Delphi, on the Serpent Column (see 28/863En), which P. would know well, and, according to Pausanias (5.23.1–2), at Olympia. The conference reported by Thucydides took place at Sparta: P. either assumes that Sparta had its own memorial and list, or he overlooks the problem.

E **on Salamis ... the following elegy:** for the attribution of these and the following verses see 36/869Cn. This piece of evidence is almost decisive for P.'s argument (not wholly, because in proclaiming the achievement of the Corinthians in general it does leave space for doubt about a particular one of them). Part of the first couplet has been found on Salamis: the stone is in the Epigraphic Museum in Athens. Corinthian dialect and Corinthian letter forms are used appropriate to the period (see *M–L* 24 for a discussion which deals with the objections of Rhys Carpenter in a review in *AJPh* 84 (1963) 81–3). The verses are also quoted by Favorinus, a writer of Hadrian's day ([Dio Chrysostom] 37.18).
the cenotaph at the Isthmus ... the following: a longer version of this is quoted by Aristeides (ed. W. Dindorf (3 vols.) Leipzig 1829, II 512), who lived about two generations after P.: his third couplet makes explicit the connection with Corinth, which otherwise depends here on P.'s statement of where the inscription was. The cenotaph was in the sanctuary of Poseidon where the Isthmian games were celebrated, just south of where the Corinth canal now emerges into the Saronic gulf.

F **temple of Leto:** this has not been identified, and the verses are not quoted elsewhere. Without P.'s context we would not know that Diodorus was a Corinthian.

As for Adeimantus himself: now P. moves to clinch his argument. These verses are also quoted by Favorinus ([Dio Chrysostom] 37.19).

871A **to name his daughters ... and his son:** Nausinice means 'Victory-by-boats', Acrothinium 'Pick-of-the-booty', Alexibia 'Averter-of-violence', and Aristeus 'Champion'.

the women of Corinth ... their men: P. understands the men to be the women's husbands (the Greek word means both 'man' and 'husband'), and so does the scholiast on Pindar *Ol.* 13.32a quoting the verses. Athenaeus 13.573 quoting them thinks the women are the famous temple prostitutes of Aphrodite, and the men their Greek clientèle. This view is the likelier, since a group of women commanding a set of bronze statues would be exceptional both in status and in wealth. It is curious that P. overlooks the possibility, despite knowing where the statues were and despite noting H.'s silence (see next note).

the ignorance of Herodotus and his contemporaries: H. (1.199) expresses strong disapproval of temple prostitution, reporting its existence in Babylon and in parts of Cyprus. He may have thought it better to be silent about Corinth. See Salmon 398–400.

B Simonides ... an epigram ... as follows: he is probably mentioned here by name to underline the importance (as P. saw it) of this evidence.

the temple they say ... Medea built: Euripides' play *Medea* shows the conversion of Medea's passion for Jason into hatred and revenge; as for Thetis, the tale is (*FHG* 4.345) that she and Medea were in a beauty competition in Thessaly, Jason's part of the world; Idomeneus judged, Medea lost, and presumably Jason agreed with him. Of the classical temple nothing survives (B.H. Hill, 'Excavations at Corinth 1926' *AJA* 31 (1927) 70).

rather than drag in Ameinocles: see 30.

40.

C round and round the islands enriching himself: P. uses the story in *Life of Themistocles* 21. Frost's note there (180–84) on P.'s methods is useful. Had P. quoted Timocreon of Ialysus here as he does there, H. would be vindicated! Themistocles' reputation for avarice was well established, as H.'s account shows; but H. names only three island communities, Andros, Paros and Carystus: all three had medized. Allied action against medizers had been promised (H. 7.132.2): against medizing islands it was likely to be led by Athens. Compare the action of Miltiades after Marathon (6.132–6), and the attempted land action against Thessaly led by the Spartan king Leotychides (6.72, and 21/859D). Themistocles managed things better. One reason for the quick growth of the Delian league may be the need for defence against this sort of reparatory raid: better to join them, and pay.

the victors' crown away from the Athenians: H. himself, in his estimate of Athens' contribution to the war at 7.139 (see 29/864Bn), makes it easy to think of the Athenians not just as the most numerous of the allies at sea and led by the wiliest strategist, but as also the best fighters. Isocrates a century later (*Panegyric* 71–98, especially 72) is quite clear about it. P. is following that tradition, which glorifies Athens to the exclusion of the others; in doing so he fails to notice the anti-Aeginetan bias in H.'s tale.

"he demanded the prize for valour": in 8.93.1 H. speaks merely of the reputation of Aegina for having fought the best; there is no mention of a prize. The story P. cites here is perhaps of Athenian origin, designed to besmirch a state long hostile to them; but after 457, when Athens at last got control of Aegina, the propaganda would be less needed. By 431 it might have been revived: in that year the Athenians expelled the native Aeginetans and put in settlers of their own (Thuc.

2.27). See 33/867An and 39/870Bn for other events of this late date which find place in H.'s *Histories*.

H.'s Greek here is ambiguous, as the translation represents: it could mean that the god asked not for the prize already awarded to the Aeginetans, if any, but for the Aeginetans to award the prize for valour to him. Their reaction, to put three gold stars on a bronze mast and to set it up at Delphi (8.122) near Croesus' mixing bowl (see 1.51.1–2), may support that. But one would expect Apollo to ask such a thing of the allies as a whole. Despite having advised defeat in the war, the god retained the respect of most of the Greeks. For prizes of valour in general, and the remarkable number of them in H., see Pritchett (1971) II ch 14.

Scythians and Persians and Egyptians: mention of the Scythians is a reminder that though P. cites no passages from book four, he knew it. See 19/858Fn.

D **Aesop:** Aesop is rather like Homer: someone called Aesop may have given definitive form to at least some of the stories attributed to him. H. speaks of him in 2.134 as a real person; he would belong to the first part of the sixth century. No information after H. is reliable. P. tells Aesop's story in 556F–557B, and refers to him and his fables nearly fifty times.

he uses the Pythian god: objection to Herodotean misuse of Delphi occurs also in 23/860D.

H. ought to have ... envy: perhaps H. had more tact. Inter-state rivalries occupy much of his *Histories* as it is. Hornblower (1983) ch 2 has a good discussion of envy in Greek politics.

41.

E **then they stopped bothering ... and held festivals:** P.'s plural is an exaggeration, and he has slightly misrepresented H.'s sequence: the Hyacinthia was under way before the wall was finished and before the Athenian delegation reached Sparta to protest, and it lasted three days only. It was a festival of early summer, but in 479 adjustment to the Spartan calendar had delayed it (see *H & W* II 288/9).

wasted the time ... prevaricating: the fortnight that passed after the protest of the Athenian delegation clearly puzzled H., and he offers his own explanation without conviction (9.8.2). P. grabs at it too eagerly. Better reasons lie to hand: it was necessary to deceive the Argives (hence the route via Orestheium, 9.11.2, and see 9.12); and not all the Peloponnesians mobilised as desired (9.77); see Cartledge (1979) ch 11. The ephors may have decided not to acquaint the Athenians with either or both of these problems while they tried to solve them; if H.'s only source of information was a survivor or two of the Athenian delegation, then his puzzlement is explained.

five thousand: P. quotes the figure as though it was impressively large. A possible maximum of 9,000 for the Spartiates is in P.'s *Life of Lycurgus* 8: 9,000 lots of land were allocated to them. More reliably, Demaratus tells king Xerxes (H. 7.234.2) that Sparta held 8,000 men as good as those at Thermopylae. It seems from Thucydides (2.10 and 3.15) that mobilisation of two thirds was standard procedure; H. (7.206.1) mentions the fact that some fraction would remain as garrison. Hence the 5,000 who went to Plataea: neither large nor small. But in 457 only 1,500 fought at Tanagra (Thuc. 1.107.2); at Leuctra in 371 only 700 were present (Xen. *Hell.* 6.4.15; see 6.4.17 for the fraction that had stayed behind); in *Life of Agis* 5.4 P. says that the Spartiate families then (mid third century) were no more than 700 all told. P. is comparing the 5,000 with the figures nearer his own day.

so many thousands: Mardonius is said to have asked for 300,000 (8.100.6), and got them (113.2–3); P. will not have shared the modern view that the figure is much too large.

F **Cheileos:** he has the same role in giving the Spartans their justification for action as Mnesiphilus does for Themistocles (37/869Dn). P.'s jibe about his importance is witty, but Cheileos is a figure of the storyteller's art as much as a figure of history: he makes a single contribution, from a slightly detached standpoint, and by timing it right solves a seeming dilemma and releases the action.

close friends: the relationship is the same as that of Demaratus and Attaginus mentioned in 31/864E.

42.

This is P.'s longest chapter. H.'s account of Plataea, despite his efforts to place events precisely by giving geographical detail which mostly now escapes us, has problems of patchy information, of misunderstanding, and of bias, both in his sources and to some extent in himself. P. does not distinguish the different problems, and constructs his own complaints; his case labours somewhat in consequence.

872A **they quarrelled with the Tegeans:** this is a curious episode. It was late to be debating the disposition of the forces when they were already moving into place, and a debate attended by all the ten thousand Spartans (9.28.1) is unlikely! P., however, does not specify his objections. Whatever problem H.'s tale reflects between the Athenians and the Tegeans, at least Pausanias solved it brilliantly, since both were placed on the left, the Athenians on the left of the whole line and the Tegeans left of the Spartans. P.'s own version of the incident in *Life of Aristeides* 12 is very different.

Heracleidae ... Amazons ... Cadmeia: H.'s order is Heracleidae, Peloponnesians (Argives), and Amazons. The difference suggests that P. was working casually, and that is confirmed by his failure to see that H.'s detail about the Argives, their burial at Eleusis, in territory controlled by Athens, is necessary to the Athenians' argument; the Cadmeia was the Theban acropolis. See *H & W* II 297.

B **Pausanias ... conceded ... own position:** some important manoeuvre lurks half-remembered in H.'s story. P.'s dismissal of it will not do. It may be that the Thebans are the problem and not the Persians: if the Thebans found themselves opposite the Spartans in the fight instead of opposite the Athenians their bitter enemies, their determination might not be so fierce; H. says that the failure of the manoeuvre was due to the Boeotians (9.47). He may be victim again of some information designed to stress Theban medism. P. makes no objection here on behalf of the Thebans: the record against them was too secure.

P. copies H. in speaking of Spartiates, not Spartans, but whatever the manoeuvre was it is hard to imagine the Spartiates moving without the rest of the Spartans. This is not discussed by Dascalakis (see 31/864Fn).

As for the rest of the Greeks: P. refers to those who started the withdrawal on the eve of the battle, the central section of the army as then drawn up, from the Corinthians at the right centre to the Megarians at the left centre: 18,600 men. There is much in H.'s account of the role of this central section which is patently distorted; P. has used it for his purposes without trying to make sense of it.

"they fled to Plataea": flight which ends in an orderly halt at the desired position is simply a brisk withdrawal. P. perceives the slander, but has not looked patiently enough at the text to undo it. From their new position it appears that the old central section was now able to move to support both right and left as appropriate: take away the slander that on the day of battle they were loath to move, and that is just what they did.

treachery: P. tells a remarkable story in *Life of Aristeides* 13 of traitors among the Athenians; but it finds no place in H. It would spoil P.'s aim in this work to observe that H. had omitted some treachery. For the reliability of P.'s treachery tale, see Sansone 190.

C **the other cities ... deprived of their glory:** part of H.'s problem was the difficulty of telling the tale of the battle in all its parts at once. But to take the performance of the Spartans and Tegeans right through to their rout of the Persians and to the Persian flight to their camp across the Asopus without bringing in the Corinthian contribution at all is, at best, misleading. It seems that here H. failed to obtain a Corinthian or other source to counteract the hostile version of his own day coming from the Athenians. See 23/860Fn.

they sat by, beside their weapons: like obedient soldiers waiting for orders.

Late in the day the Phliasians and Megarians heard: P.'s 'late in the day' is not unjust, as H.'s narrative goes. But 'heard' is unjust since it suggests something accidental, and misses what H. says of a deliberate Spartan message sent to the reserve forces; when it was received, moreover, the reserve moved without further instruction: they knew their role; see W.J. Woodhouse, 'The Greeks at Plataea' *JHS* 18 (1898) 51/2.

Pausanias (1.43.3) records a grave in Megara for her dead of the Persian wars, and a couplet, attributed to Simonides, has been found on a stone of *c*.400 A.D. put up in restoration of an older one (see Campbell XVI). P.'s silence about it is a little surprising when in vindication of the Corinthians he quotes such epitaphs several times. See 39.

and were simply destroyed: H. says (9.69.2) the Megarians lost 600 dead, which is 20% of their original 3,000 (28.6). The rest, he says, fled, pursued by the Theban cavalry – which is difficult to fit with the activity of the Boeotian cavalry in 68, but not impossible, given that H.'s battle-narrative goes forward and then back in time.

the Corinthians were not in the battle: in the Greek text the negative has been accidentally omitted. It is restored in the translation.

avoided ... the Theban cavalry: P.'s distinction between the Corinthians and the others for promptitude of reaction is unwarranted: he makes H.'s bias seem greater than it is. The Corinthians' route 'through the hills' was a diagonal one east-north-east across the little streams which feed the Oëroë (see *PG* 518): hills is rather a big word for what are undulations (but nuisance enough to hurrying soldiers). As for avoiding contact with the Theban cavalry, the Corinthians would have had to turn straight down hill to make contact with them, and it was not their job. P.'s slur can only come from someone who has not tried to make sense of the battle.

D **the Thebans ... rode in protection:** H. attributes this manoeuvre to the Boeotian cavalry as a whole (9.68).

their thankyou for being branded: see 33/866Fn and 867Bn. The rhetoric of exaggeration has taken over.

what Simonides wrote: see 36/869Cn. The text of the verses is not well preserved. They seem to be part of a longer poem, rather than an extended epigram, and not consecutive.

'Ephyra': this was the name of the Homeric city at the Isthmus. Its Homeric and Ionic form Ἐφύρη, accepted into the text by Hansen, shows that the form printed in Lachenaud's and other texts is wrongly accented: it should be Ἐφύραν. Presumably the corruption into γέφυραν (see *App. Crit.*) caused the error.

'the battle's core': this probably refers to the fact that the Corinthian entry into the fight plugged the dangerous gap between the Spartans and Tegeans on the right and the Athenians and Plataeans on the left, a gap which arose when the left wing moved too slowly to its new position (9.61.1).

'Glaucus': see *Iliad* 6.154.

E **'the honoured gold'':** Simonides means the sun. This application of the word 'gold' appears to be unique; the word 'honoured', τιμήεις, accompanies the noun χρυσός three times in Homer: *Iliad* xviii 475 and *Odyssey* viii 393 and xi 472.

not ... for a choir ... for the city: the occasion for the poem is not known. Presumably it was commissioned; but if so, not publicly, or not for a public event. **common graves ... burials ... memorials:** after Marathon the Athenians and Plataeans buried their dead under mounds on the battlefield, according to custom; see Pritchett (1971) IV ch 2, especially 249/50; Thucydides' well-known statement in 2.34 appears to be true only after *c*.465.

H.'s narrative of the burials after Plataea details three Spartan mounds and three others; the rest he says were empty, mere cenotaphs; then comes the detail of the Aeginetan cenotaph, which may be due to a malicious Athenian source (see 40/871Cn). Hostility between Athens and Aegina developed in the early days of medism: see H. 5.79–89, 6.49–50 and 73, 85–93, and 7.144–5. The invasion of Xerxes suppressed it a while (see 8.41 and 92), but it arose again, and its fruits of malice may be seen in the story in 9.78–9 and in the silliness in 9.80.3.

Athenian malice on this occasion may be a matter of misinterpretation without falsehood. H.'s figures for the Greek dead at Plataea, incomplete as they obviously are, suggest that the worst losses were suffered by those who buried their dead on the battlefield: Spartans, Tegeans, Athenians, Megarians and Phliasians. The other contingents had perhaps lost fewer, and their dead could be taken home after incineration; memorial mounds could be raised in due course. It is surprising that the Aeginetans delayed ten years; perhaps they were only provoked to build by just such an accusation of not having taken part as H. reports. At least their five hundred had attended, not like the Mantineans and Eleans; they may have felt, too, that their contribution had been made principally at sea and was adequately acknowledged.

(In 479 the allied fleet met at Aegina (8.131), 110 ships in all. H. gives no details of its composition; in the fighting at Mycale only certain of the contingents are named; the Aeginetans are not among them, but the fewness of their men at Plataea suggests that their contribution at sea was large. H.'s silence about it might be due to more Athenian malice.)

the people of Plataea still make offerings: in *Life of Aristeides* 21 P. says that the ceremonies established in 479 were still performed in his own day, and Pausanias confirms it (9.2.6), despite the disasters suffered by the Plataeans themselves in 427 and 373.

873A **Straight after the battle ... scrapping:** P. repeats the story in *Life of Aristeides* 20. In H. Pausanias appears very much in control. M.E. White, 'Some Agiad dates: Pausanias and his sons' *JHS* 84 (1964) 140–52, shows that he was probably not thirty years old!

B **these verses on the altar:** P. quotes them also in *Life of Aristeides* 19, in the three-verse form of the MSS. The extra verse, a pentameter put in after the first verse to produce a pair of regular elegiac couplets, occurs in the quotation of the epigram in the Palatine Anthology (6.50):. What the lines show is that enough Greek states were present for 'the Greeks' to be a tolerable generalisation.

C **'Pausanias ... the Medes he slew':** Thucydides includes this in his completion of the tale of Pausanias (1.132.2). It is also known from other sources. P.'s 'megalomania' is delicately mentioned by H. elsewhere rather than in book nine: 5.32 and 8.3.2.

the Greeks ... complained: as with the lines on the altar, 'the Greeks' is too imprecise for the argument P. wants to make.

the Spartans ... erased his words: they did so not simply to meet the demands of the allies but because they too were offended.

D **either the Greeks ... should not ... or:** P.'s alternatives are at the extremes, and are not the only ones possible.

Sochares: H.'s MSS have the name as Sophanes (9.73.1). P. uses the form Sochares in *Life of the elder Cato* 29.2, but in *Life of Cimon* 8 he mentions a Sophanes of Decelea, who should be the same man as H. mentions.
Aeimnestus: this is the form of the name in H.'s MSS (9.64.2); P.'s MSS here show Deipnestus and in *Life of Aristeides* 19.1 they have Arimnestus. Aeimnestus is probably right, Deipnestus arising from a misreading of capital alpha as capital delta.
the Cythnians and the Melians: for the Cythnians see 28/863E. The Melians provided two penteconters at Salamis (8.48).

43.

This chapter summarises. The arguments which underlie the points made here have been considered mostly where they first occur. P. concentrates on the big battles; these are the glories of Greece which H. has sullied. For Artemisium see 34, for Thermopylae 31–33, for Salamis 36–39, and for Plataea 41/2.

E **they stayed ... at home:** 'they' now means the Spartans; P. is writing loosely, as in 'at Plataea they sat by' below.
more on queen Artemisia: the narrative of the fighting at Salamis starts at 8.84 and ends at 93. The exploits of Artemisia occupy 87 and 88, with a brief further mention in 93. In Hude's text the whole takes 131 lines; 87 and 88 take 32, a quarter. But P. is right in a way: hers is the most memorable part of the narrative.
frog-mice fight: just such a poem survives, couched in 304 Homeric hexameters, and attributed to Homer in a footnote at the end which adds 'Some say it is the work of Tigres (*sic*) the Carian'. T.W. Allen editing the Oxford Classical text (Homer vol. V, 1912) calls it a comic and puerile imitation of Homer, impossible to place. Apart from P.'s attribution, there is that in the *Suda*, the erratic Byzantine encyclopaedia of *c*. 1000 A.D. The *Suda* says Pigres was Artemisia's brother.

874A **"lack of armour":** the Persians were not able to use the lesson of Marathon.
B **grace and force and freshness:** in 1092E P., seeking a ready example of intellectual pleasure, picks on history, 'which provides hours of enjoyable occupation and leaves our constant desire for truth insatiable and uncloyed by pleasure'. Truth, he continues, is as desirable as life itself; it can cause pain; but 'when the story and its narrative contain nothing harmful or painful, and when its great and glorious deeds attract a language of power and grace (δύναμιν καὶ χάριν), like that of Herodotus in his Greek history ... then our delight is not only great and abundant but also clean and without regrets'.
like a Homer: P. quotes most of a line from the *Odyssey*, xi 368, where king Alcinous is complimenting Odysseus: 'You told your tale like a bard, with a good understanding'. The line is simply part of P.'s cultural furniture, like the quotations from Plato and Sophocles at the start of this work. And yet, comparison of H. with Homer in understanding of events, in language, and in narrative art is regularly made nowadays (see for instance Gould 60, 76–7 and 119–20); Lachenaud (107) may well be right to suggest that P. intends some such comparison here: then, in line with a Platonic view of the poets (see *Rep.* 398A), H. with his corrupted understanding would be better in P.'s eyes with myrrh and a crown on his head, and a one-way ticket to somewhere else.
the rose-beetle: *cetonia aurata*, in the grub state very destructive of a rose's vegetation. This simile in the closing sentence of the last paragraph matches the one of the winds at the end of the first paragraph.
false ... out of place ... best ... greatest ... cities ... heroes: P.'s penchant for pairs of words (see Intro. 36) gives force to his peroration.

Indexes

Index of Plutarch's citations from Herodotus

This list contains all passages quoted or paraphrased, including very brief quotations (see Intro. 18 & 19), in Plutarch's order of use. Paraphrases are indicated by (P). It does not include references with very little or no authentic wording. Since Plutarch follows Herodotus' order of events almost entirely (see Intro. 14), the list virtually serves as a reverse index of passages of Herodotus cited by Plutarch.

11. 1.1.1; 1.4.2
12. 2.119.2–3
13. 1.135; 2.58; 2.61; 2.171.1; 2.146.1
14. 6.53.2
15. 1.29.1; 1.32.1
16. 1.61.1 (P)
17. 1.82.8
18. 1.92.4 (P); 1.96.2
19. 1.143.3; 1.146.2; 1.146.3; 1.147.2
20. 1.160.2
21. 3.47.1 (P)
22. 3.48 (>P); 3.55 (P)
23. 5.63.1; 5.70.1; 5.66.1; 5.57.1; 5.91.2; 3.49.2
24. 5.97.3; 5.100.1 (P)
25. 6.108.3
26. 6.106.3–107.1; Prologue
27. 6.115–116; 6.124.2; 6.121.1
28. 7.150.3–151; 7.152.1 and 3
29. 7.139.5; 7.139.3–4
30. 7.190
31. 7.172.1; 7.139.3 and 4; 7.222; 7.220.2; 7.220.4
33. 7.233; 6.129
34. 8.4.1(>P); 8.18; 8.23.1; 8.21.2
35. 8.30
36. 8.46.3 (P)
37. 8.57–58
38. 8.86 β–γ
39. 8.94 (part P); 8.5.1 (P)
40. 8.122
42. 9.52; 9.85.3
43. 9.62.3; 9.63.2

Index of Plutarch's references to other literature

1. Plato *Republic* 2 361A
   Sophocles fr.781 (A. Nauck
   Tragicorum Graecorum
   fragmenta Leipzig 1926^2)
   Theopompus (*FGrH* 115 T25)

2. Thucydides 7.50.4 and 4.28.5

3. Thucydides 8.73.3
   Philistus (*FHG* I xlv–xlix)
   trag. anon. fr.388 (Nauck, v.sup.)

5. Ephorus (*FGrH* 70 F189)

6. Aristophanes *Ach*.524ff and *Pax*
   605ff (unattributed)

9. Aristoxenus fr.55 (F. Wehrli Die
   Schule des Aristoteles (texte)
   Basel 1967 26)

20. Charon of Lampsacus (*FGrH* 262
    F9)

21. 'other writers'

22. Antenor the Cretan (*FGrH* 463
    F2)
    Dionysius of Chalcis (*FHG* IV
    396 F13)

24. Lysanias of Mallos (*FGrH* 426)
    Charon of Lampsacus (*FGrH*
    262 F10)

26. Diyllus of Athens (*FGrH* 73 F3)

28. Euripides *Andromache* 448
    (unattributed)

31. Aristophanes the Boeotian
    (*FGrH* 379 F5)

33. Aristophanes the Boeotian
    (*FGrH* 379 F6)
    Nicander of Colophon (*FGrH*
    271/2 F35)

34. Pindar fr.65 (C.M. Bowra
    Oxford 1947^2)
    [Simonides] (Campbell XXIV)

36. Hellanicus (*FGrH* 4 F183)
    Ephorus (*FGrH* 70 F187)
    Naxian chroniclers (*FGrH* 501
    F3)
    Simonides (Campbell XIX)

39. Thucydides 1.73–78
    [Simonides] (Campbell XI)
    [Simonides] (Campbell XII)
    [Simonides] (Campbell XIII)
    [Simonides] (Campbell X)
    Simonides (Campbell XIV)

42. Simonides (Campbell eleg. 10 &
    11)
    [Simonides] (Campbell XV)
    [Simonides] (Campbell XVII)

43. Pigres (v. ad loc.)
    Homer *Od*. xi 368

Index of all capitalised words in the Greek text

References are to Plutarch's chapters; bracketed numbers indicate how often a word occurs in that chapter.

Printed and bound by CPI Group (UK) Ltd, Croydon, CR0 4YY

09/06/2025

14685950-0001